The Lincoln-Douglas Debates and
the Making of a President

The American Declaration of Independence

When in the Course of human events, it becomes necessary for one people to dissolve the political bands which have connected them with another, and to assume among the powers of the earth, the separate and equal station to which the Laws of Nature and of Nature's God entitle them, a decent respect to the opinions of mankind requires that they should declare the causes which impel them to the separation.

We hold these truths to be self-evident, that all men are created equal, that they are endowed by their Creator with certain unalienable Rights, that among these are Life, Liberty and the pursuit of Happiness....

July 4, 1776

The Lincoln-Douglas Debates and the Making of a President

Timothy S. Good

McFarland & Company, Inc., Publishers
Jefferson, North Carolina, and London

LIBRARY OF CONGRESS CATALOGUING-IN-PUBLICATION DATA

Good, Timothy S. (Timothy Sean)
    The Lincoln-Douglas debates and the making
of a president / Timothy S. Good.
        p.   cm.
    Includes bibliographical references and index.

    ISBN-13: 978-0-7864-3065-9
    (softcover : 50# alkaline paper) ∞

    1. Lincoln-Douglas Debates, Ill., 1858.   2. Lincoln, Abraham,
1809–1865 — Political career before 1861.   3. Lincoln, Abraham,
1809–1865 — Political and social views.   4. Douglas, Stephen Arnold,
1813–1861.   5. Slavery — Political aspects — United States — History —
19th century.   6. United States — Race relations — Political aspects —
History — 19th century.   7. African Americans — Civil rights —
History — 19th century.   8. United States — Politics and
government — 1849–1861.   9. Presidents — United States —
Biography.   I. Title.
E457.4.G66   2007
973.6'8 — dc22   2006103507

British Library cataloguing data are available

©2007 Timothy S. Good. All rights reserved

No part of this book may be reproduced or transmitted in any form or by any means, electronic or mechanical, including photocopying or recording, or by any information storage and retrieval system, without permission in writing from the publisher.

Cover photographs ©2007 Clipart

Manufactured in the United States of America

McFarland & Company, Inc., Publishers
  Box 611, Jefferson, North Carolina 28640
    www.mcfarlandpub.com

To my dad,
Thanks for the history lessons
at the dinner table.

Acknowledgments

I am extremely grateful to the following for their assistance: Gene Finke, Park Ranger, Lincoln Home National Historic Site; Meredith Berg, Professor of History, Valparaiso University; Gaines Foster, Professor of History, Louisiana State University; John Marszalek, Professor Emeritus, Mississippi State University; Tim Townsend, Historian, Lincoln Home National Historic Site; Tom Trimborn, Professor, Truman State University, and author of *Encounters with Lincoln: Images and Words*; Linda Ray, Librarian, Bellevue Public Library; my dad; and of course, my wife.

Table of Contents

Acknowledgments vi

Preface 1

1. Before '58 — 5
2. A House Divided: Springfield, Illinois — 23
   June 16, 1858
3. The Campaign Begins: Chicago, Illinois — 37
   July 9–10, 1858
4. Douglas Fires Back: Bloomington, Illinois — 51
   July 16, 1858
5. The Second Round: Springfield, Illinois — 63
   July 17, 1858
6. A Challenge Made, a Challenge Accepted: The Lincoln-Douglas Letters — 77
   July 1858
7. The First Debate: Ottawa, Illinois — 87
   August 21, 1858
8. The Second Debate: Freeport, Illinois — 103
   August 27, 1858
9. The Third Debate: Jonesboro, Illinois — 115
   September 15, 1858
10. The Fourth Debate: Charleston, Illinois — 127
    September 18, 1858

Table of Contents

11. The Fifth Debate: Galesburg, Illinois 139
    October 7, 1858
12. The Sixth Debate: Quincy, Illinois 153
    October 13, 1858
13. The Last Debate: Alton, Illinois 163
    October 15, 1858

Epilogue 181
Appendix A: After '58 183
Appendix B: The Last Rebuttal 186
Chapter Notes 189
Bibliography 201
Index 205

Preface

This is the first book-length narrative on the Lincoln-Douglas debates.

I have had the pleasure of serving at three National Park Service sites that are dedicated to Abraham Lincoln's memory: Ford's Theatre National Historic Site, the Lincoln Memorial, and Lincoln Home National Historic Site. The idea for my first book, *We Saw Lincoln Shot: One Hundred Eyewitness Accounts* came to me while working at Ford's Theatre. The idea for this book came to me while I was employed at Lincoln Home.

While in Springfield, I was surprised to discover that there was no book-length narrative on the debates. When visitors asked for a book on this topic, I had to refer them to a chapter in one book, or a chapter in an out-of-print book, or an article somewhere else. I could have suggested the debate texts themselves, which are readily accessible, but they are not easily read.

Saul Sigelschiffer's *The American Conscience: The Drama of the Lincoln-Douglas Debates* and Richard Allen Heckman's *Lincoln vs. Douglas: The Great Debates Campaign* come closest as book-length narratives. However, Sigelschiffer devotes only a portion of his book to the debates while Heckman focuses far more on Steven A. Douglas's campaign than the debates themselves. He considers the Senator's efforts to lay the foundation for his future presidential campaign more important than the debates.

There are many fine books that cover the debates such as Don E. Fehrenbacher's *Prelude to Greatness: Lincoln in the 1850s*, Lionel Crocker's *Analysis of Lincoln and Douglas as Public Speakers*, Harry V. Jaffa's *Crisis of the House Divided: An Interpretation of the Issues of the Lincoln-*

Preface

Douglas Debates, and David Zarefsky's *Lincoln, Douglas and Slavery: In the Crucible of Public Debate.* These provide excellent analyses of the many issues that were debated, but they all conclude that Lincoln's political strategy was fully developed before 1858, and was consistent throughout the debates, an interpretation with which I disagree. I believe that a careful study of the record shows that Lincoln's campaign strategy evolved throughout his debates with Douglas, a point that is best appreciated through a narrative approach that focuses on Lincoln's struggles.

The main issue of the debates was the candidates' interpretation of the Declaration of Independence, specifically the phrase "all men are created equal." Douglas consistently maintained that the phrase applied only to "white men," but Lincoln vacillated, sometimes arguing that "all men" applied to "all men" while at other times asserting that it did not apply to African Americans. Therefore, it is Lincoln, not Douglas, who should be the historians' focus, because it is Lincoln who changed during the debates, and it is this transformation that made 1858 a watershed year in Lincoln's life.

This leads me to my second reason for writing this book — a new interpretation of the debates.

I maintain that Lincoln expressed his true opinions before audiences that were favorable to him, but when faced with audiences of opposing viewpoints, he, as one would expect from a politician, modified his stance. This strategy obviously does not reflect the character of a statesman, but at the last debate, when faced with an audience that did not accept the universality of "all men are created equal," and whose support he needed to win the election, Lincoln ignored the natural instinct of a politician, and spoke not as an opportunist, but as a statesman. The importance of 1858 to Lincoln was not whether he won the election, but whether he would display the courage to speak in favor of his interpretation of the Declaration of Independence before *all* audiences, whether or not they supported him.

It is my contention that, although he began the campaign speaking as a statesman, as the debates progressed, Lincoln descended to the level of a politician, and fell victim to the racism of his day. But at the end, at the last debate, he rose above it, and made the transformation from a politician into a statesman once more.

The definitions of a statesman and a politician that I apply to the

Preface

debates are not arbitrary, nor personal, nor do I define these words by twenty-first century standards. Rather, I took nineteenth century definitions, that were provided by Lincoln himself, at the last debate. Although his demarcation between a politician and a statesman may appear rather stark in that it appears to preclude the possibility of a "good" politician, I have faithfully applied it as Lincoln had defined these two terms, and although his definitions may not be applicable for all times and all places, they are, at least according to Lincoln, appropriate definitions for the America of the 1850s. In the first six debates, Lincoln never attempted to define statesmanship, but in the seventh one he did. Douglas had "intimated," Lincoln claimed, that all the nation's "difficulty in regard to the institution of slavery" was nothing more than the "mere agitation of office seekers and ambitious Northern politicians." But Northern politicians had not caused the problem of slavery, Lincoln argued. Politicians, by Lincoln's definition, were the ones who avoided discussing slavery. It was the proslavery forces, or as Lincoln put it, that "irresistible power" which, for fifty years, had "agitated the people to be stilled and subdued by pretending that it [slavery] is an exceedingly simple thing" that should not be discussed. He questioned the "statesmanship" that assumed

> that you can quiet that disturbing element in our society which has disturbed us for more than half a century, which has been the only serious danger that has threatened our institutions — I say, where is the philosophy or the statesmanship based on the assumption that we are to quit talking about it [slavery], and that the public mind is all at once to cease being agitated by it? Yet this is the policy here in the north that Douglas is advocating — that we are to care nothing about it! I ask you if it is not a false philosophy?

Lincoln accused Douglas and his followers of "false statesmanship" for creating "a policy upon the basis of caring nothing about *the very thing that every body does care the most about*? — a thing which all experience has shown we care a very great deal about?"

By Lincoln's own definition, a statesman was the one who constantly and consistently spoke against slavery. For Lincoln, nothing better proved the immorality of slavery than the words of the Declaration of Independence. At the last debate, he boldly and without reservation asserted that "all men" applied to "all men" — and he made his argument

Preface

without the encumbrances of the "superior" and "inferior" races he had mentioned at previous debates. He spoke at Alton far differently than he had at any of the debates; he spoke with the same courage and conviction that he would later display as President. He spoke as a statesman.

At Alton, one sees the Lincoln who would write the First Inaugural Speech, the Emancipation Proclamation, the Gettysburg Address, the Second Inaugural Address, and his last public address in which he called for the extension of the suffrage to African Americans. In the debates, one sees the signs of the greatness that is to come.

The final debate was his epiphany.

At Alton, he became a statesman, and this is the central story of the debates.

1

Before '58

His moment had finally come, or so he thought.

In the late 1840s, Lincoln was, for the first time, a congressman in the United States House of Representatives. He would proudly represent his Whig party on Capitol Hill.

His hopes proved greater than his successes; after a single term he departed Washington distinguished with only a new nickname, "Spotty Lincoln," for his continuous demand to know the "spot" where American troops had been fired upon by Mexican forces at the commencement of the Mexican War. Lincoln believed that the United States Army was not on American soil when initially engaged, that it had illegally invaded Mexico. Few agreed, or cared.

The summation of his life and his accomplishments, as he would later write:

> Born, February 12, 1809, in Hardin County, Kentucky.
> Education defective.
> Profession, a lawyer.
> Have been a captain of volunteers in Black Hawk war.
> Postmaster at a very small office.
> Four times a member of the Illinois legislature, and was a member of the lower house of Congress.[1]

"Upon his return from Congress he went to the practice of the law with greater earnestness than ever before," he wrote in an autobiographical statement.[2] He considered his political career dead.

In 1854, it was resurrected. Stephen A. Douglas, a Democratic Senator from Illinois, successfully championed the passing of the Kansas-Nebraska Act through Congress. The act repealed the Missouri Compromise of 1820 and allowed the possibility of slavery in territories where it had once been prohibited. Lincoln was "astounded," "thunderstruck," and "stunned" when he heard of the act. Lincoln wrote in the third person, "His profession had almost superseded the thought of politics in his mind, when the repeal of the Missouri compromise aroused him as he had never been before."[3]

Less than six months after the passage of the Kansas-Nebraska Act, Lincoln seized the opportunity to attack it publicly. He gave two speeches, one at Springfield and another at Peoria. Many of his statements in these speeches would become the foundation for his arguments in the Lincoln-Douglas debates. Unlike the Springfield speech, which was not recorded in its entirety, or in the first person, the Peoria speech was, and its transcription is therefore the more accurate of the two.

Lincoln began his speech in Peoria by praising the Declaration of Independence, and more specifically, its author. He noted that Thomas Jefferson was "a chief actor in the revolution; then a delegate to Congress; afterwards twice President" and perhaps the "most distinguished politician of our history." He acknowledged that Jefferson had also been a "slave-holder," but that he was also the one who conceived the idea of preventing slavery from "ever going into the north-western territory." The result of banning slavery from the Northwest territory was precisely what Jefferson "foresaw and intended — the happy home of teeming millions of free, white, prosperous people, and no slave amongst them." The author of the Declaration of Independence, Lincoln continued, had originated the "policy of prohibiting slavery in new territory" and that policy had through "sixty odd of the best years of the republic" worked to the nation's "great and beneficial end."

In contrast, Douglas had justified the Kansas-Nebraska Act based on the principle of popular sovereignty, the idea that the people of the territory should determine whether slavery should be permitted. Lincoln assailed that proposition. He claimed that the sacred right of self government is "grossly violated" by granting the "liberty of making slaves of other people," a concept that Jefferson had never conceived. Lincoln held that the Missouri Compromise directly applied to the Nebraska Territory and therefore prohibited slavery within it. Although Douglas claimed that his act had no effect on the application of the compromise, Lincoln emphatically believed that the act was "the repeal of the Missouri Compromise" and that it was simply wrong. He considered it "wrong in its direct effect" by allowing slavery into Kansas and Nebraska and "wrong in its prospective principle" by allowing slavery to spread beyond its current boundaries.

He was appalled at Douglas's apparent indifference to his act's effect. Lincoln confessed that he "can not but hate" this "covert real zeal for the spread of slavery." He expressed his "hate" of it "because of the monstrous injustice of slavery itself ... because it deprives our republican example of its just influence in the world — enables the enemies of free institutions, with plausibility, to taunt us as hypocrites — causes the real friends of freedom to doubt our sincerity, and especially because it forces so many really good men amongst ourselves into an open war with the very fundamental principles of civil liberty — criticising the Declaration of Independence."

However, Lincoln admitted a particular point that would also prove critical in the later senatorial debates of 1858. Lincoln confessed that his "own feelings" would not permit him to free the slaves and make them his political and social equals. He admitted that he was not arguing for the "establishment of political and social equality between whites and blacks." He did, though, admit the possibility that "gradual emancipation might be adopted."

Lincoln also rejected use of Douglas's popular sovereignty doctrine as a solution to the problem of slavery, for if the white man "governs himself that is self-government; but when he governs himself, and also governs another man, that is more than self-government — that is despotism," something Lincoln termed the "Divine right of Kings." Lincoln further argued that if the "negro is a man" and "all men are created equal" then "there can be no moral right" to make "a slave of another." He added, "No man is good enough to govern another man, without that other's consent," and this is the "leading principle — the sheet anchor of American republicanism." Lincoln warned that no one should be deceived, the "spirit of seventy-six and the spirit of Nebraska, are utter antagonisms; and the former is being rapidly displaced by the latter."

Lincoln called for the opposition to the Nebraska Act to unite. The act had, he said, "soiled" the republican robe and "trailed [it] in the dust. Let us turn and wash it white, in the spirit, if not the blood, of the Revolution." He pleaded for the people to return slavery "to the position our fathers gave it" and let "us re-adopt the Declaration of Independence."

His hope was that both "north and south — let all Americans— let all lovers of liberty everywhere — join in the great and good work. If we do this, we shall not only have saved the Union; but we shall have so saved it, as to make, and to keep it, forever worthy of the saving. We shall have so saved it, that the succeeding millions of free happy people, the world over, shall rise up, and call us blessed to the latest generations."[4]

A year later, Lincoln had another opportunity to fight the Nebraska Act. After the fall 1854 elections, the Illinois State Legislature assembled in early 1855 to choose a new United States senator. Of the ninety-nine delegates, Lincoln had the most pledged to support him on the first ballot, a total of forty-five, but he needed five more to capture the majority. A group of five anti–Nebraska Democrats represented Lincoln's best hope, but all attempts to persuade them failed. As Democrats, they would not support a Whig and thus they remained committed to an anti–Nebraska Democrat. In the succeeding ballots, Lincoln's support dwindled from forty-five delegates to fifteen as more and more of the delegates began supporting Douglas's candidate. With no chance of prevailing himself and firmly convinced that the pro–Nebraska candidate should not win, Lincoln threw his support to an anti–Nebraska Democrat, Lyman Trumbull, who carried the election.

In summarizing the contest, Lincoln wrote that the "election is over, the Session is ended, and I am not Senator." He had to content himself "with the honor of having been the first choice of a large majority" of the fifty-one legislators who chose Trumbull, but he admitted that it "was rather hard for the 44 to have to surrender to the 5 — and a less good humored man than I, perhaps would not have consented to it — and it would not have been done without my consent. I could not, however, let the whole political result go to ruin, on a point merely personal to myself."[5] The episode illustrated the statesmanship that Lincoln would later exhibit in the last debate. He threw aside personal political aspirations for the benefit of what he considered the greater political goal. To Lincoln, it was more vital that an anti–Nebraska Senator prevail than it was for him personally to prevail.

An excerpt from one of Lincoln's letters provides further evidence of his personal philosophy, what he considered his political foundation. In 1855, with the collapse of the Whig party, one of Lincoln's friends asked him where he stood politically, especially whether he supported

1. Before '58

the Know-Nothing party, which was vehemently anti-immigrant and anti–Catholic. Lincoln wrote to his friend: "I am not a Know-Nothing. That is certain. How could I be? How can any one who abhors the oppression of negroes, be in favor of degrading classes of white people? Our progress in degeneracy appears to me to be pretty rapid. As a nation, we begin by declaring that 'all men are created equal.' We now practically read it 'all men are created equal, except negroes.' When the Know-Nothings get control, it will read 'all men are created equal, except negroes, and foreigners, and catholics.' When it comes to this I should prefer emigrating to some country where they make no pretence of loving liberty — to Russia, for instance, where despotism can be taken pure, and without the base alloy of hypocracy [sic]."[6]

Just as Lincoln was reengaging in politics, he suffered another blow. The political party he loved collapsed. The Whig party could no longer bridge the differences between North and South, and its resulting disintegration left many without a political home. Some Whigs joined the anti-immigrant Know-Nothing party and some affiliated with anti–Nebraska groups, while others stood on the edge of the political process refusing to join with anyone. Lincoln was one of the last Whigs to leave. In 1856, he found a new home in a young party, the Republicans, a collection of Americans primarily brought together by their hatred of the Kansas-Nebraska Act. The nation was experiencing a momentous change in the political landscape. The Whigs were disappearing, and the Republicans were rising. William H. Herndon, Lincoln's law partner, blamed Douglas's Act: "It sounded the death-knell of the gallant old Whig party; it drove together strange, discordant elements in readiness to fight a common enemy; it brought to the forefront a leader in the person of Lincoln."[7]

At times, though, Douglas's Act did not always seem to have the force and pressure necessary to hold the young Republican party together. The same year that Lincoln joined it, the Illinois Republicans appeared to be dividing just like the Whigs. The cause for this internal strife was one man, one who sought the Republican nomination for the Third Congressional District, the outspoken Owen Lovejoy.

The Lincoln-Douglas Debates and the Making of a President

The name Lovejoy was synonymous with abolitionism. It had become a rallying cry for abolitionists nationwide ever since Elijah Lovejoy, Owen's brother, had been gunned down in Alton, Illinois, because of his stance on a number of issues, particularly slavery. Although not as radical or as anti–Catholic as his brother, Owen Lovejoy was still anathema to many Republicans. He preached abolitionism both as a pastor and as a political candidate. He openly operated an illegal station on the Underground Railroad and had once brazenly placed this advertisement in a local newspaper: "The subscriber would very respectfully inform the ladies and gentlemen of color of the South, who wish to travel North for the benefit of their condition, or any excursion of pleasure to the falls of Niagra [sic], that the above line of stages will be in action, and efficient operation during the summer." Lovejoy added that "Passengers will be carried all the way through for Nothing" and "For further particulars inquire of the subscriber at his residence in Princeton, Bureau County." He signed the advertisement with his name and with the title "Gen. Agent." He concluded with the statement that at "any hour of the day or night" he would provide "articles of clothing" for those who had "fallen among Southern Banditti and been stripped."[8]

Lovejoy operated his house as a station throughout the 1850s with all the dangers that this service entailed. When a pro-slavery man attempted to recapture an escaped slave, Lovejoy slammed his front gate on him and barred his entrance. Another time, when a large crowd assembled before his house, knowing that an escaped slave was inside, Lovejoy stood before them and preached an impromptu antislavery sermon. He thereby distracted the crowd, and the slave escaped unnoticed. These actions made him a hero to some, an enemy to many. The conservative Republicans, who were united in opposing slavery's spread but not in calling for slavery's end, either eventual or immediate, considered his actions abhorrent.[9]

The Republican who most publicly opposed Lovejoy was Judge David Davis of Bloomington, Illinois. Davis was a mammoth of a man, over three hundred pounds, and had earned respect equal to his size. Raised on a Maryland slave plantation, he went on to study law at Yale University and became a devoted Whig politician. The Judge firmly believed that slavery should be restricted and joined the Republican party to further this cause.

1. Before '58

The Judge had come to know Lincoln over numerous years on the judicial circuit, when, in spring and fall, Lincoln would join the band of lawyers traveling across central Illinois to hear a variety of cases in many local courthouses. Davis had become so impressed with Lincoln that he allowed the lawyer to preside over cases when he was unable.

Although against the spread of slavery, Davis was no abolitionist and had no love for the abolitionists. He wrote that "every feeling of his nature, and every aspiration of his heart, was at war with the wild and disorganizing schemes of the political abolitionists."[10] Most Americans of the 1850s agreed. The abolitionists' claims that the races were equal in all respects had few supporters. In operating the Underground Railroad and in opposing all laws regarding the return of fugitive slaves, the abolitionists gained the ire of those who supported the Constitution. And finally, the abolitionists were blamed for inciting slave rebellions. The most notable one, named after Virginia slave Nat Turner, had resulted in the death of fifty-five white people who were stabbed, shot, or clubbed.

Davis was determined to prevent Lovejoy from securing the Republican nomination for the Third Congressional District, and he had a significant ally in Judge T. Lyle Dickey. Dickey, born in Kentucky like Lincoln, opposed slavery's spread but also disliked the abolitionists even more. A former Whig, a friend of Davis and Lincoln, he collaborated with the conservative Republicans to prevent the abolitionist from becoming a member of Congress.

On July 2 the Republican delegates for the Third Congressional District met, and nominated Lovejoy — by one vote. Davis and Dickey were shocked. Lincoln, favoring a far more conservative candidate, was not pleased with Lovejoy's nomination either. Lincoln had no desire to speak on behalf of a party whose members were considered abolitionists. But in traveling through the Third Congressional District, he recognized Lovejoy's immense popularity. The party needed supporters, of which Lovejoy had an abundance. The trip had a profound influence on Lincoln's thinking toward Lovejoy. He wrote Davis, admitting that when he heard of Lovejoy's nomination "it turned me blind." He was "by invitation" on his "way to Princeton," Lovejoy's district, but had "really thought of turning back. However, on reaching that region, and seeing the people there — their great enthusiasm for Lovejoy — considering the activity they will carry into the contest with him — and their great disappointment, if he should now be torn from them, I really think it best to let the matter stand. It is not my business to advise in the case; and if it were, I am not sure I am capable of giving the best advice; but I know, saying what I do, will not be offensive to you."[11]

Davis reluctantly agreed with Lincoln, but Dickey did not. He concocted a plan to run against Lovejoy, believing that more Republicans would support him. On July 16, in Bloomington, Illinois, he arranged a meeting to nominate himself instead of Lovejoy for Congress. Dickey spoke, an uninspiring speech by one account, followed by one of his supporters who gave a more rousing speech in which he accused Lovejoy of being a "nigger thief." Dickey's nomination now seemed assured, and the meeting appeared at an end, but to the surprise of those present, Lovejoy stood and began to speak.

Lovejoy, described by one of his contemporaries as a "man of powerful physique, intense feeling and of great magnetism as a speaker," lived up to his reputation that night.[12] The federal government, Lovejoy began, could not abolish slavery where it then existed, but could do so in the territories. He supported weakening the Fugitive Slave Law and, in response to the "nigger thief" comment, replied: "If it is meant by that that I go to Kentucky or Missouri to entice slaves to run away, it is not true.... It is not necessary for me to do that. But if you mean by that charge that when a man or woman comes to my door and asks for a cup of water and a crust of bread and that I point them to the North star, if that is what you mean, and I have had such women come to my door as white as your wife or mine, if that is what you mean, then I plead guilty.... And who of you would not do the same thing?"[13]

Lovejoy won the day. The audience responded with great applause, and further efforts to oppose Lovejoy's nomination failed. Despite this setback, Dickey would not abandon his opposition and decided to run as an independent. Davis, however, recognized the futility of any further opposition, and two days after the Bloomington convention, he wrote his fellow judge: "Now, my dear friend, I am not stating these things by way of any justification for those who so act, but simply as reasons (unsatisfactory as they may be) why the people are pre-disposed to vote for Lovejoy. I think the grand reason after all is that his views and opinions are becoming the views and opinions of a majority of the people. It would not profit us to inquire in this letter what has brought this about, but I am led to the conclusion that it is a melancholy fact."[14]

Dickey ignored Davis's counsel. He described his crusade in a letter to his son: "We are in the midst of a political tornado. The congressional convention of Fremont men met at Ottawa on the 2d of this month nominated for Congress Rev. Owen Lovejoy, a rank old-fashioned Abolitionist. About half the delegates bolted the nomination and called another convention to nominate another candidate who would not only oppose the introduction of slavery into Kansas, but would at the same time be true to the acknowledged rights of the South under the Constitution, embracing their right to recapture runaway slaves—and who in general would exercise a spirit of fidelity and fraternity to the people of the South and avoid all unnecessary cause of difference. That convention put me in nomination. And I am now a candidate for Congress in the midst of the hurricane, preaching peace, fraternity and fidelity. I am stemming a terrible current without any reasonable certainty of success."[15]

Lincoln campaigned throughout Illinois in 1856 with other party leaders speaking on behalf of the Republican presidential candidate John C. Frémont, and it was during this campaign, on September 12, in Bloomington, Illinois, that he first made public a statement that would later make him famous, or to some, infamous. In the speech that day, he expressed his belief that the government could not last, part slave and part free—that either slavery would be abolished everywhere or it would be made legal everywhere. One of the people who also made a speech on Fremont's behalf that day, and heard Lincoln's words, was Dickey.

Dickey, always sensitive to any remarks that appeared abolitionist, was appalled by Lincoln's statement and confronted him that night in a hotel room. The judge asked the lawyer, "What in God's name could induce you to promulgate such an opinion?" and "What good is to be accomplished by inculcating that opinion ... in the minds of the People?" To Dickey, Lincoln's statements only made "Abolitionists of all the people of the North & slavery protagonists of all [the] South." Further, the Judge feared that Lincoln's speech would "precipitate a struggle which may end in disunion." Dickey's argument was effective. Lincoln agreed not to mention the phrase for the remainder of the 1856 campaign, a case of politics trumping conviction.[16]

The deal may have included reciprocation. The next day, Dickey ended his campaign against Lovejoy. And that fall, the preacher easily won his district by over six thousand votes.

The campaign concluded with Frémont's defeat. The anti–Democratic, anti–Nebraska votes were split between the Republicans and the Know-Nothings. The Republicans hoped that the Know-Nothing sentiment would evaporate before the 1858 Senate election. The combination of Know-Nothings and Republicans would give the Republicans a fair chance at defeating the Democratic Senator, Stephen A. Douglas.

After the election, perhaps looking ahead to 1858, Lincoln wrote a brief fragment comparing his life and his accomplishments to the life and accomplishments of Douglas. While these comparisons might seem unfair — Douglas was then representing Illinois in the United States Senate and Lincoln was practicing law in a two-man firm — they both began their careers as lawyers in Illinois and Lincoln had met Douglas "twenty-two years ago." He remembered that they "were both young then; he a trifle younger than I. Even then, we were both ambitious; I, perhaps, quite as much so as he. With me, the race of ambition has been a failure — a flat failure; with him it has been one of splendid success. His name fills the nation; and is not unknown, even, in foreign lands."

Lincoln understood the larger issue that eclipsed personal fame. He held no contempt for the "high eminence" that Douglas had achieved. He only desired such "elevation" for himself if the "oppressed of my species" could have shared it with him. If that were the situation, Lincoln would have preferred to "stand on that eminence, than wear the richest crown that ever pressed a monarch's brow." The Declaration of Independence and the hypocrisy of American slavery remained his focus. He was still willing to sacrifice his political career for the greater good, as he had done in 1855.[17]

1. Before '58

Lincoln's hopes for his nation suffered another setback on March 6, 1857. The Supreme Court issued its Dred Scott decision, with Chief Justice Roger Taney writing the majority opinion that declared that African Americans were not citizens, and could therefore not sue in federal court. Furthermore, Congress did not have the power to prohibit slavery from the territories, thereby nullifying the 1820 Missouri Compromise, which had prohibited slavery from the northern part of the Louisiana Purchase.

The events leading to this watershed decision began in 1836, when an army surgeon traveled north on the Mississippi River to an outpost named Fort Snelling, on the west bank of the river. The territory, which would later become the state of Minnesota, had come under the jurisdiction of the United States through the Louisiana Purchase. The trip itself was not worthy of note, except for the fact that the surgeon brought with him, into a territory that prohibited slavery, a slave named Dred Scott.

Scott lived there for a year before his surgeon-owner was transferred again. The surgeon returned to Fort Snelling for two years from 1838 to 1840 and again brought Scott with him. Twice in the span of four years, Scott was taken into free territory, but kept as a slave.

The court case for the freedom of Scott and his wife began in 1846. Four years later, the first court ruled in Scott's favor. The decision was appealed, and in 1852 the Missouri state supreme court reversed the first ruling and determined that Scott was still a slave. When it was again appealed, the United States circuit court for the district of Missouri issued its decision in 1854, declaring that if Missouri determined that Scott was a slave, then he would remain a slave despite any other laws. The last appeal landed the case before the United States Supreme Court, and in February 1856, the Court heard the first arguments. Ten months later, the Court, having been unable to come to agreement, heard four more days of reargument.

On March 6, 1857, just two days after James Buchanan's inauguration as the fifteenth President of the United States, the Supreme Court issued one of the most controversial decisions in its history. Chief Justice Taney's opinion proved devastating to those who agreed with Lincoln's interpretation of the Declaration of Independence.[18]

The Court fundamentally had to decide one simple issue: whether Dred Scott as a citizen of Missouri had the right to bring suit in federal court. Taney seized on the opportunity of this issue to redefine it, and to lay the foundation for a far broader decision. The Chief Justice determined that "the question is simply this: Can a negro, whose ancestors were imported into this country and sold as slaves, become a member of the political community formed and brought into existence by the Constitution of the United States, and as such become entitled to all the rights, and privileges, and immunities" guaranteed by the Constitution? Those rights included, of course, the "privilege of suing in a court of the United States."[19] On this basis, Taney then conceived that the question before the Court was whether African Americans, slave or free, are "members of this sovereignty" or, in other words, citizens of the United States. "We think they are not," he declared, "and that they are not included, and were not intended to be included under the word 'citizens' in the Constitution, and can therefore claim none of the rights and privileges which that instrument provides for and secures to citizens of the United States." Not satisfied with simply denying citizenship, Taney declared that at the time of the Constitution African Americans were "considered as a subordinate and inferior class of beings, who had been subjugated by the dominant race, and, whether emancipated or not, yet remained subject to their authority, and had no rights or privileges but such as those who held the power and the Government might choose to grant them."[20]

Trespassing upon what Lincoln considered sacred ground, Taney then thought it necessary to interpret the Declaration of Independence in order to justify his decision. The phrase "all men are created equal," the Chief Justice argued, "would seem to embrace the whole human family" but it was "too clear for dispute that the enslaved African race were not intended to be included." As historian Don Fehrenbacher so aptly described it, Taney believed that "all slaves are Negroes; therefore, all Negroes are excluded from the rights enumerated in the Declaration."[21]

Douglas had little difficulty in accepting the Court's decision and attacked those who were assailing it, in a June 1857 speech in Chicago. He described the Supreme Court as the "highest judicial tribunal on earth" and that "whoever resists the final decision of the highest judicial tribunal, aims a deadly blow at our whole republican system of government — a blow, which, if successful, would place all our rights and liberties at the mercy of passion, anarchy and violence."[22] He further found nothing incongruous between his notion of popular sovereignty and the ruling. The right to keep slaves, Douglas contended, "remains a barren and worthless right, unless sustained, protected, and enforced by appropriate police regulations and local legislation, prescribing adequate remedies for its violation. These regulations and remedies must necessarily depend entirely upon the will and wishes of the people of the Territory, as they can only be prescribed by the local legislatures." From the Senator's perspective, the Supreme Court decision would not be binding if the local governments refused to enforce it. Therefore, he concluded that "the great principle of popular sovereignty and self-government is sustained and firmly established by the authority of this decision." Douglas welcomed the Court's determination that the Missouri Compromise was null and void, believing that the Supreme Court supported the Kansas-Nebraska Act and his principle of popular sovereignty. He also was especially pleased with the Court's "main proposition" that "a negro descended from slave parents" could never receive American citizenship. This supported Douglas's contention that in the Declaration of Independence the phrase "all men are created equal" did not apply to all men.[23]

Lincoln was stunned. The legislative branch had passed the Kansas-Nebraska Act, which repealed the Missouri Compromise. The judicial branch had then annulled the Missouri Compromise with the Dred Scott decision. And finally, the executive branch gave its support to those desiring slavery's spread by offering no challenge to these decisions. President James Buchanan's reasons for not opposing these occurrences, for supporting the Missouri Compromise's end, were best articulated three years after the decision in his third annual address to Congress. He claimed that the "right has been established of every citizen to take his property of any kind, including slaves, into the common Territories belonging equally to all the States of the Confederacy." As for the power of other institutions to prevent this "right," the President declared that neither "Congress nor a Territorial legislature nor any human power has any authority to annul or impair this vested right." Buchanan had feared that the Court might have decided that Congress or the territorial legislature would "possess the power to annul or impair the right of property in slaves," in which case "the evil would have been intolerable." The President believed that, had the Court decided otherwise, this "sacred rights of property" would have been determined simply by elections for the territorial government. Nothing could have been worse to Buchanan than to have this fundamental "right," the "right" to possess slaves in the territories, decided by the voters.[24]

On June 26, three months later, Lincoln responded, and the arguments he used in this speech, like those he had used in his 1854 speech in response to the Kansas-Nebraska Act, would form the foundation for many of his speeches in the Lincoln-Douglas debates. The Dred Scott decision would become, second only to the Kansas-Nebraska Act, the major stimulus to the refinement of Lincoln's views on slavery. The speech also highlighted what Lincoln considered especially grievous about Taney's decision: the chief Justice's erroneous interpretation of what Lincoln considered America's cornerstone — the Declaration of Independence.

In the speech in Springfield, where two weeks earlier Douglas had spoken on a variety of subjects, including the Dred Scott decision, Lincoln admitted that he had listened to Douglas's speech and he now wished to "assail (politically, not personally)" those who shared the Senator's opinions. He denied, as some had charged, that the Republicans were somehow violently resisting the Court. Lincoln claimed that the Republicans believed in "obedience to, and respect for the judicial department of government" and that the Court's "decisions on Constitutional questions, when fully settled, should control, not only the particular cases decided, but the general policy of the country, subject to be disturbed only by amendments of the Constitution" and that any actions beyond these actions "would be revolution."

While acknowledging full respect of the court and stating that the Republicans "offer no resistance to it," Lincoln asserted, "We think the Dred Scott decision is erroneous," in part, because the Taney court had made the decision on the basis of historical facts that were wrong. Taney had declared that "negroes were no part of the people who made, or for whom was made, the Declaration of Independence, or the Constitution of the United States." Lincoln noted that Judge Benjamin R. Curtis, in his dissenting opinion, had shown that in five of the thirteen states that

1. Before '58

formed the Constitution, "free negroes were voters." The people had ordained and established the Constitution and in some states, "colored persons were among those qualified by law to act on the subject."[25]

Lincoln also took issue with Taney's declaration that the "public estimate of the black man is more favorable now than it was in the days of the Revolution." Lincoln countered that this "assumption is a mistake" and that it was "grossly incorrect to say or assume." States had withdrawn the right of suffrage for free blacks. In earlier times, "our Declaration of Independence was held sacred by all, and thought to include all; but now, to aid in making the bondage of the negro universal and eternal, it is assailed, and sneered at, and construed, and hawked at, and torn, till, if its framers could rise from their graves, they could not" recognize it at all.

Taney admitted that the Declaration was "broad enough to include the whole human family," but both Taney and Douglas also claimed that it did not include African Americans, because the founders did not "place them on equality with whites." This line of argument, Lincoln argued, was committing "obvious violence to the plain unmistakable language of the Declaration. I think the authors of that notable instrument intended to include all men, but they did not intend to declare all men equal in all respects. They did not mean to say all were equal in color, size, intellect, moral developments, or social capacity. They defined with tolerable distinctness, in what respects they did consider all men created equal — equal in 'certain inalienable rights, among which are life, liberty, and the pursuit of happiness.' This they said, and this [they] meant." Lincoln recognized that these freedoms were not currently available to all, but that did not weaken the power of the Declaration. The founders "did not mean to assert the obvious untruth, that all were then actually enjoying that equality, nor yet, that they were about to confer it immediately upon them.... They meant simply to declare the right, so that the enforcement of it might follow as fast as circumstances should permit. They meant to set up a standard maxim for free society, which should be familiar to all, and revered by all; constantly looked to, constantly labored for, and even though never perfectly attained, constantly approximated, and thereby constantly spreading and deepening its influence, and augmenting the happiness and value of life to all people of all colors everywhere." The phrase "all men are created equal" was of no use in declaring independence from Great Britain, Lincoln argued, but it was created as "a stumbling block to those who" in the future "might seek to turn a free people back into the hateful paths of despotism."

Douglas held a completely counter view, Lincoln argued. To Douglas, the Declaration applied only to the "white race," specifically "British subjects on this continent." This interpretation, Lincoln believed, made a "mere wreck — mangled ruin" of "our once glorious Declaration" by placing the "French, Germans and other white people of the world" with the "Judge's inferior races."

Lincoln devoted considerable time to two other issues: amalgamation and colonization. He refuted Douglas's charge that Republican policies would cause more racial amalgamation, presenting statistics to prove that amalgamation occurred more frequently on slave plantations than among free blacks. This issue would receive some attention from both candidates in 1858, but he mentioned another which would be, for the most part, absent: colonization. Lincoln had considered it as a possible solution to the racial issue and called on Americans to pursue it. He would continue to consider this idea until in his presidency, but would eventually drop it.[26]

Lincoln concluded with a summation of the differences between the parties. The Republicans, he claimed, considered the "negro" "a man; that his bondage is cruelly wrong, and the field of his oppression ought not be enlarged." Douglas and the Democrats, he said, reject "negro" "manhood; deny, or dwarf to insignificance, the wrong of his bondage," "crush all sympathy for him," "cultivate and excite hatred and disgust against him" and then "compliment themselves as Union-savers for doing so" by describing the extension of slavery into the territories as "a sacred right of self-government."[27]

For Lincoln, the Dred Scott decision in conjunction with Douglas's Nebraska Act also represented something more sinister. Not only were the Supreme Court's decision and Congress's legislation indicative of the nation's rejection of the Declaration of Independence, but these facts also seemed — from his perspective — to point toward a conspiracy to nationalize slavery. First, Congress nullified the Compromise of 1820 with the Nebraska Act, and then Taney weighed in from the bench to not only nullify the Compromise, but also to invalidate each state's right

1. Before '58

to prohibit slavery. The final member of the conspiracy was President Buchanan, who took office the same month the Dred Scott decision was delivered. Buchanan's administration supported the Lecompton Constitution for Kansas, which would have brought that state into the union as a slave state, cementing the change that Douglas had engineered in 1854, and validating Taney's opinion. The legislative, the judicial, and now the executive branch were all conspiring to destroy the Declaration of Independence, Lincoln concluded, and his nation could not have been in greater peril.

Lincoln, though, was mistaken. There was no conspiracy. The Lecompton controversy in Kansas revealed the vast differences between Buchanan and Douglas. Kansas pro-slavery delegates, chosen in one-sided elections, had written the Lecompton Constitution for the purpose of bringing Kansas into the union quickly, and bringing it into the union as a slave state. When the constitution was presented to Congress for acceptance, Douglas faced two choices: side with Buchanan and improve his standing with the Southern wing of the Democratic party, or oppose the President and improve his standing in the North. His final decision, to oppose the constitution, stemmed from his unshakable belief in popular sovereignty and fair elections, concepts that had not been pursued in the election of the Lecompton delegates. The Buchanan administration and many Democrats were so appalled by Douglas's opposition that some Democrats, called "Danites," opposed Douglas's reelection.

Taney's decision and Douglas's policy were also incongruous. The Chief Justice, by declaring that Congress could not legislate slavery in the territories, voided Douglas's popular sovereignty by denying the right of anyone to prevent slavery in the territories. These decisions by Douglas, Buchanan, and Taney to permit slavery's expansion had all occurred independently of each other. However, Lincoln could only view the results, and it did not require a great leap of faith to believe that a conspiracy existed, and these sequential events strengthened Lincoln's resolve to halt slavery's spread. Ironically, Lincoln would defeat Douglas in the 1860 presidential election, would succeed Buchanan as president, and would take the oath of office from Taney.[28]

Although the Lecompton Constitution conflict of 1858 was not indicative of collaboration between Buchanan and Douglas, it did bring Douglas into a mutual cause with Kentuckian John J. Crittenden, and this relationship would have dramatic consequences on the 1858 Illinois senatorial campaign. In the spring of 1858, during the political maneuverings in Congress on the Lecompton issue, Crittenden offered a substitute bill proposing that Kansans be granted another opportunity to vote on the constitution in a closely supervised election. If Kansans rejected Lecompton, they would be given an opportunity to write another one. Although Crittenden's compromise was defeated, as was the proposal to accept the Lecompton Constitution, thus leaving Kansas as a territory, Douglas and Crittenden fought side by side for the Kentuckian's bill, and Douglas gained Crittenden's respect. This respect would later pay Douglas dividends in a way he could not fully fathom at the time.[29]

That same year, with Douglas running for reelection, Lincoln had his opportunity to fight the perceived pro-slavery conspiracy of Douglas, Buchanan, and Taney, when the Illinois Republicans made an unprecedented move. For the first time in the nation's history, a state party decided to nominate a senatorial candidate before the elections. The state legislatures still chose the senators, and in all previous contests, the potential candidates waited until after the state legislators had been elected before declaring their candidacies. This time, the Republicans nominated Lincoln almost five months before election day.

There was some discussion of other candidates, but no serious opposition materialized. Lincoln had been considered the prime candidate for some time.

His moment had finally come.

2

A House Divided: Springfield, Illinois

June 16, 1858

The Illinois Republicans' uniform support for Lincoln did not alleviate all of the party's problems; the party had cracks that threatened to become permanent fissures. Consequently, in commencing his campaign against Douglas, Lincoln would have to compose a speech that would bind the dissimilar elements together. He would have to find overarching principles upon which abolitionists and conservatives could share common ground. In the end, Lincoln would fail. Although he appealed to some, he would alienate others.

The problems symptomatic of a young party were evident with Congressman Lovejoy's reelection. Lovejoy remained anathema to many Republicans, among them Davis and Dickey, who again attempted to defeat the "abolitionist." The Congressman had an advantage this time: he had a new friend. Lincoln immediately came to Lovejoy's aid when he heard of Davis's plans. On March 8, Lincoln penned a secret letter to Lovejoy, the man he had once opposed: "I have just returned from court in one of the counties of your District, where I had an inside view that few will have who correspond with you; and I feel it rather a duty to say a word to you about it." Lincoln warned that there was a danger that "some republican" would "run against you without a nomination, relying mainly on democratic votes. I have seen the strong men who could make the most trouble in that way." While Lincoln believed that those men would not "consent to be so used," he feared that they had "been urgently tempted by the enemy; and I think it is still the point for you to guard most vigilantly. I think it is not expected that you can be beaten for a nomination; but do not let what I say, as to that, lull you." He ended with the request that "this be strictly confidential; not that there is anything wrong in it; but that I have some highly valued friends who would not like me any the better for writing it." Lincoln also wrote a brief postscript: "Be glad to hear from you."[1] Ignorant of Lincoln's support for Lovejoy, Davis offered himself as a candidate. Fervently, the conservative Republicans lobbied the delegates to the nomination convention to drop their support of Lovejoy and rally behind Davis. They failed. The majority of delegates remained committed to Lovejoy just as they had been two years before.

Some Republicans were still unwilling to surrender, and concocted a plan to run an independent candidate against Lovejoy. Lincoln had enough, and he publicly intervened. To one of those who had been working with Davis and Dickey, Lincoln requested that all opposition efforts cease: "Two or three days ago I learned that McLean [County] had appointed delegates in favor of Lovejoy, and thenceforward I have considered his re-nomination a fixed fact. My opinion — if my opinion is of any consequence in this case, in which it is no business of mine to interfere — remains unchanged that running an independent candidate against Lovejoy, will not do — that it will result in nothing but disaster all round. In the first place whoever so runs will be beaten, and will be spotted for life; in the second place, while the race is in progress, he will be under the strongest temptation to trade with the democrats, and to favor the election of certain of their friends to the Legislature; thirdly, I shall be held responsible for it, and Republican members of the Legislature, who are partial to Lovejoy, will, for that, oppose me; and lastly it will in the end lose us the District altogether."[2] Lincoln concluded his advice by reminding this fellow Republican that, in his opinion, while Lovejoy had "been known as an abolitionist," he was now "occupying none but common ground." This was persuasive; the conservative Republicans yielded. Congressman Lovejoy was unanimously renominated at the Third Congressional District Convention on June 30.

Lovejoy knew his reputation posed a danger to the Republicans, so in his acceptance speech he avoided abolitionist statements. He knew it was wise for him, for Lincoln, and for his party, to appear more moderate by distancing himself from those calling for immediate abolition:

2. A House Divided

"For myself, I hate slavery with a deathless and earnest hatred, and would like to see it exterminated, as some time by some means it must be. But because I thus feel towards slavery, it does not follow that I shall seek its extermination in unjustifiable modes. It does not follow that because I am opposed to monarchy that therefore I should be in favor of fitting out a naval armament to dethrone Queen Victoria. I am content to fight slavery in modes pointed out in the Constitution, and in those modes only."

He also declared his unqualified support for Lincoln: "It is asked if I am for Lincoln. My reply is that the Republican Party was not organized for the benefit of any man — it was not made for Lincoln or Lovejoy, or any one else, but it was organized for the purpose of giving political efficiency to those principles of freedom with which, in theory, our government is distinct, but which have of late in its administration been crucified. I am no hero worshipper. And now I am prepared to say that I am for Lincoln, not because he is an old line Whig — to me this is no objection and it is no commendation — but I am for him because he is a true hearted man, and that, come what will, unterrified by power, unseduced by ambition, he will remain true to the great principles upon which the Republican party is organized."[3]

These statements failed to mollify all Republicans. Judge T. Lyle Dickey remained furious that Lovejoy had prevailed, but he had little time to calm himself. Another speech would soon cause him to erupt in anger. This time, it would not be an individual whom he had long opposed, but one he had called his friend.

When composing the "House Divided" speech, Lincoln unchained himself. No longer beholden to any party leader as he had been in 1856, he now wrote freely and honestly, as a party leader himself. This was a Lincoln more like Lovejoy than Davis, more like a statesman than a politician. He spoke to no one before, or while, writing it. This was his opportunity to point out from his perspective how wrong his nation's course had become under such leaders as Douglas.

When the speech was completed, Lincoln shared it with several Republicans, none of whom approved. All expressed disappointment and condemnation; it was far too radical to them. Herndon, Lincoln's law partner, who professed a hatred of slavery but who also voted in 1848 to keep free "negroes" out of Illinois, admitted that Lincoln's statements were "true" but, he added, "is it wise or politic to say so?" One Republican declared it a "d — d fool utterance," while a more diplomatic individual described it as "ahead of its time." Lincoln patiently listened to the advice, but made no changes.[4]

On Wednesday, June 16, 1858, before a packed crowd in the Representatives Hall of the Illinois State Capitol, Lincoln delivered his "House Divided" speech. Initially, casting aside the chains of the day's political exigencies and rising above the political fray, Lincoln framed the issue dispassionately. Step by step, as was his style, he presented the salient facts of the emotional slavery issue. It was as though he was issuing a call to the conscience of the nation, reminding those within the Hall and those who would hear of his speech later that this nation, since its founding, had been placed on a course that would inevitably lead to slavery's end:

> "A house divided against itself cannot stand."
> I believe this government cannot endure, permanently half slave and half free.
> I do not expect the Union to be dissolved — I do not expect the house to fall — but I do expect it will cease to be divided.
> It will become all one thing, or all the other.
> Either the opponents of slavery, will arrest the further spread of it, and place it where the public mind shall rest in the belief that it is in course of ultimate extinction; or its advocates will push it forward till it shall become alike lawful in all the States, old as well as new — North as well as South.
> Have we no tendency toward the latter condition?

The reaction to Lincoln's statements would be far from unanimous. The abolitionists and all those who called for slavery's eventual demise would overwhelmingly applaud these statements. To those who feared living near free African Americans, to those who believed that the white race should be superior to the black race, to those who believed that Douglas's fundamental error was in just allowing slavery into the territories, these sentences were appalling. The Democrats had consistently attempted to portray the Republicans as radical abolitionists. On numerous fronts, the Republicans almost seemed determined to prove this allegation. Certainly, Lovejoy's presence in the party supported the fears

2. A House Divided

that the Republicans were becoming an abolitionist party. Likewise, William H. Seward, a Republican senator, played into the Democrats' hands by declaring in his "Higher Law" speech that Americans should hold allegiance to God above the Constitution. Lincoln's statements, in his "House Divided" speech, appeared in the same vein as these abolitionists. These conclusions were the same ones that Lincoln's advisors had so vehemently opposed.

These opening lines were also a direct affront to those Americans, like Dickey, who believed that the nation could continue half-free and half-slave, a belief that Lincoln did not share. Lincoln's remarks accurately defined his perception of the America of 1858. There was no middle ground — either one was aligned with the forces that intended to make slavery extinct, or one supported those who intended to make slavery national. Lincoln's opening lines fit perfectly with his stark definitions of politician and statesman that he would articulate at the last debate. At Alton, he would label those who sought slavery's extinction as statesmen and those who did not as politicians. One was either for the nationalization of slavery or for the ultimate extinction of slavery. One was either a politician or a statesman.

Lincoln argued that the nation, since its founding, had been placed on a course that would inevitably lead to slavery's end. Up to 1854, slavery was "excluded from more than half the States by State Constitutions, and from most of the national territory by Congressional prohibition," but Douglas's Nebraska Act had diverted the nation's course and "opened all the national territory to slavery."

To Lincoln, Douglas's Act attacked the twin pillars of the nation's philosophical and political underpinning, repudiating the African American birthright in the Declaration of Independence and invalidating that section of the Constitution that had codified this high principle. The new Act insured that "no negro slave, imported as such from Africa, and no descendant of such slave can ever be a citizen of any State, in the sense of that term as used in the Constitution of the United States."

Furthermore, Douglas had stripped from Congress and the territorial legislatures the power to "exclude slavery from any United States territory." Nothing now stood in slavery's path. It could spread unfettered throughout the nation, ensuring that "individual men may fill up the territories with slaves, without danger of losing them as property, and thus to enhance the chances of permanency to the institution through all the future."

Lincoln argued that Douglas was not solely responsible for these developments, that a conspiracy to nationalize slavery had developed. The Supreme Court was another participant in this grand scheme: Chief Justice Taney, in the Dred Scott case, and the separate opinions of all the concurring judges, expressly declared that the Constitution of the United States neither permits Congress or a territorial legislature from excluding slavery from any United States territory. Through the Court's decision and Douglas's legislation, the nation's fate had been sealed. Lincoln then brought the matter home to Illinois: "Welcome or unwelcome, such decision is probably coming, and will soon be upon us, unless the power of the present political dynasty shall be met and overthrown. We shall lie down pleasantly dreaming that the people of Missouri are on the verge of making their State free; and we shall awake to the reality, instead, that the Supreme Court has made Illinois a slave State."

Lincoln, having made his case that the nation's future was endangered, that it must revert to its pre-1854 condition, then asked: "But how can we best do it?" Some antislavery individuals, including some Republicans, believed that Douglas had shown recent signs of change, that he could undo the damage, that he was opposed to slavery's spread. Lincoln disagreed: "How can he oppose the advances of slavery? He don't care anything about it. His avowed mission is impressing the 'public heart' to care nothing about it."

Lincoln concluded with a firm conviction that slavery could be defeated if the Republicans stood united: "Two years ago the Republicans of the nation mustered over thirteen hundred thousand strong. We did this under the single impulse of resistance to a common danger, with every external circumstance against us. Of strange, discordant, and even, hostile elements, we gathered from the four winds, and formed and fought the battle through, under the constant hot fire of a disciplined, proud, and pampered enemy. Did we brave all then, to falter now?—now—when that same enemy is wavering, dissevered and belligerent? This result is not doubtful. We shall not fail—if we stand firm, we shall not fail. Wise counsels may accelerate or mistakes delay it, but, sooner or later the victory is sure to come."[5]

2. A House Divided

Lincoln gave the three thousand word speech with no notes before him and the audience responded with thunderous applause.

The speech would backfire on him in ways he could never imagine.

Lincoln must have been stunned. For all the careful planning, research and preparation that he had given his "House Divided" speech, his moment of triumph rapidly faded as he found himself in the unexpected position of having to explain what he considered self-evident.

Some people interpreted his statements as a declaration that he and his party intended to make the nation all free, by whatever means necessary. Seward, a prominent Republican with an abolitionist reputation, had declared in his "Higher Law" speech that there existed a "higher law than the Constitution"—a moral law established by "the Creator of the universe"—and that slavery was doomed. To some, Lincoln's speech was a continuation of Seward's, despite Lincoln's attempt to appear less radical and less abolitionist.

To one person who asked for a clarification, Lincoln, with some frustration, wrote back: "I am much flattered by the estimate you place on my late speech; and yet I am much mortified that any part of it should be construed so differently from any thing intended by me. The language, 'place it where the public mind shall rest in the belief that it is in course of ultimate extinction,' I used deliberately, not dreaming then, nor believing now, that it asserts, or intimates, any power or purpose, to interfere with slavery in the States where it exists. I believe that whenever the effort to spread slavery into the new territories, by whatever means, and into the free states themselves, by Supreme court decisions, shall be fairly headed off, the institution will then be in course of ultimate extinction; and by the language used I meant only this. I have declared a thousand times, and now repeat that, in my opinion, neither the General Government, nor any other power outside of the slave states, can constitutionally or rightfully interfere with slaves or slavery where it already exists.[6]

None of Lincoln's letters provide insight as to whether he considered the "House Divided" speech a success or a failure, but the debates offer some evidence. Douglas considered the speech great material for attacks on Lincoln, and referred to it often. Lincoln, on the other hand, mentioned it rarely, only choosing to debate it at those times when Douglas had attacked it.

The "House Divided" speech had other unexpected ramifications for Lincoln, in terms of its effect on one man: Judge Dickey. Dickey's hatred of Lincoln's opening lines was both political and personal. He considered the phrases too radical, and believed that they would alienate more moderate voters, especially former Whigs. He also harbored a distinct hatred of abolitionists and considered any suggestion that the nation would eventually be free of slavery to be an abolitionist dream. And finally, he believed these statements would only result in the disunion of his nation.

When Lincoln discussed this idea with Dickey two years before, the judge had argued him out of using it again. Dickey recalled, "We shook hands upon it" and "the subject was dropped." From 1856 on, Dickey "heard no more of this time [type] of thought from Mr Lincoln until the year of 1858 — when he proclaimed it in his famous Speech at Springfield — at the Opening of that year's Canvass." This time, as before, the shock of Lincoln's speech prompted Dickey into action. He joined Douglas's campaign, appeared with him at numerous sites in Illinois, and, most critically, he wrote to Senator John J. Crittenden of Kentucky, requesting that he endorse Douglas.[7]

Dickey, as a former Whig, knew that, above all, the Whigs still adored former Senator Henry Clay of Kentucky. After Clay's death, Crittenden came closest to holding the great American's mantle. Dickey knew that a letter of endorsement from the Kentucky senator would greatly assist Douglas in capturing central Illinois.

Lincoln was surprised and concerned. His former friend had not only abandoned him and the Republicans, but he was now actively assisting the opposition. The idea that Crittenden might pen a letter endorsing Douglas was especially devastating. Upon receiving the news, Lincoln immediately wrote to the Kentucky senator and, in a rare instance in all his writing, he made use of an exclamation mark:

2. A House Divided

I beg you will pardon me for the liberty in addressing you upon only so limited an acquaintance, and that acquaintance so long past. I am prompted to do so by a story being whispered about here that you are anxious for the reelection of Mr. Douglas to the United States Senate, and also of Harris, of our district, to the House of Representatives, and that you are pledged to write letters to that effect to your friends here in Illinois, if requested. I do not believe the story, but still it gives me some uneasiness. If such was your inclination, I do not believe you would so express yourself. It is not in character with you as I have always estimated you.

You have no warmer friends than here in Illinois, and I assure you nine tenths—I believe ninety-nine hundredths—of them would be mortified exceedingly by anything of the sort from you. When I tell you this, make such allowance as you think just for my position, which, I doubt not, you understand. Nor am I fishing for a letter on the other side. Even if such could be had, my judgment is that you would better be hands off!

Please drop me a line; and if your purposes are as I hope they are not, please let me know. The confirmation would pain me much, but I should still continue your friend and admirer.[8]

Three weeks later, Crittenden wrote back. The Senator apologized for not having responded sooner, but he claimed to have only received Lincoln's letter "a few days" before. He admitted that their acquaintance was "still freshly remembered" and that he had "retained" toward Lincoln "favorable sentiments of personal regard" and "respect." While Lincoln had been "frank" with him, he believed that he should also respond with "frankness."

Crittenden acknowledged that he and Douglas had "always belonged to different parties, opposed, in politics, to each other" but "at the last session of Congress" they "concurred" and "acted together in opposing the enforcement of the Lecompton Constitution upon the people of Kansas." The Kentucky senator considered the constitution "a gross violation of principle and good faith, and fraught with danger to the country." Douglas's "opposition to it was highly gratifying to me" and the "position taken by him, was full of sacrafice [sic]" and "full of hazard." Douglas had defended his position "like a Man":

For this he had my warm approbation and sympathy — and, when it was understood, that, for the very course of conduct, in which I had concurred & participated, the angry power of the Administration & its party was to be employed to defeat his re-election to the Senate, in Illinois, I could not but wish for his success—and his triumph over such a persecution—I thought that his re-election was necessary as a rebuke to the Administration, and a vindication of the great cause of popular rights & public justice.[9]

Crittenden claimed that his "present feelings in regard" to Douglas occurred "naturally" and "spontaneously." They "were entirely unconnected with mere party calculations and most certainly, did not include a single particle of personal unkindness or opposition to" Lincoln. Crittenden had "openly" and "ardently" expressed his respect for Douglas "in many conversations, at Washington and elsewhere" and confessed that he still adhered to it, but he was somewhat vague concerning his correspondence on the issue. He had "not written a single letter to any person in Illinois" since "the adjournment of Congress" and had only written "three or four" before. "But I have now on my table several letters from citizens of your State" and "I could not forbear replying without subjecting myself to imputations of insincerity or timidity.... As to the future, Sir, I can not undertake to promise or to impose any restriction upon my conduct.... But this I can truly say to you, that I have no disposition for officious intermeddling—and that I should be extremely sorry to give offence or cause mortification to you or any of my Illinois friends—Whatever my future course may be, I trust that I shall so act as to give no just cause of offence to any candid & liberal friend, even tho' he may differ with me in opinion."[10]

Lincoln could take little solace from this letter. Crittenden refused to confirm whether he had received a letter from, or whether he would write to, Judge Dickey.

The disturbing news was spreading throughout Illinois, and reached Lovejoy four days after Lincoln received Crittenden's letter, and the Congressman immediately wrote to Lincoln. Lovejoy wanted to know whether the rumor was true: was Crittenden "exerting" his influence for Douglas? He attempted to be upbeat by complimenting Lincoln—"I think you said the whole in a word when you said that the mistake of Judge D. was that he made slavery a little thing when it was a great thing"—and expressing his support ("Yours for the ultimate extinction of slavery"), but his main concern was Crittenden. Lovejoy well knew that the Kentucky senator could have a decisive impact on the election.[11]

Dickey then delivered Lincoln's campaign another blow. The *Chicago Times* published a long letter written by Dickey in which he explained his reasoning for supporting Douglas. Dickey recalled that, thirty years before, the people of the slave states were "devising plans" to "gradually and without violence rid themselves of the then conceded evil of slavery." However, the "slavery agitation" began and rendered the "subject of emancipation at once unpalatable and unsafe to the whole South. This was Abolitionism. The only fruit it ever bore was vile sectional hatred and slavery propagandism." The "element of contention" between the slavery "propagandism" and the abolitionists "annihilated the old Whig party and totally metamorphosed the old Democratic party," conservatism was "neutralized," and "The ultras ruled and held control, North and South, in both great political parties...."

In this atmosphere, Dickey said, the Lecompton Constitution was brought forward by the "Southern extremists of the Democratic party ... to force upon the people of Kansas a slavery constitution against their will." Douglas "had the sagacity to see the dangers of the measure proposed — the courage to stand up for the sentiment of Illinois, and withstand the wrong — and the ability in the very heat of the action, to roll back the tide of ultraism in his own party...." The Illinois senator did not stand alone, Dickey asserted: "A powerful body of Union-loving men from the South, under the lead of that long-tried and distinguished patriot, John J. Crittenden, of Kentucky, took position by the side of our Senator...."

While Dickey acknowledged that the Republicans in Congress had aided in this effort, he emphatically declared that "the Republican party of Illinois, unfortunately, has passed into the control of the old Abolition party." Douglas represented the "conservatism of the country" and any opposition to him "sustains, fosters, and gives strength to the propagandism in the nation, and radical revolutionary abolitionism at home."

Dickey concluded with a plea for moderation. He hoped that "there shall be in the councils of the nation men from the free States of such moderation and wisdom, of such fidelity and fraternity, that by their kindness and prudence the asperities of the conflict may soon be worn away and peace and confidence restored everywhere." The Judge feared that "in some of the older States, both North and South, the spirit of kindness and fraternity which once glowed so brightly is already too far gone to make it safe to lean upon in such a crisis." He ended the letter expressing his desire that "we may all be guided in that way which shall best subserve the peace, union and happiness of this great nation."[12]

However, Dickey made several unexpected omissions in his entire letter. Not only did he fail to mention the "House Divided" speech, but he also failed to mention Lincoln. This omission exemplifies the sincere respect with which Lincoln was held by Dickey. The Judge supported Douglas, but he would not write one ill word against his friend.

There was also another particular omission in Dickey's letter: a discussion of the immorality of slavery. Except for one passing reference to the "evil of slavery," the Judge made no other attack on the institution and made no mention of the Declaration of Independence. In this respect, Dickey exemplified Lincoln's definition of a politician. The Judge did not want to discuss the very thing that Lincoln believed everyone should be discussing. While Lincoln foresaw two possibilities, a nation all free or a nation all slave, Dickey believed that the two sections could continue divided.

And finally, there is the last and most vital omission: Dickey refused to state whether he had received a letter from Crittenden. But despite any public confirmation, Dickey did receive a response from the Kentucky senator, and he handled the letter with political savvy. He allowed rumors to spread, but he kept the endorsement private. He would wait until a week before the election, and then drop the bomb. The Republicans would not have time to respond.

Lincoln would not fully know until a week before election day just how damaging his "House Divided" speech had been.

From a political perspective, the "House Divided" speech was not a success, but from the perspective of a statesman, it was. Lincoln continually attempted to clarify his statement as a mere prediction, not a blueprint for future action. However, his contemporaries recognized that of the two futures — a nation all slave or a nation all free — one was clearly more favorable to him than the other. At a time when all forces were moving to make slavery legal, not only in the territories, but nationally, it required some courage to envision a nation where slavery no longer existed at all, which was precisely the idea that Lincoln captured

2. A House Divided

in the opening lines of his speech. The Congress, the President, and the Supreme Court were all aligned to permit slavery's expansion, the majority of the Democrats and many Republicans opposed the end of slavery, and Lincoln spoke, like the abolitionists, of a future time when slavery could be extinguished — everywhere and forever, although he never professed the manner by which that could occur. While the speech was, in most respects, a political failure, from the perspective of a statesman, as Lincoln defined the word, it was a gem.

3

The Campaign Begins: Chicago, Illinois

July 9–10, 1858

The senatorial campaign had officially begun on June 16 with Lincoln's "House Divided" speech. Just a little over three weeks later, on July 9, Douglas launched his campaign with a speech in Chicago, and Lincoln responded the following day.

For the two candidates, it was no simple task to develop a cohesive campaign strategy, because Illinois was not a monolithic entity. It resembled America in microcosm, especially in its political complexities, a fact that Lincoln had confirmed when he studied the 1856 election returns. New Englanders and European immigrants traveling along the canal system and through the Great Lakes had primarily settled Northern Illinois. These immigrants had given Frémont strong support in 1856, and Lincoln could be confident that they would support him now, or, as he wrote, "We take to ourselves, without question." Southern Illinois, settled by Kentuckians and other southerners, had overwhelmingly supported President James Buchanan, the Democratic candidate, two years before, leaving little hope for the Republicans. Lincoln summed up his chances in this area, "We give up these districts."[1]

That left nineteen districts—the central Illinois districts, former Whig districts populated with followers of Henry Clay—that would determine the next senator. The candidates, when making their speeches, could either modify their statements to conform to the voters' sensibilities in each region, or they could develop a statewide strategy that they would follow throughout the campaign regardless of whether they were addressing a crowd in northern or southern Illinois.

The candidates' first test of their campaign strategy occurred in Chicago, and it was appropriate that they first dueled there. Cook County was already the most populous county in the state, Chicago was Douglas's hometown, and it was in Chicago that Douglas first attempted to defend his Kansas-Nebraska Act in 1854, and where he had been heckled and jeered for so trying.

Chicago, though, as Lincoln had determined, was Republican country. The 2nd Congressional District included seven northern counties stretching from Cook County on the shores of Lake Michigan to Rock Island County on the banks of the Mississippi. In the 1856 congressional election, the Republican candidate garnered sixty-one percent of the vote for the entire district and fifty-four percent in Cook County. Lincoln could freely express his hatred of slavery in this region without fear of displeasing the voters, while Douglas would be under more pressure to modify his comments to conform to the pro–Republican voters.[2]

For Lincoln's conservative supporters, this speech was of great concern. The advisors who had expressed caution and reservation over his "House Divided" speech, and others, such as Davis, who advocated a more conservative position on the issues pertaining to African Americans, must have hoped that the resulting backlash from Lincoln's Springfield remarks would have made their candidate more cautious. If this was their hope, they were disappointed. In the "House Divided" speech, Lincoln had avoided direct mention of the Declaration of Independence, and its application to African Americans. He would not avoid it in Chicago. In Illinois' great city, he would boldly speak of the universality of "all men are created equal." This speech marked a change in strategy for Lincoln, as he appeared to be more accepting of Lovejoy's philosophy and that of the radical wing of the Republican party. This speech was all Lincoln the statesman.

These two speeches in Chicago were of such significance to both candidates that, when later determining locations for the debate sites, they both agreed that a debate was not necessary in this Congressional District since they both considered their speeches equal to a debate. Both candidates would speak from one of Chicago's finest hotels: the Tremont House.

However, the Democrats hoped they would persuade voters of

3. The Campaign Begins

Douglas's dominance not only by his speech in Chicago, but also by Douglas's procession into Chicago. While en route from Toledo, Ohio, he surprisingly stopped at La Porte, Indiana, instead of continuing on to his final destination. From there, by horse and buggy, he traveled to Michigan City. The Republican *Chicago Press and Tribune* claimed that he abandoned the Michigan Southern railroad at La Porte because "he did not like to land at so shabby a depot [in Chicago], and so far from the 'spontaneous' Tremont House. The effect would be better if he landed at the Grand Central Depot. So his friends say."[3]

The pro–Democrat *Chicago Times* estimated that four hundred people traveled on the train from Chicago to meet Douglas at Michigan City. As the train arrived, the Senator's supporters intended to greet it with a cannon but "some malicious person" had "secretly spiked the only gun" in town so the Democrats "obtained a large anvil, and placing it in the middle of the street, made the welkin [heavens] echo." Along the way "at every station, at almost every farmhouse and laborer's cabin — in every cornfield and at every point where laborers were engaged — there was exhibited by cheers, by waving of handkerchiefs and other demonstrations, that cordial 'welcome home' to the great representative of popular rights":

> As the train passed along the Twelfth street to the depot, crowds of ladies were assembled on the doorsteps of the residences on Michigan avenue, waving banners and handkerchiefs; the lake part was crowded by persons hastily proceeding to the depot. Long before the train could enter the station house, thousands had crossed over the breakwater, got upon the track, and climbed into the cars, and when the latter reached the depot they were literally crammed inside and covered on top by ardent and enthusiastic friends and supporters of the illustrious Illinoisan.

One hundred and fifty cannons fired, hotels, residencies, warehouses were covered with flags and crowded with people. A banner that declared "Douglas, the champion of Popular Sovereignty" was hung above the street. In all, according to the *Times*, it presented a "grand display."

Douglas traveled in an open carriage pulled by six horses escorted by a large procession including "a band of music, and two companies of militia." As the Senator approached the Tremont House, all the planning had clearly paid off. By all reports, it was a massive crowd:

The Lincoln-Douglas Debates and the Making of a President

Chicago has never before witnessed such a sight. A field of human forms parted with difficulty as the procession passed through, and closed instantly behind it, with the surge and roar of the waters of a sea; an ocean of upturned faces, extending beyond the farthest limits to which the senator's powerful voice could reach, from which broke one spontaneous burst of applause as he appeared upon the balcony before them![4]

The *Times* claimed that "over all the light of the illumination, and the glare and glitter of the fireworks, spread an appearance which is indescribable!"

In his Chicago speech, Douglas countered many of the assertions that Lincoln had made in his "House Divided" speech and in so doing he provided some indication as to what would become the central issues over which the two candidates would argue during the seven debates. He defended his actions in defeating the Lecompton Constitution, praised the Kansas-Nebraska Act as the epitome of popular sovereignty, attacked for the first time the opening lines of Lincoln's "House Divided" speech, and criticized Lincoln's opposition to the Dred Scott decision with a subtle rejection of Lincoln's interpretation of the Declaration of Independence.[5]

Douglas commenced his speech with a defense of what he considered a popular topic: his leadership in opposing the Lecompton Constitution. When he discovered an effort in Congress to "force a constitution upon the people of Kansas against their will, and to force that state into the Union with a constitution which her people had rejected by more than 10,000" voters, Douglas "felt bound as a man of honor and a representative of Illinois, bound by every consideration of duty, of fidelity, and of patriotism, to resist to the utmost of my power the consummation of that fraud. With others," he claimed, he "did resist it, and resisted it successfully until the attempt was abandoned. We forced them to refer that constitution back to the people of Kansas, to be accepted or rejected as they shall decide at an election." This was a great victory for popular sovereignty, Douglas asserted. He regarded the "Lecompton battle as having been fought and the victory won, because the arrogant demand for the admission of Kansas under the Lecompton constitution unconditionally, whether her people wanted it or not, has been abandoned, and the principle which recognizes the right of the people to decide for themselves has been submitted to its place."

3. The Campaign Begins

Douglas did admit that he was not alone in achieving this victory. The credit for this "great moral victory is to be divided among a large number of men of various and different political creeds." He had "rejoiced" when he "found in this great contest the Republican party coming up manfully and sustaining the principle that the people of each territory, when coming into the Union, have the right to decide for themselves whether slavery shall or shall not exist within their limits." Douglas knew better than this. His assertion was false, or rather a half-truth. Many Republicans had not opposed the Lecompton constitution out of a strict adherence to Douglas's popular sovereignty, but because the constitution would have brought Kansas into the union as a slave state.

Douglas then defended the Kansas-Nebraska Act which had initiated the controversy of which the Lecompton constitution had been a result. He considered the Act a "great principle of popular sovereignty as having been vindicated and made triumphant in this land as a permanent rule of public policy in the organization of territories and the admission of new states." Illinois had already given its approval when in 1851 the Illinois House of Representatives had approved a resolution in favor of popular sovereignty, a resolution that declared "the great principle of self-government as applicable to the territories and new states, passed the House of Representatives of this state by a vote of sixty-one in the affirmative, to only four in the negative." Douglas considered this "an expression of public opinion, enlightened, educated, intelligent public opinion" that approached "nearer to unanimity than has ever been obtained on any controverted question."

Precedent had been set for popular sovereignty before he introduced his controversial act, he contended. The public and the state legislature had already accepted the concept, so "when it became necessary to bring forward a bill for the organization of the territories of Kansas and Nebraska" he asked, "Was it not my duty, in obedience to the Illinois platform, to your standing instructions to your Senators, adopted with almost entire unanimity, to incorporate in that bill the great principle of self-government, declaring that it was 'the true intent and meaning of the act not to legislate slavery into any state or territory, or to exclude it therefrom, but to leave the people thereof perfectly free to form and regulate their domestic institutions in their own way, subject only to the Constitution of the United States?'" He had simply incorporated a publicly approved "principle in the Kansas-Nebraska Bill, and perhaps I did as much as any living man in the enactment of that bill, thus establishing the doctrine in the public policy of the country." The Senator "then defended that principle against the assaults from one section of the Union" and "during this last winter" he had "to vindicate it against the assaults from the other section of the Union. I vindicated it boldly and fearlessly, as the people of Chicago can bear witness, when it was assailed by Freesoilers." He pledged to "vindicate the principle of the right of the people to form their own institutions, to establish free states or slave states as they chose, and that that principle should never be violated either by fraud, by violence, by circumvention, or by any other means, if it was in my power to prevent it." Douglas's sole "object was to secure the right of the people of each state and of each territory, North or South, to decide the question for themselves, to have slavery or not, just as they chose" and he reiterated that his "opposition to the Lecompton constitution was not predicated upon the ground that it was a pro-slavery constitution" or would his action have been any different had the Kansans been forced to accept an undemocratic "free-soil constitution."

Douglas targeted President Buchanan and the many southern congressmen and senators who had supported the Lecompton Constitution. He denied the "right of Congress to force a slave-holding state upon an unwilling people," denied "the right to force a free state upon an unwilling people," and denied "their right to force a good thing upon a people who are unwilling to receive it. The great principle is the right of every community to judge and decide for itself, whether a thing is right or wrong, whether it would be good or evil for them to adopt it; and the right of free action, the right of free thought, the right of free judgment upon the question is dearer to every true American than any other under a free government." His "objection to the Lecompton contrivance" was undertaken because the President and the Congress were attempting to "put a constitution on the people of Kansas against their will, in opposition to their wishes, and thus violated the great principle upon which all our institutions rest."

Douglas also mentioned a speech to which he would refer throughout the campaign, not because he was impressed with the oratory, but because he knew that Lincoln had used language that most people, especially the vital former Whig voters, would associate with abolitionists.

3. The Campaign Begins

He noted that the Republicans had assembled in Springfield and nominated a candidate for the United States Senate. He first, though, took time to compliment his opponent. He claimed to "take great pleasure in saying that I have known, personally and intimately, for about a quarter of a century, the worthy gentleman who has been nominated for my place, and I will say that I regard him as a kind, amiable, and intelligent gentleman, a good citizen and an honorable opponent; and whatever issue I may have with him will be of principle, and not involving personalities." However, it was a gesture that Lincoln would never return. Apparently, Douglas's actions, such as his Kansas-Nebraska bill, so upset Lincoln that he could not bring himself to speak with the same complimentary language of his opponent as Douglas did of him.

The "House Divided" speech was the topic Douglas chose for his first attack against Lincoln. By using the speech as his first topic on which to assail Lincoln, Douglas indicated the high value that he placed on Lincoln's remarks for propelling his campaign, and for damaging Lincoln's campaign. He believed that Lincoln's "House Divided" speech had been "evidently well prepared and carefully written" and that Lincoln had put forth "two distinct propositions," upon which Douglas intended to "take a direct and bold issue with him." The Senator stated that Lincoln's "first and main proposition," which he agreed to quote in Lincoln's own language, and with "his exact language" was the opening: "'A house divided against itself cannot stand.' I believe this government cannot endure, permanently, half slave and half free. I do not expect the Union to be dissolved. I do not expect the house to fall; but I do expect it to cease to be divided. It will become all one thing or all the other." The Senator belligerently interpreted that phrase, claiming that in these words his opponent advocated "boldly and clearly a war of sections, a war of the North against the South, of the free states against the slave states — a war of extermination — to be continued relentlessly until the one or the other shall be subdued and all the states shall either become free or become slave."

Douglas argued that Lincoln's desire to have the South conform to the North violated American principle and precedent. It was "neither desirable nor possible," he said, "that there should be uniformity in the local institutions and domestic regulations of the different states of the Union." The Constitution's framers had not intended this conformity, knowing "that each locality, having separate and distinct interests, required separate and distinct laws, domestic institutions, and police regulations adapted to its own wants and its own condition." Therefore, Lincoln had "totally misapprehended the great principles upon which our government rests," Douglas believed, and further, "Uniformity in local and domestic affairs would be destructive of state rights, of state sovereignty, of personal liberty and personal freedom. Uniformity is the parent of despotism the world over."

He turned the attack on the "House Divided" speech into a defense of popular sovereignty. In order to "maintain our liberties," Douglas asserted, "we must preserve the rights and sovereignty of the states, we must maintain and carry out that great principle of self-government incorporated in the compromise measures of 1850: endorsed by the Illinois legislature in 1851; emphatically embodied and carried out in the Kansas-Nebraska Bill, and vindicated this year by the refusal to bring Kansas into the Union with a constitution distasteful to her people."

Douglas switched his focus to Lincoln's "other proposition," his "crusade against the Supreme Court of the United States on account of the Dred Scott decision." Douglas defended the Dred Scott decision on two points. First, he expressed his support for the decision, not specifically on the merits of the case, which may have led him to contradict popular sovereignty, but rather because he held the institution of the Supreme Court in high esteem. He respected the "decisions of that august tribunal" and would "always bow in deference to them" because he was a "law-abiding man" and would "sustain the Constitution of my country as our fathers have made it." Douglas promised to "yield obedience to the laws" whether he supported them or not. He would sustain "the judicial tribunals and constituted authorities in all matters within the pale of their jurisdiction as defined by the Constitution."

He also defended the Dred Scott decision by arguing that the "negro" had no guaranteed rights, an issue that would prove critical throughout the campaign. In his opinion, the government was "founded on the white basis" and "was made by the white man, for the benefit of the white man, to be administered by white men, in such manner as they should determine." This argument obviously refuted Lincoln's position that African Americans were included in the Declaration of Independence.[6]

Lincoln had been present and heard the entire speech. He prepared

3. The Campaign Begins

to respond to Douglas the following day. At this stage in the campaign, Lincoln had one advantage and one disadvantage in terms of following Douglas's remarks. He had the advantage of listening to the Senator's arguments and then countering them with a subsequent speech, but the renowned senator attracted far larger crowds, which gave Douglas the opportunity to persuade more voters. Douglas's larger audiences also gave the perception that Douglas was the more popular candidate.

As opposed to the celebratory atmosphere that greeted Douglas, that around Lincoln was far more subtle. There was no great procession, no cannons or fireworks. People did crowd the windows, balconies and streets around the Tremont House, but even the Republican *Press and Tribune* had to admit that the audience was "in point of numbers about three-fourths as large as that of the previous evening."[7]

To open his remarks on the following day, July 10, Lincoln noted that "yesterday evening" at the Senator's reception he had been "furnished with a seat very convenient" to hearing him, and was "very courteously treated by him and his friends, and for which I thank him and them." But these were Lincoln's last amiable comments about his opponent.

Lincoln attacked popular sovereignty. Referring to the Declaration of Independence, he questioned Douglas's claims concerning the Lecompton Constitution's defeat. He then defended the "House Divided" speech, assailed slavery in regard to the phrase "all men are created equal," and reiterated his belief in the conspiracy to make slavery national. He first attacked Douglas's proposition that his popular sovereignty was a new principle. Lincoln questioned whether the "right of the people to form a State Constitution as they please, to form it with Slavery or without Slavery" was "anything new, I confess I don't know it. Has there ever been a time when anybody said that any other than the people of a Territory itself should form a Constitution?" He quoted from the Declaration of Independence — "We hold these truths to be self-evident that all men are created equal; that they are endowed by their Creator with certain inalienable rights; that among these are life, liberty, and the pursuit of happiness" — to substantiate that in order to "secure these rights, governments are instituted among men, deriving their just powers from the consent of the governed." In those words, Lincoln insisted, one could find the "origin of Popular Sovereignty." He asked, "Who, then, shall come in at this day and claim that he invented it?"

Lincoln took special exception to Douglas's comments regarding the defeat of the Lecompton Constitution. He agreed that Douglas was right to oppose it, but he believed the Senator had failed to tell the whole story of its defeat. The Senator was not alone in fighting it, "all the Republicans in the nation opposed it, and they would have opposed it just as much without Judge Douglas' aid, as with it. They had all taken ground against it long before he did."

Lincoln also disagreed with Douglas's assertion as to who actually defeated that constitution, pointing out that, in fact, the Republicans were primarily responsible for the defeat of the constitution. He admitted that the defeat was a "good thing"; however, Douglas and the other Democrats in the Senate who opposed it cast only "three votes" against, while "the Republicans furnished twenty." In the House of Representatives, the discrepancy was even greater, with the Republicans providing "ninety odd" votes against and Douglas's friends "some twenty votes."

However, the Lecompton Constitution was of minor importance compared to Douglas's attacks on the "House Divided" speech. The Senator's characterization of Lincoln's remarks necessitated a response. Lincoln denied that he was "in favor of making war by the North upon the South for the extinction of slavery; that I am also in favor of inviting (as he expresses it) the South to a war upon the North, for the purpose of nationalizing slavery." He argued that if one carefully read his words they did not indicate that he was "in favor of anything in it." It was a "prediction only" and, in one of the rare instances where Lincoln came close to admitting that the words in his speech may have been politically unwise, he confessed, "It may have been a foolish one perhaps." He further asserted that he had not even expressed a desire "that slavery should be put in course of ultimate extinction."

Lincoln took special offense at Douglas's additional remarks, especially those comments that questioned his knowledge of American history. Lincoln wanted to be clear that he was not "unaware that this Government has endured eighty-two years, half slave and half free. I know that. I am tolerably well acquainted with the history of the country, and I know that it has endured eighty-two years, half slave and half free." The nation had endured, Lincoln asserted, because the "public

3. The Campaign Begins

mind" had rested in "the belief that slavery was in course of ultimate extinction" until the "introduction of the Nebraska Bill." He always "hated slavery" as much as "any Abolitionist," although he considered himself "an Old Line Whig." Lincoln confessed that he had "always been quiet" about his hatred of slavery until the "new era of the introduction of the Nebraska Bill began."

Douglas claimed that not only did Lincoln oppose slavery, but that he was also prepared to abolish slavery where it then existed. Lincoln disagreed. His opposition to slavery did not indicate that he or "the people of the free States" had a legal right "to enter into the slave States, and interfere with the question of slavery at all. I have said that always. Judge Douglas has heard me say it — if not quite a hundred times, at least as good as a hundred times." Lincoln reiterated this point, stating that, as to whether he was in "favor of setting the sections at war with one another," he had "never meant any such thing, and I believe that no fair mind can infer any such thing from anything I have ever said."

For Lincoln, the key difference between the candidates lay in their view of slavery. Douglas "looks upon all this matter of slavery as an exceedingly little thing — this matter of keeping one-sixth of the population of the whole nation in a state of oppression and tyranny unequalled in the world." The Senator "looks upon it as being an exceedingly little thing ... as something having no moral question in it." It was this interpretation by Douglas that Lincoln considered the foundation of the Senator's mistake, because there was a "vast portion of the American people that do not look upon that matter as being this very little thing. They look upon it as a vast moral evil."

In response to Douglas's charges concerning Lincoln's hostility to the Dred Scott decision, Lincoln repeated his opposition to it, but said he had no intention to "resist it." His opposition to the decision was not based on a disrespect to the Supreme Court, rather it was a refusal to "obey it as a political rule." If he were in Congress, and "a vote should come up on a question whether slavery should be prohibited in a new territory, in spite of that Dred Scott decision, I would vote that it should."

Douglas had spent considerable time describing how Illinois had insisted that he support his act. Lincoln claimed that "nobody instructed him to introduce the Nebraska bill. There was nobody in that legislature ever thought of such a thing."

The Lincoln-Douglas Debates and the Making of a President

Lincoln then returned to his paramount issue, the issue of slavery. Supporting Douglas, Lincoln argued, would indicate acceptance of the Senator's position that "you do not care whether slavery be voted up or down." The Republicans were those who would through peaceful actions "oppose the extension of slavery" and would "hope for its ultimate extinction." Douglas, believing that this "government was made for white men," had narrowly defined the nation's freedoms by stating "that the people of America are equal to the people of England." Lincoln attacked this proposition and took the opportunity to expound on his universal egalitarian understanding of the Declaration of Independence. He noted that, in addition to those who had immigrated from England, the United States has received others who had immigrated "from Europe — German, Irish, French and Scandinavian." Descendants of these immigrants, if traced through history in an attempt to discover a genealogical link with the American Revolution, would "find they have none." These Americans "cannot carry themselves back into that glorious epoch and make themselves feel that they are part of us, but when they look through that old Declaration of Independence they find that those old men say that, 'We hold these truths to be self-evident, that all men are created equal,' and then they feel that that moral sentiment taught in that day evidences their relation to those men, that it is the father of all moral principle in them, and that they have a right to claim it as though they were blood of the blood, and flesh of the flesh of the men who wrote that Declaration." For Lincoln, that was the "electric cord" in the Declaration that linked "the hearts of patriotic and liberty-loving men together" and "will link those patriotic hearts as long as the love of freedom exists in the minds of men throughout the world."

The totality of Douglas's philosophy was a direct threat to the nation, Lincoln charged. The Senator's philosophy of "'don't care if slavery is voted up or voted down,'" his support for the Dred Scott decision, and his position that the "Declaration of Independence did not mean anything at all" were endangering the foundation of the nation. Douglas's opinions would "rub out the sentiment of liberty in the country" if these sentiments were "ratified," "confirmed," "endorsed," "taught to our children, and repeated to them." At their base, Lincoln considered these arguments the same as those "kings have made for enslaving people in all ages of the world." There was significant danger, Lincoln

3. The Campaign Begins

believed, "in taking this old Declaration of Independence, which declares that all men are equal upon principle, and making exceptions to it, where will it stop.[7] If one man says it does not mean a negro, why not another say it does not mean some other man?"

Contradicting Douglas's claims concerning the slaveholding nature of the founding fathers, Lincoln, as he had done in his June 16 speech, turned to Scripture. He recalled "one of the admonitions of the Lord, 'As your Father in Heaven is perfect, be ye also perfect.' The Savior, I suppose, did not expect that any human creature could be perfect as the Father in Heaven; but He said, 'As your Father in Heaven; be ye also perfect.' He set that up as a standard, and he who did most towards reaching that standard, attained the highest degree of moral perfection." Lincoln saw a direct parallel between the scriptural passage and the Declaration. "So I say in relation to the principle that all men are created equal, let it be as nearly reached as we can. If we cannot give freedom to every creature, let us do nothing that will impose slavery upon any other creature. Let us then turn this government back into the channel in which the framers of the Constitution originally placed it." If they failed to halt Douglas's progression, Lincoln predicated that America would become "one universal slave nation" as he had predicted in his "House Divided" speech.

In his conclusion, Lincoln attacked the idea of "superior" and "inferior" races. He asked that the nation "discard all this quibbling about this man and the other man — this race and that race and the other race being inferior, and therefore they must be placed in an inferior position," and "discard all these things, and unite as one people throughout this land, until we shall once more stand up declaring that all men are created equal."[8] It would be a stance that he would not consistently uphold at all the debates.

Douglas and Lincoln both argued the issues based on the principles that they had previously advocated. Douglas, having good reason to modify his statements, had passed the test and stood firm to the ideas he had long advocated. Lincoln, having no political reason to change his principles in a pro–Republican Congressional District, had not modified his position, as would have been expected. Both would face another test, as they moved south, into the highly competitive central Illinois region, where the election would be decided. Springfield, Lincoln's hometown, would serve as the next city where both candidates would deliver significant speeches of the campaign. This time, it was Lincoln who would be tested, as the voters in the central Illinois area were more supportive of the Democrats than the Republicans. But before the two tangled again, Douglas gave one of the most critical speeches of his campaign in Judge Davis's hometown of Bloomington, Illinois.

4

Douglas Fires Back: Bloomington, Illinois

July 16, 1858

Bloomington offered Douglas his first opportunity to respond to Lincoln's Chicago remarks, and Douglas's speech would so please the Democrats that eighty thousand copies of it would be printed for circulation throughout Illinois. None of the Senator's other speeches would receive such publicity.[1]

However, Douglas's journey from Chicago to Bloomington proved to be as eventful as his speech. From the descriptions provided by the pro–Douglas Chicago *Times*, the people of Illinois seemed to be receiving him with the same pageantry that would be customary for a conquering military hero. At Chicago, Douglas's supporters had almost completely covered the locomotive with flags. Banners with the inscription of "Stephen A. Douglas, the Champion of Popular Sovereignty" adorned the railroad cars. As the train traveled through the countryside, people shouted greetings of "God speed" and crowds along the route gave parting cheers. The *Times* declared that "at every station on the road — at Brighton Cross, Summit, Athens, and Lockport — the people were out waiting an opportunity to testify their respect to their patriot Senator." Artillery sounded at Joliet, and at Elwood "cheer after cheer went up, whilst two or three individuals expressed their enthusiasm by the discharge of their revolvers." A platform car with thirteen flags and a cannon (named "Popular Sovereignty") was added to the train at Joliet. As the locomotive approached Wilmington, "Popular Sovereignty" announced the Senator's arrival and a brass band welcomed Douglas to the town. At all the other stations people "were out awaiting the train and greeted Senator Douglas with loud hurrahs." When Douglas finally arrived at Bloomington, five thousand people "on horseback, in vehicles, and on foot" cheered him. "The train was overrun with people who clambered on top of the cars and tumbled in on all sides" and "the thunder of the guns, the music of the band, and the shouts of the multitude filled the air." A crowd escorted him to a hotel where he waited until evening. An hour before his speech, the town came alive again with the "roar of the cannon and the firing of the rockets" and "the ringing of the court house bell." Ten thousand people filled the square, a number that would have been much greater, according to the *Times*, had many of Douglas's supporters not been prevented from attending "by the heavy rain which fell in this neighborhood all last night and to-day."[2]

Douglas had spoken for a relatively brief time in Chicago, and he even admitted toward the conclusion of his remarks that he had "spoken without preparation and in a very desultory manner" and that he "may have omitted some points." The typically energetic, fiery Senator confessed to the Chicago audience that he had "exhausted" himself and that it had been "two nights" since he had "been in bed" and that he thought he had "a right to a little sleep."[3]

Now, in Bloomington, he was back in full form. The Senator spoke for nearly twice as long as he had in Chicago, responded to Lincoln's points, and laid the foundation for his upcoming address in Springfield. Douglas's strategy was simple: he intended to convince the audience that their prejudices were his prejudices, that their fears were his fears, that their hopes for the nation were his hopes for the nation.

Although it can be presumed that the majority in attendance were Douglas supporters, not all were, for Lincoln was also present.

The Senator added several crucial arguments to his speech at Bloomington that he had not included in Chicago. He upheld his attack on the Lecompton Constitution as proving that he was a man of great principle but, unlike his Chicago speech, he gave substantial credit to one man, Senator John J. Crittenden, who had suddenly become one of Douglas's favorite people. In defending popular sovereignty, Douglas claimed that he was acting on behalf of the popular will of the people of Illinois. He once again assailed the opening lines of Lincoln's "House

4. Douglas Fires Back

Divided" speech, and criticized Lincoln's opposition to the Dred Scott decision. But the other major change in this speech, as compared to Chicago, involved his attack on Lincoln's interpretation of the Declaration of Independence. In that part of his speech, Douglas proclaimed not only the crucial difference between himself and Lincoln, but he also described his future for America, a future far different from the one his opponent had described a week before.

Of all the topics Douglas covered, the one theme that served as the basis for most of his attacks was Lincoln's call for rejecting the discussion of "superior" and "inferior" races. The Senator seized on his opponent's request to "discard all this quibbling about this man and the other man — this race and that race and the other race being inferior" as the perfect foundation upon which to undermine Lincoln's campaign. Douglas was baiting his opponent. The Senator wanted to pressure Lincoln into either again substantiating his Chicago remarks, which Douglas believed were far too radical for those in central Illinois, or reversing his position, which would provide Douglas with a new attack on Lincoln's consistency. Douglas's Bloomington speech, more than any other, would represent the beginning of Lincoln's slide from statesman to politician, as Douglas forced Lincoln to reject the statesmanlike remarks that he had so eloquently made at Chicago.

The Senator opened his speech with the Lecompton Constitution issue, specifically defending the actions that he took to defeat it. Douglas had "from the beginning to the end" maintained "bold, determined, and unrelenting ground in opposition to that Lecompton Constitution" because that constitution "was not the act and deed of the people of Kansas, and did not embody their will." His attack on the Lecompton Constitution was based on the "fundamental principle in all free governments — a principle asserted in the Declaration of Independence, and underlying the Constitution of the United States, as well as the Constitution of every State of the Union — that every people ought to have the right to form, adopt, and ratify the Constitution under which they are to live." According to Douglas, popular sovereignty was the key point that Lecompton violated, a point that his Nebraska bill had substantiated. Douglas's bill distinctly stated "that the people of Kansas should be left not only free, but perfectly free to form and regulate their own domestic institutions to suit themselves." He "did not oppose the Lecompton Constitution" because it permitted slavery, as "it made no difference" to him whether slavery was prohibited or permitted. He was only asserting "a principle, under which you have no more right to force a free State upon them without their consent."[4]

While he had made a passing reference to Crittenden in his Chicago remarks, the Senator now heaped praise upon him. Douglas had either seen the letter that Dickey had received from Crittenden, or he was confident that the letter would soon be received, and he took this opportunity not only to publicly recognize Crittenden, but also to place him on a pedestal from which the dissatisfied Whigs might take direction. "My friends, I do not desire you to understand me as claiming for myself any special merit for the course I have pursued" concerning the defeat of Lecompton. He had done his "duty, a duty enjoined by fidelity, by honor, by patriotism." However, he had not acted alone: "There were others, men of eminent ability, men of wide reputation renowned all over America, who led the van and are entitled to the greatest share of the credit. Foremost among them all, as he was head and shoulders above them all, was Kentucky's great and gallant statesman, John J. Crittenden." Douglas believed that "By his course upon this question he has shown himself a worthy successor of the immortal Clay, and well may Kentucky be proud of him."

Not only had other politicians supported Douglas in his defense of popular sovereignty, but his home state rallied behind him years before. "Illinois stands proudly forward as a State which early took her position in favor of the principle of popular sovereignty as applied to the Territories of the United States." The Senator acknowledged that "when the compromise measure of 1850 passed, predicated upon that principle" he reminded the audience of "the excitement which prevailed throughout the northern portion of this State." Douglas, in rising to the challenge of 1850, "vindicated those measures then, and defended" himself "upon the ground that they embodied the principle that every people ought to have the privilege of forming and regulating their own institutions to suit themselves—that each State had that right, and I saw no reason why it should not be extended to the Territories." Referring

4. Douglas Fires Back

again to the 1851 resolution of the Illinois legislature, Douglas claimed that the state representatives had "endorsed" the principle of popular sovereignty as "a principle vindicated by our revolutionary fathers" and upon which "no limitation should ever be placed upon it, either in the organization of a Territorial government or the admission of a State into the Union."[5]

Douglas assailed Lincoln's "House Divided" speech as a direct attack upon popular sovereignty. Lincoln had declared "the fundamental principle" of his campaign in the opening lines of that speech and Douglas rejected Lincoln's principle. The nation, the Senator claimed, had "existed from 1789 to this day, divided into free States and slave States, yet we are told that in the future it cannot endure unless they shall become all free or all slave." Lincoln wanted "to go to the Senate of the United States in order to carry out that line of public policy which will compel all the States in the south to become free." Douglas cleverly turned Lincoln's proclamation into a mandate for war. "How is he going to do it? Has Congress any power over the subject of slavery in Kentucky, or Virginia, or any other State in the Union? How, then, is Mr. Lincoln going to carry out that principle which he says is essential to the existence of this Union: to wit, that slavery must be abolished in all the States of the Union, or must be established in them all." The only way, Douglas argued, that Lincoln's policy could be enacted was by convincing "the South that they must either establish slavery in Illinois, and in every other free State, or submit to its abolition in every Southern State." This policy would bring "warfare upon the Northern States in order to establish slavery, for the sake of perpetuating it at home. Thus, Mr. Lincoln invites, by his proposition, a war of sections, a war between Illinois and Kentucky, a war between the free States and the slave States, a war between the North and the South, for the purpose of either exterminating slavery in every Southern State, or planting it in every Northern State." Lincoln demands that "the States must all be free or slave, for a house divided against itself cannot stand," Douglas declared.[6]

Douglas asserted that Lincoln's divisive policies were a direct result of the Republican's sectional nature. The Senator opposed the organization of any "sectional party" which only appealed to "Northern pride, and Northern passion and prejudice" and only opposed "Southern institutions." This policy served no other purpose than to stir "up ill feeling and hot blood between brethren of the same Republic. I am opposed to that whole system of sectional agitation, which can produce nothing but strife, but discord, but hostility and finally disunion. And yet, Mr. Lincoln asks you to send him to the Senate of the U.S., in order that he may carry out that great principle of his that all States must be slave or all must be free."[7]

Douglas assailed Lincoln's position on the Dred Scott decision, the issue over which the two would argue more than any other. Douglas described his opponent's opposition to the decision as "a crusade against the Supreme Court of the United States." The Senator claimed to "have no issue to make with the Supreme Court," to "have no crusade to preach against that august body" and to "have no warfare to make upon it." He claimed great respect of the Court and received its decision "as the final adjudication upon all questions within their jurisdiction." As a lawyer before the Court, in arguing a case, Douglas considered it "perfectly legitimate and proper for Mr. Lincoln, myself, or any other lawyer to go before the Supreme Court and argue any question that might arise there ... but when the decision is pronounced, that decision becomes the law of the land, and he, and you, and myself, and every other good citizen, must bow to it, and yield obedience to it." The Senator warned, "Unless we respect and bow in deference to the final decisions of the highest judicial tribunal in the country, we are driven at once to anarchy, to violence, to mob law, and there is no security left for our property, or our own civil rights."

But the Dred Scott decision was moot and not worthy of discussion, Douglas claimed. The real issue was not the opinion of the justices, the laws of Congress, or the laws of the territorial government, but the opinion of those residing in a state or territory. "If the people of a Territory want slavery they will encourage it" by "laws, and the necessary police regulations, patrol laws and slave code," while if the local population opposes slavery "they will withhold that legislation, and by withholding it slavery is as dead as if it was prohibited by a Constitutional prohibition." In a short span of time, he predicted, "They could pass such local laws and police regulations as would drive slavery out in one day, or one hour, if they were opposed to it." For this reason, the Senator alleged, "It matters not how the Dred Scott case

4. Douglas Fires Back

may be decided with reference to the Territories." From Douglas's perspective, it was not the Supreme Court or Congress which should determine the legal existence of slavery.... "Whether slavery shall exist or shall not exist in any State or Territory," he argued, "will depend upon whether the people are for it or against it, and which ever way they shall decide it in any Territory or any State, will be entirely satisfactory to me."[8]

The Dred Scott issue proved a perfect transition for Douglas to discuss the fundamental issue of the debates, and the fundamental difference between the two opponents: their interpretation of the Declaration of Independence. The two disparate interpretations represented two futures for America: one in which American would bestow equality on only Europeans descendants, and another that envisioned equality bestowed on all. Lincoln had argued for an egalitarian interpretation of the Declaration at Chicago, and it was precisely on that point that Douglas pounded away. Lincoln rejected the Court's decision, the Senator insisted, because it "deprives the negro of the benefits of that clause of the Constitution of the United States which entitles the citizens of each State to all the privileges and immunities of citizens of the several States." The Senator acknowledged that "by deciding that a negro is not a citizen, of course it denies to him the rights and privileges awarded to citizens of the United States. It is this that Mr. Lincoln will not submit to." Lincoln objected to the Court's decision, Douglas argued, "for the palpable reason that he wishes to confer upon the negro all the rights, privileges, and immunities of citizens of the several States." Lincoln "conscientiously believes that a negro ought to enjoy and exercise all the rights and privileges given to white men."

Douglas disagreed. This "government of ours," the Senator asserted, "was founded on the white basis. I believe that it was established by white men by men of European birth or descended of European races for the benefit of white men and their posterity in all time to come. I do not believe that it was the design or intention of the signers of the declaration [sic] of Independence or the framers of the Constitution to include negroes, Indians or other inferior races with white men as citizens." There was ample historical justification for his stance, Douglas claimed: "Our fathers had at that day seen the evil consequence of conferring civil and political rights upon the Indian and Negro in the Spanish and French colonies on the American continent and the adjacent islands. In Mexico, in Central American, in South America and in the West India islands, where the Indian, the Negro, and men of all colors and all races are put on an equality by law, the effect of political amalgamation can be seen." Once amalgamation took hold, the nation would collapse, Douglas predicted: "Amalgamation there, first political, then social, has led to demoralization and degradation, until it has reduced that people below the point of capacity for self-government. Our fathers knew what the effect of it would be, and from the time they planted foot on the American continent, not only those who landed at Jamestown, but at Plymouth Rock and all other points on the coast, they pursued the policy of confining civil and political rights to the white race, and excluding the negro in all cases." Despite the historical precedent, Lincoln still "conscientiously believes that it is his duty to advocate negro citizenship. Lincoln, Douglas alleged, wanted to "give the negro an equality under the law, in order that he may approach as near perfection or an equality with the white man as possible."

Douglas further stoked the audience's racial fears that Lincoln's policy would result in a mass migration of "negroes" into Illinois and that they would be granted full political rights. Lincoln would eliminate from the state constitution "that clause which prohibits negroes from coming into this State, and making it an African colony, and permit them to come and spread over these charming prairies until in midday they shall look black as night." The mass migration to Illinois would be followed with full suffrage. "When our friend Lincoln gets all his colored brethren around him here," Douglas predicted, "he will then raise them to perfection as fast as possible, and place them on an equality with the white man, first removing all legal restrictions, because they are our equals by Divine law, and there should be no such restrictions. He wants them to vote. I am opposed to it." Lincoln's position granted "negroes" "the right to vote" and "under the Divine law and the Declaration of Independence, to be elected to office, to become members of the Legislature, to go to Congress, to become Governors, or United States Senators, or Judges of the Supreme Court; and I suppose that when they control that Court they will probably reverse the Dred Scott Decision. He is going to bring negroes here, and give them the right of

4. Douglas Fires Back

citizenship, the right of voting, and the right of holding office and sitting on juries, and what else?"[9]

Douglas argued, contrary to Lincoln's interpretation, that the Declaration of Independence had limited, narrow applicability, especially in regards to the phrase of "all men are created equal." "I do not believe that the signers of the Declaration of Independence had any reference to negroes when they used the expression that all men were created equal, or that they had any reference to the Chinese or Coolies, the Indians, the Japanese, or any other inferior race." The Founding Fathers, Douglas asserted, "were speaking of the white race, the European race on this continent, and their descendants, and emigrants who should come here. They were speaking only of the white race and never dreamed that their language would be construed to include the negro." Douglas alleged that when "the Declaration of Independence was put forth, declaring the equality of all men, every one of the thirteen colonies was a slaveholding colony, and every man who signed that Declaration represented a slaveholding constituency." He then asked, "Did they intend, when they put their signatures on that instrument, to declare that their own slaves were on an equality with them; that they were made their equals by divine law, and that any human law reducing them to an inferior position was void, as being in violation of divine law?" The Senator inquired as to whether Thomas Jefferson or "any of the signers of that instrument, or all of them, on the day they signed it give their slaves freedom?" Douglas answered, "History records that they did not." He then questioned whether the signers "put the negro on an equality with the white man throughout the country? They did not. And yet if they had understood that the Declaration as including the negro, which Mr. Lincoln holds they did, they would have been bound, as conscientious men, to have restored the negro to that equality which he thinks the Almighty intended they should occupy with the white men. They did not do it."

Further, there was no dominant abolition sentiment at the founding of America, Douglas declared, because "slavery was abolished in only one State before the adoption of the Constitution in 1789" and although it had been abolished "gradually" since the founding, not one state had abolished slavery since the "abolition agitation began." The "whole history," Douglas declared, "confirms the proposition that from the earliest settlement of the colonies down to the Declaration of Independence and the adoption of the Constitution of the United States, our fathers proceeded on the white basis, making the white people the governing race, but conceding to the Indian and negro, and all inferior races all the rights and all the privileges they could enjoy consistent with the safety of the society in which they lived."

As opposed to Lincoln's policy of "political warfare," of creating "strife between North and South," of hoping to elect "a sectional President" which will reduce the South to "dependent colonies," Douglas recommended respect between the two sections: "Let us recognize the sovereignty and independence of each State, refrain from interfering with the domestic institutions and regulations of other States, permit the Territories and new States to decide their institutions for themselves, as we did when we were in their condition; blot out these lines of North and South, and resort back to these lines of State boundaries which the Constitution has marked out, and engraved upon the face of the country; have no other dividing lines but these, and we will be one united, harmonious people, with fraternal feelings, and no discord or dissension."[10]

To maintain the "fraternal feelings" and to rally the support of the Whigs in central Illinois, the Senator evoked the memory of Henry Clay. "These are my views and these are the principles to which I have devoted all my energies since 1850, when I acted side by side with the immortal Clay and the God-like Webster in the memorable struggle in which Whigs and Democrats united upon a common platform of patriotism and the Constitution, throwing aside partizan [sic] feelings in order to restore peace and harmony to a distracted country." Clay supported Douglas's popular sovereignty as the rightful descendant of his philosophy. The Great Compromiser "looked upon the principle embodied in the great Compromise measures of 1850, the principle of the Nebraska bill, the doctrine of leaving each State and Territory free to decide its institutions for itself, as the only means by which the peace of the country could be preserved and the Union perpetuated." Douglas had "pledged" to Clay "on that death bed of his, that so long as I lived my energies should be devoted to the vindication of that principle, and of his fame as connected with it."

In conclusion, Douglas, believing that, above all, the maintenance

4. Douglas Fires Back

of the Union was the paramount goal, reiterated his belief that only by respecting the rights of the individual states could the nation endure: "The Union can only be preserved by maintaining the fraternal feeling between the North and the South, the East and the West. If that good feeling can be preserved, the Union will be as perpetual as the fame of its great founders. It can be maintained by preserving the Sovereignty of the States, the right of each State and each Territory to settle its domestic concerns for itself, and the duty of each to refrain from interfering with the other in any of its local or domestic institutions." If this policy of state sovereignty is respected, Douglas argued, than "the Union will be perpetual ... and this Republic, which began with thirteen States and which now numbers thirty-two; which when it began only extended from the Atlantic to the Mississippi, but now reaches to the Pacific, may yet expand North and South, until it covers the whole Continent, and becomes one vast ocean-bound confederacy. Then, my friends, the path of duty, of honor, of patriotism is plain.... Bear in mind the dividing line between State rights and federal authority; let us maintain the great principles of popular sovereignty, of State rights, and of the Federal Union as the Constitution has made it, and this republic will endure forever."[11]

Douglas had slightly changed his arguments in this speech. Compared to his Chicago remarks, he more freely expounded on his interpretation of the Declaration of Independence, and, for the first time, used the issue of miscegenation to his advantage, two ideas he had not expressed in northern Illinois. However, Douglas's main points were entirely consistent with his Chicago speech: he attacked the "House Divided" speech, defended popular sovereignty, the Kansas-Nebraska Act, and the Dred Scott decision.

At the conclusion, the *Bloomington Pantagraph* reported that "loud calls were made for Hon. Abraham Lincoln." Lincoln "held back for a little while, but the crowd finally succeeded in inducing him to come upon the stand." "Three rousing cheers," which the pro–Lincoln newspaper claimed were "much louder than those given to Judge Douglas," greeted the Republican candidate. But no speech would come: "'This meeting,' said Mr. Lincoln, 'was called by the friends of Judge Douglas, and it would be improper for me to address it.'" Lincoln "then retired amid loud cheering."[12]

The Lincoln-Douglas Debates and the Making of a President

He would respond the next day and provide the first hint as to whether he would, in his hometown and in the crucial central area of Illinois, proclaim the same egalitarian vision of America as he had in Chicago. But Douglas would speak first at Springfield, and that speech would give further indication as to whether the Senator intended to hold to one philosophy throughout the campaign, or whether he would embrace a new one as he moved further south.

5

The Second Round: Springfield, Illinois

July 17, 1858

On July 17, Douglas and Lincoln jousted again, this time in Springfield, Illinois, a central Illinois district, Lincoln's hometown and an area of different political attitudes than the northern part of the state. While the 2nd Illinois Congressional District that included Chicago leaned Republican, the 6th Illinois Congressional District leaned Democratic. In the 1858 congressional election the voters had given the Democratic candidate a 58 percent majority, with no counties voting Republican. The closest vote was within Lincoln's home county, Sangamon, where the two candidates would next speak. In that county, the Democrats squeaked out a majority with just under 51 percent.[1]

By all indications, Douglas's railroad trip to Bloomington had been a huge success. This, of course, disturbed the Republicans and the *Chicago Press and Tribune* thought it necessary to respond, taking issue with the reaction at Joliet. "The appearance in our streets of an organ-grinder with a monkey to catch the pennies would call together as large a crowd and create full as much enthusiasm as did the visit of Mr. Douglas today." But the Republican criticism had no effect. Douglas thoroughly enjoyed the attention that he had received, and his journey to Springfield was no less dramatic than his trip to Bloomington. The seven car train departed Bloomington covered with flags and banners, with a band and the Senator's cannon. The banner inscriptions all supported the Democratic candidate: "Illinois welcomes Douglas," "Stephen A. Douglas, the people's choice," and "State Sovereignty, Popular Union."

This intense attention toward Douglas must have been somewhat demoralizing for at least one of the passengers; Lincoln was also riding this train.

At Atlanta, Douglas's cannon, "Popular Sovereignty," announced the Senator's arrival, and two cannons from the town fired in reply. The crowd called for Douglas to speak, but he declined and Lincoln, having been asked to speak, declined as well. The citizens of the next town, Lincoln, had assembled a "large triumphal arch" decorated with "leaves, flowers, evergreens, flags, and small banners" over one of their main streets. On the arch's top in "very large letters" were the words "Douglas forever," while one of the houses hung a banner inscribed "Douglas, the Champion of Popular Sovereignty." More cars were added to the train at Lincoln to accommodate the "hundreds" of additional people who wanted to ride to Springfield. The rain began to pour as the train approached Williamsville but the cannon still "thundered" Douglas's arrival and "several bands" greeted the Senator.

At Springfield, despite the "drenching rain," thousands assembled to cheer. The cannon "boomed in response to cannon on the ground." Flags and pennants decorated the grove. Other trains from the south and the east, covered with Douglas banners and filled with Douglas supporters, converged on the city.[2]

A little after three o'clock, at the grove where the train had stopped, the Senator gave his speech.

Despite the differences between the 2nd and 6th Congressional Districts, Douglas's Springfield speech followed many of the same themes as his Chicago speech. He defended popular sovereignty—especially in relation to the recent Lecompton crisis—the Dred Scott decision, states' rights, and attacked Lincoln's interpretation of the Declaration of Independence. The Senator described the Lecompton Constitution as "an attempt to violate one of the fundamental principles upon which our free institutions rest." Forcing the Lecompton Constitution on "the people of Kansas against their will" would have been, Douglas argued, "subversive of the great fundamental principles upon which all our institutions rest." To Douglas, "the right of the people to form and ratify the constitution under which they are to live" is the "one principle more sacred and more vital to the existence of a free government than all others." While Lincoln contended that the Declaration of Independence

5. The Second Round

was America's cornerstone, Douglas asserted that popular sovereignty was "the corner stone of the temple of liberty" and "the foundation upon which the whole structure rests." In the Lecompton crisis, Douglas had deemed it his duty, "as a citizen and as a representative of the state of Illinois, to resist, with all my energies and with whatever of ability I could command, the consummation of that effort to force a constitution upon an unwilling people." He again reiterated his indifference to the constitution's slavery provision, claiming that his opposition was solely based "upon the fact that it was not the act and deed of that people, and that it did not embody their will."[3]

Douglas considered popular sovereignty "the highest privilege of our people," which allowed the residents of a territory or state to decide "for themselves what kind of institutions are good and what kind of institutions are bad." There is no right, he asserted, for anyone to "force a free state upon an unwilling people" or to "force a slave state upon them against their will." This freedom, Douglas admitted, would allow those people in a "different latitude and different climate, and with different productions and different interests" to decide the slavery issue for themselves "in order to adapt their institutions to the wants and wishes of the people to be affected by them."[4]

Douglas recalled, for the third consecutive speech, that the 1851 Illinois House of Representatives resolution had supported "the great principle of self-government," noting that the resolution was supported by all Whigs and all Democrats. The four votes cast in the negative were the "Abolitionists, of course." It was his responsibility following the will of the people of Illinois, Douglas asserted, to incorporate that principle in the Kansas-Nebraska Act. Yet, for supporting that resolution and his principle of popular sovereignty, he had suffered as a martyr. After the Kansas-Nebraska bill passed, he "could then travel from Boston to Chicago by the light of my own effigies, in consequence of having stood up for it. I leave it to you to say how I met the storm ... whether I did not 'face the music,' justify the principle and pledge my life to carry it out."

Lincoln's claim that a conspiracy existed to nationalize slavery, and that Douglas was a coconspirator, perplexed the Senator. He noted that the conspiracy was supposedly composed of "political tricksters," namely "Chief Justice Taney and his eight associates, two Presidents of the

United States, and one Senator of Illinois." Douglas dismissed the conspiracy charge with the words "no comment" and further added that he did not "think so badly of the President of the United States and the Supreme Court of the United States, the highest judicial tribunal on earth, as to believe that they were capable in their action and decision of entering into political intrigues for partisan purposes."

Douglas then, once again, attacked the "House Divided" speech and characterized his opponent as an abolitionist. Lincoln, claimed Douglas, "does not think this Union can continue to exist composed of half slave and half free states" and that he had one intention: "to go to the Senate in order to carry out this favorite patriotic policy of his, of making all the states free, so that the house shall no longer be divided against itself." Lincoln would accomplish this goal by "lawful and constitutional means" by "amending the Constitution so that slavery can be abolished in all the states of the Union." This would result in a "uniformity," Douglas argued, but one that was not "of liberty" but "of despotism." Lincoln would cause sectional conflict — a "war of the North against the South, a warfare of the free states against the slaveholding states."

In order to preserve the Union, the Senator professed a different philosophy. Douglas believed that the Union could "only be preserved by maintaining inviolate the Constitution of the U.S. as our fathers have made it." While Lincoln sought "consolidation and uniformity," Douglas advocated the continuation of the "confederation of the sovereign states under the Constitution, as our fathers made it, leaving each state at liberty to manage its own affairs and own internal institutions" and avoiding "a warfare upon the Supreme Court of the United States because of the Dred Scott decision."

Douglas again responded to those who feared that Kansas would become a slave state. Slavery could not "exist a day in the midst of an unfriendly people with unfriendly laws." Although the laws supported slavery in Kansas, the majority's opposition to the institution had resulted in fewer slaves than existed when "the Nebraska Bill passed and the Missouri Compromise was repealed." The Dred Scott decision was therefore a "theoretical question" not worthy of consideration. The Republicans had only engaged this issue as a means to gain political office or to produce "political capital." They were only campaigning on issues simply for political effect, and not out of a sincere ideology.

5. The Second Round

Douglas finally attacked Lincoln's "main objection to the Dred Scott decision." In so doing, he outlined the crucial issue of the debates, the most substantive difference between him and Lincoln: their interpretation of the Declaration of Independence. Lincoln primarily objected to the decision, Douglas claimed, because it "intended to deprive the negro of the right of citizenship in the different states of the Union." The court's decision ran counter to Lincoln's belief that the "negro ought to be permitted to have the rights of citizenship." Douglas defined "negro citizenship" as support for "negro" suffrage. He claimed that he, unlike his opponent, was not in "favor of negro citizenship," because he disagreed with the premise "that a negro is a citizen or ought to be a citizen." Douglas then made an assertion that he would often repeat, although here at Springfield, he dropped the word "European" that he had used in Bloomington, preferring to use the word "white": "I believe that this government of ours was founded, and wisely founded, upon the white basis. It was made by white men for the benefit of white men and their posterity, to be executed and managed by white men." As to the "nature and extent of the rights which a negro ought to have," Douglas answered that this was "a question for each state and each territory to decide for itself."

In the case of Illinois, Douglas reminded the audience that "a negro is not a slave, but we have at the same time determined that he is not a citizen and shall not enjoy any political rights." The Senator concurred "in the wisdom of that policy" and claimed that he was "content with it." The main issue was not whether the "negro" should have further rights, but whether the states should have the independence to confer those rights. Douglas asserted that "the sovereignty of Illinois had a right to determine that question as we have decided it" and denied "that any other state has a right to interfere with us or call us to account for that decision." He discussed the state of Maine, noting that the citizens of that state had "decided by their constitution that the negro shall exercise the elective franchise and hold office on an equality with the white man." Douglas did not consider these actions in "good sense or correct taste," but he had "no disposition to quarrel with her," because it is the business of Maine, and not that of Illinois. "If the people of Maine desire to be put on an equality with the negro, I do not know that anybody in this state will attempt to prevent it. If the white people of Maine think a negro their equal, and that he has a right to come and kill their vote by a negro vote, they have a right to think so, I suppose, and I have no disposition to interfere with them." He could not help mentioning the example of another state, that of New York, recalling that there the citizens had determined "that a negro may vote provided he holds $250 worth of property, but that he shall not unless he does; that is to say, they will allow a negro to vote if he is rich, but a poor fellow they will not allow to vote. In New York they think a rich negro is equal to a white man."[5]

Lincoln's interpretation was not limited to "negroes," Douglas argued. While Lincoln's interpretation of the Declaration was inclusive of "all men," such as "negroes, Indians, and all inferior races," Douglas noted, it was Lincoln's statements on African Americans to which he gave special attention. The Senator referred to Lincoln's Chicago speech to connect Lincoln with abolitionists such as Lovejoy. He reminded the audience that his opponents argued that "negroes" "were endowed by the Almighty with the right of equality" and that the "law of God makes them equal to the white man, and therefore that the law of the white man cannot deprive them of that right":

> This is Mr. Lincoln's argument. He is conscientious in his belief. I do not question his sincerity, I do not doubt that he, in his conscience, believes that the Almighty made the negro equal to the white man. He thinks the negro is his brother. I do not think that the negro is any kin of mine at all. And here is the difference between us. I believe that the Declaration of Independence, in the words "all men are created equal," was intended to allude only to the people of the United States, to men of European birth or descent, being white men, that they were created equal ... but the signers of that paper did not intend to include the Indian or the negro in that declaration, for if they had would they not have been bound to abolish slavery in every state and colony from that day?[6]

While Lincoln had interpreted the Declaration of Independence's clause "all men" to include "negroes, Indians, and all inferior races," Douglas rejected "negro equality" and "Indian equality." He was "opposed to putting the coolies, now importing into this country, on an equality with us, or putting the Chinese or any other inferior race on an equality with us." The "white race, the European race," including the Irish, German, French, Scotch and English are "our equals," Douglas declared. "The Declaration of Independence only included the white

5. The Second Round

people of the U.S." and "the Constitution of the U.S. was framed by the white people" and should "be administered by them" only. However, adhering to his popular sovereignty, Douglas asserted that all matters involving the "negro" should be deferred to the states, granting each state independent authority to determine the degree to which the "negro" should receive political and civil rights.

As he had done in Bloomington, Douglas again stoked the audience's racial fears. Lincoln would "strike out of the constitution of Illinois that clause which prohibits free negroes and slaves from Kentucky or any other state coming into Illinois." The alteration of the state's constitution, Douglas claimed, would open "the gate for all the negro population to flow in and cover our prairies in mid-day they will look dark and black as night" and Lincoln would then "apply his principles of negro equality" by changing the state constitution again to "allow negroes to vote and hold office, and will make them eligible to the legislature so that thereafter they can have the right men for U.S. Senators." These actions would result in "negro" judges who would "not refuse his judge the privilege of marrying any woman he may select!" Interracial marriage, Douglas believed, was "the inevitable conclusion." Douglas objected "to any political amalgamation or any other amalgamation on this continent" because the result of equality, Douglas asserted, was "social amalgamation, demoralization and degradation, below the capacity of self-government."

Lincoln's philosophy represented a threat to the nation, Douglas believed. He argued that "if we wish to preserve this government we must maintain it on the basis on which it was established, to wit: the white basis." The Senator believed that the nation's leaders "must preserve the purity of the race not only in our politics but in our domestic relations." This could only be attained by preserving the "sovereignty of the states," the federal Union, and "the federal constitution inviolate." Harkening to his passion for manifest destiny, Douglas claimed that the preservation of these ideals would perpetuate the Union and would give hope that it may "spread over the entire continent."

Douglas summarized the campaign as a "contest of principle" in which either "the radical Abolition principles of Mr. Lincoln must be maintained, or the strong, constitutional, national Democratic principles with which I am identified must be carried out."[7]

That evening Lincoln responded, under much different circumstances than his opponent had spoken:

> A few handbills had been posted about the city during the day, announcing that Lincoln would speak in the State House at 8 o'clock in the evening. There were no clap-trap arrangements to draw a crowd. There was no music, no guns and no fireworks. There was only the quiet, simple announcement that Lincoln would speak. But evening came, and with it came the people from all parts of the city, until the Representatives' Hall was filled and crowded.
> Mr. Lincoln ascended the stand amid cheers....
> — *Chicago Press and Tribune*[8]

Lincoln's speech also covered familiar ground: attacking Douglas's role in the Lecompton defeat, defending the "House Divided" speech, repudiating the Kansas-Nebraska Act, and advocating the egalitarian principles of the Declaration of Independence. He opened his remarks not with a discussion of the issues, but with his assessment of the Republican party's electoral possibilities in Illinois. While Lincoln was confident that the party would elect its statewide candidates, the Republicans' victory in the state legislature was uncertain because of three disadvantages. Lincoln noted that the population in northern Illinois had increased substantially relative to that of southern Illinois. However, the current apportionment predated 1855 when the population in northern Illinois had not been as substantial, which Lincoln described as a "very great disadvantage." He reminded the audience that a census had occurred in 1855 and that, if a new apportionment had been fairly distributed, the Republican party would gain "from six to ten more members." The Democrats, though, "holding the control of both branches of the Legislature, steadily refused to give us such an apportionment as we were rightfully entitled to have upon the census already taken."[9]

Lincoln pointed to a second disadvantage under which the Republicans labored, namely those senators in the legislature whose seats were not up for election. He believed that there were "one or two Democratic Senators who will be members of the next Legislature, and will vote for the election of Senator, who are holding over in districts in which we could, on all reasonable calculation, elect men of our own, if we only had the chance of an election." To those who would claim that one or two votes were insubstantial, Lincoln countered that with only "twenty

5. The Second Round

five Senators in the Senate, taking two from the side where they rightfully belong and adding them to the other, is to us a disadvantage not to be lightly regarded."

The final disadvantage concerned Lincoln in comparison to Douglas. Lincoln realized that his opponent had "world wide renown." Democrats viewed Douglas, due to his prestige and reputation, as a future "President of the United States," while Lincoln admitted that "nobody has ever expected me to be President."

Because of the disadvantages under which the Republicans labored, Lincoln argued, this battle must be fought "upon principle, and upon principle alone." And the first principle with which Lincoln took issue was Douglas's popular sovereignty. The Senator narrowly construed popular sovereignty to apply only to "the question of negro slavery" and not "to other minor domestic matters of a territory or state." By this definition, Lincoln asserted, Douglas was not "sustaining popular sovereignty, but absolutely opposing it." The Senator "sustains the [Dred Scott] decision which declares" that the residents of the territories have "no constitutional power to exclude slavery during their territorial existence," which Lincoln logically concluded was precisely the policy that Douglas "has fought for or is fighting for," a policy which, by prohibiting the residents of a territory from excluding slavery, did not support popular sovereignty but rather "annihilates and crushes [it] out."

Lincoln believed that the Lecompton Constitution was unpopular among people in Illinois, so he sought to blunt the image of Douglas as the great champion who destroyed it and instead to show that it was the Republicans who had furnished the majority of the opposition. He wanted "to know what there is in the opposition of Judge Douglas to the Lecompton constitution" that entitled "him to be considered the only opponent to it — as being par excellence the very quintessence of that opposition." Lincoln agreed with the "rightfulness of his opposition" but found that Douglas and his followers numbered only three in the United States Senate and "formed a number of about twenty" in the House of Representatives. "It took one hundred and twenty to defeat the measure against one hundred and twelve. Of the votes of that one hundred and twenty, Judge Douglas's friends furnished twenty, to add to which there were six Americans and ninety-four Republicans."

Douglas also failed to mention that "our Republican Senator Trumbull made a speech against Lecompton, even before he did."

Lincoln then defended his "House Divided" speech. In response to Douglas's charges that he would make war, he wanted the audience to know that he had stated "again and again" that he "would not enter into any of the states to disturb the institution of slavery" and his prophetic statement was not indicative of his personal wish or purpose, but simply his "expectation." Slavery "ought to be placed in the very attitude where the framers of this Government placed it, and left it," Lincoln argued. He admitted that at Chicago he expressed his "wish" that "the spread of slavery" would be "arrested" and "placed where the public mind shall rest in the belief that it is in course of ultimate extinction." To Lincoln, once the public was satisfied that slavery was permanently restricted, then "we shall have peace on the slavery question." The "public mind did rest in that belief up to the introduction of the Nebraska Bill."

Douglas's bill had disrupted the nation's course in regard to slavery, Lincoln asserted. The "mind of the great majority, had rested in that belief up to the repeal of the Missouri Compromise." Lincoln personally attested that with the passage of the Kansas-Nebraska Act he became convinced that he had either "been resting in a delusion, or the institution was being placed on a new basis—a basis for making it perpetual, national and universal." He believed that subsequent events only provided more justification that the bill was "the beginning of a conspiracy" for the purpose of expanding slavery. Lincoln argued that the public mind would remain agitated over this question until the power of Congress to restrict its spread was once again "acknowledged and exercised" or if "all resistance" to slavery was "entirely crushed out."

In countering his opponent's comments on the Dred Scott decision, Lincoln argued that Douglas approved of the decision because "it tends to nationalize slavery." Douglas considered this result "a very small matter at most—that it has no practical effect; that at best, or rather, I suppose, at worst, it is but an abstraction," while Lincoln considered the proposition "which determines whether a man is free or a slave" a "concrete" result rather than an "abstract" one. Lincoln thought that it would be important to anyone if their "liberty depended upon it, and so would Judge Douglas if his liberty depended upon it."

5. The Second Round

Lincoln saved his most crucial comments, those that related to the issue of the Declaration of Independence, for the later part of his speech. He recalled that the night before Douglas had "tormented himself with horrors about my disposition to make negroes perfectly equal with white men in social and political relations. He did not stop to show that I have said any such thing, or that it legitimately follows from any thing I have said, but he rushes on with his assertions." Lincoln declared, "I adhere to the Declaration of Independence" and if "Judge Douglas and his friends are not willing to stand by it, let them come up and amend it. Let them make it read that all men are created equal except negroes. Let us have it decided, whether the Declaration of Independence, in this blessed year of 1858, shall be thus amended." Lincoln noted that Douglas had, the previous year, interpreted the freedoms of the Declaration as making "Americans in America" "equal to Englishmen in England. Then, when I pointed out to him that by that rule he excludes the Germans, the Irish, the Portuguese, and all the other people who have come amongst us since the Revolution, he reconstructs his construction. In his last speech he tells us it meant Europeans."

Lincoln pressed Douglas further on the Declaration, asking him if "it meant to include the Russians in Asia? Or does he mean to exclude that vast population from the principles of our Declaration of Independence?" Douglas "is satisfied with anything which does not endanger the nationalizing of negro slavery. It may draw white men down, but it must not lift negroes up. Who shall say, 'I am the superior, and you are the inferior?'"

My declarations on "negro slavery may be misrepresented" by Douglas, Lincoln claimed, but they "cannot be misunderstood." In a major departure from his Chicago remarks, Lincoln admitted that he did not "understand the Declaration to mean that all men were created equal in all respects. They are not our equal in color; but I suppose that it does mean to declare that all men are equal in some respects; they are equal in their right to 'life, liberty, and the pursuit of happiness.' Certainly the negro is not our equal in color — perhaps not in many other respects; still, in the right to put into his mouth the bread that his own hands have earned, he is the equal of every other man, white or black."

In the closing paragraphs, Lincoln reiterated what he considered two crucial points. First, he repeated his belief that slavery had been on a course of ultimate extinction. The founding fathers provided Congress with the ability to abolish the slave trade, they prohibited slavery in the territories where it then did not exist, and simply "yielded to the necessity for the rest." Countering those who considered him a radical abolitionist, he confessed his desire for a "separation of the white and black races." Second, Lincoln also repeated his belief that Douglas was a member of a "conspiracy to perpetuate and nationalize slavery" and he explicitly charged "him with having been a party to that conspiracy and to that deception for the sole purpose of nationalizing slavery."[10]

Douglas and Lincoln had slightly modified their comments for their Springfield audiences. Of the two, Douglas exhibited more consistency. Compared to his Chicago remarks, he more freely espoused his interpretation of the Declaration of Independence, and used the issue of miscegenation to his advantage, two ideas he had not expressed in northern Illinois, but which he had covered in Bloomington. However, Douglas's main points were entirely consistent with his Chicago and his Bloomington speeches: he attacked the "House Divided" speech, defended popular sovereignty, the Kansas-Nebraska Act and the Dred Scott decision. These arguments were nearly identical to those he had made at the commencement of the campaign.

Lincoln, on the other hand, had shifted, too, although only slightly, on the issue of race. He again attacked the concept of "superior" and "inferior" races, but he qualified his statements concerning the Declaration of Independence. He had not specifically mentioned the Declaration of Independence in the "House Divided" speech, but he had attacked Douglas's Act for banning the hope that African Americans could ever attain citizenship, and enjoy the benefits of "all men are created equal." In his Chicago speech, he had been more blatant in claiming that African Americans were included in the Declaration. But now, in the same city where he had given his "House Divided" speech just one month before, and just one week after his Chicago speech, Lincoln posited that the African American was not equal in all respects. The slight on African American equality was a significant change. Lincoln had traveled two hundred miles south, and had not completely maintained the position he had held in the pro–Republican part of Illinois, or in his opening campaign speech. On its own, the subtle change would not warrant notice; but it became crucial in the context of the entire

5. The Second Round

campaign. It signified Lincoln's willingness to change his statements for the sake of appealing to the electorate, at the expense of adhering to his personal convictions on the Declaration of Independence.

Several factors pressured Lincoln to retreat from his statements on African American equality. He had begun the campaign with a high degree of personal confidence, as exhibited by the manner in which he handled the "House Divided" speech. Lincoln wrote it without consultation, and when he finally shared the speech with a few hand-picked advisors, and all of them suggested changes, he ignored their advice, and gave the speech as he had composed it. But Lincoln was sensitive to his campaign's poor start, and Douglas's criticisms. The "House Divided" speech was now more popular with Douglas than with Lincoln; it had resulted in Dickey's defection, and Douglas used the speech to cast Lincoln as an abolitionist. These factors must have placed incredible pressure on Lincoln to answer his critics and modify his statements. He desperately wanted to win election, and he knew he could not prevail if cast as an abolitionist. The Springfield speech marked the first, but certainly not the last, time that the politician displaced the statesman.

6

A Challenge Made, A Challenge Accepted: The Lincoln-Douglas Letters

July 1858

Lincoln's troubles continued. The negative reaction to the "House Divided" speech, the Dickey defection, and the rumored Crittenden endorsement were followed by another problem. Lincoln had developed a strategy by which he followed Douglas throughout the state, a strategy that he had employed at Chicago and Springfield.[1] When Douglas spoke, Lincoln would encourage those who listened to the Senator to assemble later that same day or the next day to hear his response. While it permitted him the opportunity to answer Douglas's charges, it also made Lincoln appear incapable of attracting an audience on his own, a perceived weakness that proved fertile ground for his opponent's attacks. The criticisms forced Lincoln to develop a new strategy, which would result in a dramatic change in the conduct of the campaign, and would place both candidates under renewed pressure to modify their public positions before the deeply divided Illinois electorate.

Lincoln's staunch ally in Chicago, the *Chicago Press and Tribune*, felt pressure to defend Lincoln's campaign strategy in an article that was published two days after Lincoln's Chicago speech. The July 12 *Tribune* article was entitled "Speech of Hon. Abraham Lincoln in Reply to Senator Douglas," with the subtitle "Enthusiastic Reception of Mr. Lincoln by the Republicans of Chicago." The newspaper admitted what Lincoln's critics had stated, that the "audience assembled to hear Hon. Abraham Lincoln on Saturday evening was in point of numbers, about three-fourths as large as that of the previous evening, when Douglas held forth." Although Lincoln had attracted the smaller audience, the *Tribune* asserted "in point of enthusiasm" the audience was "about four times as great." Further, it represented a great mass of humanity because the "crowd extended from the corner of Lake and Dearborn Streets the whole length of the Tremont House, and as on the evening previous, the balconies, windows and roofs of the adjoining buildings were filled with attentive spectators—ladies and gentlemen." This was not the result of substantial publicity, because the "only advertisement of the meeting consisted of a notice in the Saturday morning papers, and a few handbills distributed during the day. The essential difference in the two demonstrations was simply that the Lincoln audience was enthusiastically for Lincoln," and the Douglas audience was not "qualified in favor of anybody. This will be admitted by any fair-minded man who witnessed both demonstrations." The *Tribune* acknowledged that Douglas's supporters had estimated their "crowd of Friday evening at 30,000" but noted that this estimate was "something more than the whole male adult population of the city. We presume that 12,000 is a liberal reckoning for that evening, and that 9,000 would about cover the gathering of Saturday night."

The *Tribune* emphasized the passion of the audience more than its number. "During the progress of Mr. Lincoln's speech a procession of four hundred men from the Seventh ward including the German Republican Club, arrived on the ground, preceded by a band of music, and carrying the Seventh ward banner. They were received with loud and continued cheers from the audience." When Lincoln was introduced and "made his appearance he was greeted with a perfect storm of applause. For some moments the enthusiasm continued unabated. At last, when by a wave of his hand partial silence was restored, Mr. Lincoln spoke."[2]

On July 23, the pro–Douglas *Chicago Times* fired back at the *Tribune* by again attacking Lincoln's strategy, an easy target for any of Lincoln's opponents, and poked fun at Lincoln in an article entitled "An Audience Wanted":

6. A Challenge Made, A Challenge Accepted

There are but few of our readers who have not known, or at least heard of physicians unable, even in the midst of sickness, to obtain patients, lawyers unable to obtain clients, and actors unable to draw houses. But we venture to say that never before was there heard of in any political canvass in Illinois, of a candidate unable to obtain an audience to hear him! But such is the fact. Abe Lincoln, the candidate of all the Republicans, wants an audience. He came up to Chicago, and, taking advantage of the enthusiasm of Douglas' reception, made a speech here; he went to Bloomington, and, at the Douglas meeting, advertised himself for a future occasion; at Springfield he distributed handbills at the Douglas meeting imploring the people to hear him. The Springfield attempt was a failure. He came to Chicago, and declared it impossible for him to get people to turn out to hear him, and then it was resolved to try and get him a chance to speak to the crowds drawn out to meet and welcome Douglas. That proposition was partially declined and another substituted; but yet the cringing, crawling creature is hanging at the outskirts of Douglas' meetings, begging the people to come and hear him. At Clinton he rose up at the Democratic meeting, and announced his intention to speak at night, but only 250 persons could be inducted to attend his meeting.

The *Times* described Lincoln as a "poor, desperate creature" who traveled to Monticello "in Douglas's train." He "wants an audience; the poor unhappy mortal," the *Times* continued, but "people won't turn out to hear him, and he must do something, even if that something is mean, sneaking and disreputable!" The newspaper had a "suggestion to make to Mr. Judd," whom it described as "the next friend of Lincoln": "There are two very good circuses and menageries traveling through the State; these exhibitions always draw good crowds at country towns. Mr. Judd, in behalf of his candidate, at a reasonable expense, might make arrangements with the managers of these exhibitions to include a speech from Lincoln in their performances. In this way Lincoln could get good audiences, and his friends be relieved from the mortifications they all feel at his present humiliating position."

The *Illinois State Journal*, based in Springfield, responded to these complaints of the *Chicago Times*. The *Journal* described its competitor's article as "a personal attack upon Mr. Lincoln for presuming to be present when Mr. Douglas speaks." The *Journal* believed the *Times* was erroneously suggesting that "Mr. Douglas has a patent right to audiences in Illinois. We hope that Mr. Lincoln will continue to follow up Senator Douglas with a sharp stick, even if it does make his organ howl with rage."

The *Chicago Journal*, another Republican paper, also attacked the

Times. The *Journal* wrote that the "*Times* growls because Mr. Lincoln made a speech at Clinton at night, in reply to that of Senator Douglas, delivered in the afternoon, and that he 'went to Monticello in Douglas' train.' We suppose Douglas owns neither the railroad trains he travels on, nor the people whom he addresses."

Even newspapers outside of Illinois picked up on this controversy. The *New York Herald* stated that Douglas and Lincoln met at Clinton on July 27, and that Douglas had spoken for three hours while Lincoln had replied in the evening. The *Herald* described the *Times* as indulging "in a tirade against Mr. Lincoln, an extract from which will serve to indicate the bitterness of feeling that enters into this contest":

> Lincoln was present during the delivery of the speech, sitting immediately in front of Senator Douglas, but rendered invisible from the stand by a gentleman in green goggles, whom he used as a shield and cover. After Senator Douglas had concluded, and the cheers which greeted him ceased, green goggles rose and proposed three cheers for Lincoln, which were given by ten men who stood immediately around him. Mr. Lincoln then gradually lengthened out his long, lank proportions until he stood upon his feet, and with a desperate attempt at looking pleasant, said that he would not take advantage of Judge Douglas' crowd, but would "sich" as liked to hear him in the evening at the Court House. Having made this announcement in a tone and with an air of a perfect "Uriah Heep," pleading his humility, and asking for forgiveness of Heaven for his enemies, he stood washing his hands with invisible soap in imperceptible water, until his friends, seeing that his mind was wandering, took him in charge, and bundled him off the ground....

The *Herald* noted that "Mr. Lincoln's course in following Senator Douglas is condemned here even by his friends." The newspaper claimed that Lincoln "explains it by saying that he challenged Judge Douglas to meet the people and address them together, which challenge had not been accepted. This unfairness and untruth of this statement made in Chicago you who have seen the correspondence know."

Two other out-of-state newspapers commented on this issue. The *Philadelphia Press* wrote that "Lincoln, unable to gather a crowd himself, follows up Douglas and attempts to reply; but they are mere attempts. His hearers soon become satisfied and by the time he is done begging for a seat in the Senate he finds himself minus an audience." The *Journal and Courier* of Lowell, Massachusetts, trying to put a positive spin on Lincoln's

6. A Challenge Made, A Challenge Accepted

strategy, concluded that "Douglas and Lincoln are stumping the state and a right merry time they have of it; wherever the Little Giant happens to be, Abe is sure to turn up and be a thorn in his side."

Even after the debates had begun, Lincoln continued to receive criticism for "following" Douglas. In September, the *Illinois State Register*, a pro–Douglas paper, jumped into the fray with an article entitled "Who Furnishes the Audiences?":

> Under this caption the *Chicago Press and Tribune*, of the 23d inst., proceeds to argue that at the joint discussions between Douglas and Lincoln thus far, the friends of the latter have been largely in the ascendant — hence Mr. Lincoln draws the greatest crowds. This conclusion is characteristic of the logical proclivities of that paper, and only lacks one feature — truth.
>
> If this assertion is true, why then does Mr. Lincoln persist in following up Judge Douglas for the ostensible purpose of taking advantage of the large audiences assembled to hear him? For instance look at his last demonstration at Sullivan, where, through his uncourteous behavior, a riot was almost precipitated.
>
> The fact is, Mr. Lincoln can't draw large crowds — the sympathy of the people is not with him — consequently he resorts to this highly disreputable course to make a show. The Chicago organ cannot palm off such logic upon the people of Illinois.[3]

The partisanship of the *Times* and many of the papers is patently obvious, but the analysis of Lincoln's tactics, although predictably exaggerated, held some truth that even Republicans recognized. In July, approximately one week after his Springfield speech, Lincoln sought the advice of a man that some considered a traitor, Norman B. Judd.

Judd had once been a fervent member of the Democratic party and had fought with great passion against the Whigs, until Douglas's Nebraska Act. He did not abandon the Democratic Party immediately, though; he waited until 1856 to join the Republicans. In the interim, he had been one of five state legislators who had refused to support Lincoln for the Senate in 1855. His stubbornness in that election had caused many of Lincoln's supporters, including Davis, to distrust Judd, but Lincoln did not. He never wrote an ill word of Judd or any of the other Democrats who had opposed him in 1855, and who had kept him from the Senate. Lincoln believed that Judd had genuinely converted to the Republican cause, and he not only admired Judd's convictions and his candidness, but also his keen political mind.

The Lincoln-Douglas Debates and the Making of a President

Judd and Lincoln met a week before the *Times* published the article entitled "An Audience Wanted." Apparently arriving at the same conclusion as had the *Times*, the two men devised a new strategy. They concluded that Lincoln's appearances at Douglas's rallies were not successful. However, appearing with Douglas might work to Lincoln's advantage if he could persuade Douglas to share the same stage with him.

This was an ingenious decision, although not for the reasons that Lincoln and Judd had considered, but for the ramifications that this new strategy would have beyond 1858. There was no individual whom the Republicans despised more than Douglas, the author of the Nebraska Act and the destroyer of the Missouri Compromise. In fact, the hatred of Douglas was perhaps the most significant common bond among all Republicans. By having Lincoln on the platform with Douglas, he would appear as the ultimate archrival and nemesis of Douglas, in a manner that no one else could imitate. It did not matter whether he won the debates, or even if he won the election, Lincoln would be known as the Republican's champion against Douglas. This exposure would be more valuable to Lincoln's political career than multiple terms as a senator or a governor. Every newspaper article that reported on the campaign that had Lincoln's name with Douglas's name would reinforce Lincoln's image as the great defender of the Missouri Compromise and the great assailer of the Nebraska Act. This would launch Lincoln's presidential career more than any other event of 1858.[4]

My Dear Sir:
  Will it be agreeable to you to make an arrangement for you and myself to divide time, and address the same audiences during the present canvass? Mr. Judd, who will hand you this, is authorized to receive your answer; and, if agreeable to you, to enter into the terms of such arrangement.
  Your Obt. Servt
  A. Lincoln[5]

This offer must have surprised Douglas. He had served two terms in the House of Representatives, two terms in the United States Senate,

6. A Challenge Made, A Challenge Accepted

had passed the Nebraska Bill through the Halls of Congress, had traveled overseas, was well known throughout Washington and the nation, had debated against and prevailed against hostile audiences, and was considered the leading contender for his party's nomination for president. And despite Douglas's stature and unquestioned public speaking skill, Lincoln proposed to debate him.

Douglas knew his opponent's campaign had not started well. Lincoln had played into his hands by the extremism of the "House Divided" speech. Dickey had abandoned Lincoln and supplied a wonderful endorsement from Crittenden, and now Lincoln wanted to debate him. Douglas must have found it amusing how Lincoln popped up from the crowd at the end of the speeches, begging the audience to come hear him speak either later that day or the next one, and then to have only a fraction of a crowd appear.

The Senator knew the wisest course: turn down the offer. Although he was not fond of Lincoln speaking after him, or, as he described it, Lincoln having the opportunity to "close" on him, Douglas, as historian David Donald described it, "had nothing to gain" from debating this upstart, and "much to lose." But Douglas had a weakness, and the letter had hit its mark. The Senator's ego would not allow him to back down from a fight, even if conventional wisdom cried against it. He would not be called a coward:[6]

Dear Sir:
Your note of this date, in which you inquire if it would be agreeable to me to make an arrangement to divide the time and address the same audiences during the present canvass, was handed me by Mr. Judd....

I cannot refrain from expressing my surprise, if it was your original intention to invite such an arrangement that you should have waited until after I had made my appointments, inasmuch as we were both here in Chicago together for several days after my arrival, and again at Bloomington, Atlanta, Lincoln and Springfield, where it was well known I went for the purpose of consulting with the State Central Committee and agreeing upon the plan of campaign.

While under these circumstances I do not feel at liberty to make any arrangements which would deprive the Democratic candidates for congress, State officers and the Legislature from participating in the discussion at the various meetings designated by the Democratic State Central Committee, I will, in order to accommodate you as far as it is in my power to do so, take the responsibility of making an arrangement with you for a discussion between us at one prominent point in each congressional district in the state, excepting the second and sixth districts, where we have both spoken and in each of which cases you had the concluding speech. If agreeable to you, I will indicate the following places as those most suitable in the several congressional districts at which we should speak, to wit, Freeport, Ottawa, Galesburg, Quincy, Alton, Jonesboro and Charleston.

I will confer with you at the earliest convenient opportunity in regard to the mode of conducting the debate and the times of meeting at the several places subject to the condition that where appointments have already been made by the Democratic State Central Committee at any of those places I must insist upon you meeting me at the time specified.

Very respectfully, Your Obd't Servant
S.A. Douglas[7]

Dear Sir:
Yours of the 24th, in relation to an arrangement to divide time and address the same audiences, is received; and, in appology [sic] for not sooner replying, allow me to say that when I sat by you at dinner yesterday I was not aware that you had answered my note, nor certainly, that my own note had been presented to you. An hour after I saw a copy of your answer in the Chicago Times; and, reaching home, I found the original awaiting me....

I agree to an arrangement for us to speak at the seven places you have named, and at your own times, provided you name the times at once, so that I, as well as you, can have to myself the time not covered by the arrangement. As to the other details, I wish perfect reciprocity, and no more. I wish as much time as you, and that conclusions shall alternate. That is all. Your obedient Servant,
A. Lincoln

P.S. As matters now stand, I shall be at no more of your exclusive meetings; and for about a week from to-day a letter from you will reach me at Springfield.[8]

Dear Sir:
Your letter, dated yesterday, accepting my proposition for a joint discussion at one prominent point in each Congressional district as stated in my previous letter was received this morning.

The times and places designated are as follows:

6. A Challenge Made, A Challenge Accepted

Ottawa, La Salle Co.	August	21	1858
Freeport, Stephensen [sic] Co.	"	27	"
Jonesboro, Union Co.	September	15"	"
Charleston, Coles Co.	"	18"	"
Galesburg, Knox Co.	October	7"	"
Quincy, Adams Co.	"	13"	"
Alton, Madison Co.	"	15"	"

I agree to your suggestion that we shall alternately open and close the discussion. I will speak at Ottawa one hour, you can reply, occupying an hour and a half, and I will then follow for half an hour. At Freeport you shall open the discussion and speak one hour, I will follow for an hour and a half and you can then reply for half an hour. We will alternate in like manner in each successive place. Very resp' Y'r ob't Serv't,
 S.A. Douglas[9]

Dear Sir
 Yours of yesterday, naming places, times, and terms, for joint discussions between us, was received this morning. Although, by the terms, as you propose, you take four openings and closes to my three, I accede, and thus close the arrangement. I direct this to you at Hillsboro; and shall try to have both your letter and this, appear in the Journal and Register of Monday morning.
 Your Obt. Servt.
 A. Lincoln[10]

Three weeks after Lincoln wrote this letter, the most famous political debates in American history began and, more importantly, so did the forging of an American statesman.

7

The First Debate: Ottawa, Illinois

August 21, 1858

Ottawa was, for Lincoln, a new hope. The "House Divided" speech, his strategy of following Douglas throughout the state, and the Dickey defection had all given Lincoln the appearance of a young, inexperienced upstart attempting to defeat a more established and more mature politician. Ottawa was Lincoln's opportunity to stand on the same stage with Douglas, to battle with the Senator, and to show the electorate that he was Douglas's equal. It would be an opportunity lost. Lincoln would fail in all respects.

Lincoln's political career was filled with carefully refined speeches, before either a jury or a favorable audience, but he had no experience with political debates or hostile audiences. He had never been placed in a situation — as a lawyer, as a candidate, or as a congressman — where he had to respond quickly to an opponent or to a crowd. He had been comfortable in sedate surroundings where careful preparation provided him with an advantage. Research and writing were his forte.

Two law cases illustrate Lincoln's skill and experience. Before his brief time in Congress, a widow of an American Revolutionary War soldier, who had been cheated out of a part of her pension, came to him for help. Lincoln, hoping to avoid a court case, first approached the man who had committed the disservice and asked that he correct the wrong. To Lincoln's surprise, the man refused, and Lincoln took the case. He prepared for his courtroom speech by researching the American Revolution. The resulting speech to the jury illustrated his detailed research and his ability to draw on emotion: "Time rolls by, the heroes of '76 have passed away and are encamped on the other shore. The soldier has gone to rest, and now, crippled, blinded, and broken, his widow comes to you and to me, gentlemen of the jury, to right her wrongs. She was not always thus. She was once a beautiful young woman. Her step was as elastic, her face as fair, and her voice as sweet as any that rang in the mountains of old Virginia. But now she is poor and defenceless. Out here on the prairies of Illinois, many hundreds of miles away from the scenes of her childhood, she appeals to us, who enjoy the privileges achieved for us by the patriots of the Revolution, for our sympathetic aid and manly protection."[1]

The speech brought tears, indignation, and victory. Lincoln's notes to which he referred during his presentation were simple: "No contract.— Not professional services.— Unreasonable charge.— Money retained by Def't not given by Pl'ff.— Revolutionary War.— Describe Valley Forge privations.— Ice — Soldiers bleeding feet.— Pl'ff's husband.— Soldier leaving home for army.— Skin Def't.— Close."[2]

And skin him he did. He won the case, and he covered all the widow's costs, including her hotel bill and her transportation home.

In another case, in 1858, Lincoln defended William Armstrong, who was accused of murder. Armstrong's parents had befriended Lincoln during his early years in Illinois and Lincoln agreed to defend their son. The chief evidence against Armstrong was an eyewitness, who claimed that from one hundred fifty feet away, by the light of the moon shining overhead, he had seen Armstrong strike another man. At the trial, Lincoln produced an almanac that proved the moon was at the horizon at the time, and could not have possibly produced much light. Armstrong was found innocent, and Lincoln charged his parents no fee.

Lincoln was at his best in these cases, but they were poor preparation for political debates. Juries were not large hostile crowds. They did not banter with him nor did they cheer his opponent. Before a jury, Lincoln was confident, experienced and dominant. Before a crowd, he was not.

While Lincoln was the consummate lawyer, Douglas was a masterful debater. His skill had been honed through two terms in the House of Representatives and two terms in the Senate. Douglas had also gathered valuable experience through the hundreds of speeches he had given throughout the nation. He was quick, forceful, and articulate in his public addresses, and he knew how to grab the attention of a crowd and how to stand his ground before a hostile audience. When debating on the Senate floor, he consistently attracted a crowd in the galleries. It was not so much the importance of his speeches or the logic within, but his performance. It was theatre with all the drama that the Little Giant — all five feet four inches of him — could muster. His speeches bore evidence to his intelligence and his grasp of the issues, but it was his outbursts — "God damns" and "by Gods" — and his tone that made for a gripping show. Senators and visitors equally applauded his speeches.[3]

Before hostile crowds, Douglas was equally dramatic. His most famous encounter occurred in Chicago, the city he called home. On September 1, 1854, a violent crowd gathered to express their outrage at the Kansas-Nebraska Act. The crowd jeered, yelled, and threw objects at Douglas. The Little Giant could not speak above the noise, and he did lose his temper, but rather than immediately retreating, he stood on that stage for over two hours before finally retiring. They may have hindered his speech, but he did not surrender easily.[4]

Douglas and Lincoln differed in more crucial respects than their experience and abilities. Their political motivations and future goals for the nation were fundamentally dissimilar as well. Douglas firmly believed in manifest destiny; it had been his decades-long hope that the United States would stretch from the Atlantic to the Pacific. Slavery and all other issues were simply a hindrance to American expansion. His motivation was best expressed in an 1854 letter: "How are we to develop, cherish and protect our immense interests and possessions on the Pacific, with a vast wilderness fifteen hundred miles in breadth, filled with hostile savages, and cutting off all direct communication? The Indian barrier must be removed. The tide of emigration and civilization must be permitted to roll onward until it rushes through the passes of the mountains, and spreads over the plains, and mingles with the waters of the Pacific. Continuous lines of settlement with civil, political and religious institutions all under the protection of the law, are imperiously demanded by the highest national considerations. These are essential, but they are not sufficient. No man can keep up with the spirit of this age who travels on anything slower than the locomotive, and fails to receive intelligence by lightning. We must therefore have Rail Roads and Telegraphs from the Atlantic to the Pacific, through our own territory. Not one line only, but many lines, for the valley of the Mississippi will require as many Rail Roads to the Pacific as to the Atlantic, and will not venture to limit the number. The removal of the Indian barrier and the extension of the laws of the United States in the form of Territorial governments are the first steps toward accomplishment of each and all of those objects."[5]

As opposed to Douglas's emphasis on manifest destiny, Lincoln's decade-long passion was encapsulated in the phrase "all men are created equal." On August 17, just four days before the first debate, he gave one of his greatest speeches on the Declaration of Independence before a supportive audience in Lewistown, in central Illinois. Lincoln argued that the colonial communities, speaking through "their representatives in old Independence Hall, said to the whole world of men: 'We hold these truths to be self-evident: that all men are created equal; that they are endowed by their Creator with certain unalienable rights; that among these are life, liberty, and the pursuit of happiness.' This was their majestic interpretation of the economy of the Universe. This was their lofty, and wise, and noble understanding of the justice of the Creator to His creatures."

This right was not limited, Lincoln contended; it was to be granted "to all His creatures, to the whole great family of man. In their enlightened belief, nothing stamped with the Divine image and likeness was sent into the world to be trodden on, and degraded, and imbruted by its fellows. They grasped not only the whole race of man then living, but they reached forward and seized upon the farthest posterity. They erected a beacon to guide their children and their children's children, and the countless myriads who should inhabit the earth in other ages. Wise statesmen as they were, they knew the tendency of prosperity to breed tyrants, and so they established these great self-evident truths, that when in the distant future some man, some faction, some interest should set up the doctrine that none but rich men, or none but white men, were entitled to life, liberty, and the pursuit of happiness, their posterity might look up again to the Declaration of Independence and take courage to renew the battle which their fathers began — so that truth, and justice, and mercy, and all the humane and Christian virtues might not be extinguished from the land; so that no man would hereafter dare to limit and circumscribe the great principles on which the temple of liberty was being built."

7. The First Debate

The Declaration was not safe, though, Lincoln believed. It was under attack, and had already been damaged. "Now, my countrymen [Mr. Lincoln continued with great earnestness] if you have been taught doctrines conflicting with the great landmarks of the Declaration of Independence; if you have listened to suggestions which would take away from its grandeur, and mutilate the fair symmetry of its proportions; if you have been inclined to believe that all men are not created equal in those inalienable rights enumerated by our chart of liberty, let me entreat you to come back. Return to the fountain whose waters spring close by the blood of the Revolution. Think nothing of me — take no thought for the political fate of any man whomsoever — but come back to the truths that are in the Declaration of Independence. You may do anything with me you choose, if you will but heed these sacred principles. You may not only defeat me for the Senate, but you may take me and put me to death. While pretending no indifference to earthly honors, I do claim to be actuated in this contest by something higher than an anxiety for office. I charge you to drop every paltry and insignificant thought for any man's success. It is nothing; I am nothing; Judge Douglas is nothing. But do not destroy that immortal emblem of Humanity — the Declaration of American Independence."[6]

The speech as it was reprinted in the *Collected Works of Abraham Lincoln* is preceded with the following paragraph, which may have been written by the person who recorded the speech, and which provides insight into the passions of those who supported Lincoln in 1858: "I cannot close this letter without giving your readers a passage from Mr. Lincoln's noble and impressive apostrophe to the Declaration of Independence. This was truly one of the finest efforts of public speaking I ever listened to. It gave to his auditors such an insight into the character of the man as ought to carry him into the Senate on a great surge of popular affection. In my poor opinion, Mr. Lincoln is not only one of the foremost men in the Northwest in the nobility and excellence of his character, the clearness and scope of his intellect, but the peer of any man who has sat in the Senate since the mighty shadows of Webster and Clay ceased to darken the threshold of the Capitol."[7]

Best evidence suggests that Horace White recorded this speech, which was later widely reprinted. White had been assigned by Joseph Medill, the editor of the *Chicago Press* and *Tribune*, to cover Lincoln's campaign. The young twenty-three-year-old reporter had been an avid abolitionist. He viewed the debates in terms of the larger battle against slavery, applauded the "House Divided" speech, and cheered Lincoln's egalitarian statements. White traveled with Lincoln throughout the campaign, attended all the debates, most of the speeches and most of the rallies. Unfortunately, he never wrote a book on his first-hand experiences. His remembrances would have been completely lost had Herndon not requested that White compose the chapter on the debates for his Lincoln biography. White's quotes are from this valuable chapter.[8]

The debates were expected to attract thousands of people from a wide area around each location. The newspapers encouraged attendance for their favored candidate, including the pro–Lincoln *Chicago Press and Tribune*:

THE GREAT DEBATE AT OTTAWA

The first grand encounter between the champions of Slavery and Freedom, — Douglas and Lincoln — takes place at Ottawa on Saturday afternoon, Aug. 21st.

A special train will leave the Rock Island depot at 8 A.M., passing Blue Island at 8:45, Joliet at 9:55, Morris at 10:50, and Ottawa at 11:45, which will give plenty of time for dinner, to arrange the preliminaries, and to prepare the polemic combatants for the contest. The train will leave Ottawa on its return at 6 P.M. and will be back in Chicago at 9:45.

Passengers will be carried the round trip for half-fare from all the stations above named. How big a crowd is going from this city? The Lincoln boys should be on hand.[9]

— *Chicago Press and Tribune*, August 18, 1858

HO! FOR OTTAWA

The gallant Lincoln will enter the lists at Ottawa today, with Douglas. The meeting will be a memorable one, and the first of the present campaign.

A large delegation will be in attendance from this city, leaving here by the 8 A.M. train on the Chicago & Rock Island Railroad, returning this evening. Let there be a good attendance of our Republicans.

The Press and Tribune of Monday will contain a full Phonographic verbatim report of the speeches of Lincoln and Douglas. Let all who can be present hear the champions, and all who cannot should read and judge for themselves.[10]

— *Chicago Press and Tribune*, August 21, 1858

7. The First Debate

The next stage brought us to Ottawa, the first joint debate, August 21st. Here the crowd was enormous. The weather had been very dry and the town was shrouded in dust raised by the moving populace. Crowds were pouring into town from sunrise till noon in all sorts of conveyances, teams, railroad trains, canal boats, cavalcades, and processions on foot, with banners and inscriptions, stirring up such clouds of dust that it was hard to make out what was underneath them. The town was covered with bunting, and bands of music were tooting around every corner, drowned now and then by the roar of cannon. Mr. Lincoln came by railroad and Mr. Douglas by carriage from La Salle. A train of seventeen passenger cars from Chicago attested [to] the interest felt in that city in the first meeting of the champions. Two great processions escorted them to the platform in the public square. But the eagerness to hear the speaking was so great that the crowd had taken possession of the square and the platform, and had climbed on the wooden awning overhead, to such an extent that the speakers and the committees and reporters could not get to their places. Half an hour was consumed in a rough-and-tumble skirmish to make way for them, and, when finally this was accomplished, a section of awning gave way with its load of men and boys, and came down on the heads of the Douglas committee of reception. But, fortunately, nobody was hurt.[11]
— Horace White

Only two newspapers consistently published the debates in their entirety: the *Chicago Times* and the *Chicago Press and Tribune* (henceforth referred to as the *Tribune*). The *Times* supported Douglas while the *Tribune* backed Lincoln. Allegations flew from Republicans and Democrats throughout the debates that each paper recorded the debates in a manner favorable to their candidate, and in a manner unfavorable to their candidate's opposition. There are numerous discrepancies between the candidates' statements as recorded in the two newspapers, which presents an obvious challenge to the historian. Lincoln had an edition of the debates published and, when faced with this predicament, he arrived at an equitable solution. He chose to print Douglas's comments as they were recorded in the newspaper that supported Douglas, the *Times,* and chose to print his own comments as they were recorded in the newspaper that supported him, the

The Lincoln-Douglas Debates and the Making of a President

Tribune. The editors of the *Collected Works of Abraham Lincoln* decided to follow Lincoln's decision, and the text reprinted in this study follows that methodology.[12]

Each debate lasted three hours and covered a variety of topics; but the key issue between the two candidates was their interpretation of the Declaration of Independence as to whether "all men are created equal" applied to all men.[13]

The debate at Ottawa, in Dickey's hometown, provided the Judge with another opportunity to publicly show his support for Douglas. When Lincoln and Douglas stood upon the Ottawa stage, accompanying Douglas was Dickey, and standing with Lincoln was the congressman of the Third Congressional District, the renowned abolitionist, and one of Dickey's enemies, Owen Lovejoy.

This district was a safe Republican area. In the 1856 congressional election Lovejoy had won nearly 60 percent of the vote, with all but one of the thirteen counties giving him a majority, and two supporting him at almost 80 percent. It would be an electorate before which Lincoln should have expected strong support for his interpretation of the Declaration of Independence, but he would still straddle the fence on this issue, and not discuss the Declaration with the same boldness that he had in earlier speeches of the campaign.[14]

> At an early hour Ottawa was alive with people. From daylight till three o'clock in the afternoon the crowds came in, by train, by canal-boat, and by wagon, carriage, buggy, and on horseback. Morris, Joliet, and all the towns on the railroad, above and below Ottawa, sent up their delegates. Lincoln on Friday night left Peoria, and passed up the road to Morris, where he staid [*sic*] over, in order that he might have the appearance of being escorted to Ottawa by the crowds who filled the special train on Saturday morning. Douglas left Peru in the morning in a carriage, escorted by a large delegation on horseback, and in vehicles. The procession as it passed along the road received new accessions at every cross-road and stopping place, and when it reached Ottawa it was nearly a mile in length. As it passed through the streets the people from the sidewalks, from

7. The First Debate

windows, piazzas, house-tops, and every available standing point, cheered and welcomed him.[15]
— Chicago *Times*, August 26, 1858

At two o'clock the multitude gathered in the public square, the sun shining down with great intensity, and the few trees affording but little shade. It would seem that the most exposed part of the city was selected for the speaking.[16]
— *Chicago Press and Tribune*, August 23, 1858

If any Illinoians had doubts concerning the *Times'* partisanship, the headline for the article on the Ottawa debate left no room for doubt:

THE CAMPAIGN — DOUGLAS AMONG THE PEOPLE
Joint discussion at Ottawa.— Lincoln Breaks Down.— Enthusiasm of the People!— The Battle Fought and Won.— Lincoln's Heart Fails Him!— Lincoln's Legs Fail Him!— Lincoln's Tongue Fails Him!— Lincoln's Arms Fail Him!— Lincoln Fails All Over!!— The People Refuse to Support Him!— The People Laugh at Him!— Douglas the Champion of the People!— Douglas Skins the "Living Dog."— The "Dead Lion" Frightens the Canine.— Douglas "Trotting" Lincoln Out.— Douglas "Concludes" on Abe[17]

From the first debate, Douglas's campaign strategy was clear, and unlike his opponent he never wavered from it. Although the debate was held in a northern Illinois city, in a district that had overwhelmingly supported Lovejoy for Congress, Douglas spoke frankly on the issue that he knew was Lincoln's weaknesses: the perception that Lincoln supported "negro citizenship." Douglas asked the assembled whether they were "in favor of conferring upon the negro the rights and privileges of citizenship? Do you desire to strike out of our State Constitution that clause which keeps slaves and free negroes out of the State, and allow the free negroes to flow in, and cover your prairies with black settlements? Do you desire to turn this beautiful State into a free negro colony, in order that when Missouri abolishes slavery she can send one hundred thousand emancipated slaves into Illinois, to become citizens and voters, on an equality with yourselves? If you desire negro citizenship, if you desire to allow them to come into the State and settle with the white man, if you desire them to vote on an equality with yourselves, and to make them eligible to office, to serve on juries, and to adjudge your rights, then support Mr. Lincoln and the Black Republican party, who are in favor of the citizenship of the negro. Douglas opposed "negro citizenship in any and every form" because "this government was made on the white basis" and it was "made by white men, for the benefit of white men and their posterity for ever." The Senator favored "confining citizenship to white men, men of European birth and descent, instead of conferring it upon negroes, Indians, and other inferior races."[18]

This exemplified Douglas's strategy. He knew that the central area of Illinois would determine the election and that those in that area held far different views on the racial issue than those in northern Illinois. Douglas would repeat these statements consistently throughout the campaign. He knew he would not convince those who supported Lovejoy, but he also knew that these comments would gain the support of those who did not.

Douglas further expounded on his "negro citizenship" statements with an attack on Lincoln's interpretation of "all men are created equal." His opponent had followed "the example and lead of all the little Abolition orators, who go around and lecture in the basements of schools and churches," reading from the "Declaration of Independence, that all men were created equal, and then asks how can you deprive a negro of that equality which God and the Declaration of Independence awards to him. He and they maintain that negro equality is guaranteed [sic] by the laws of God, and that it is asserted in the Declaration of Independence. If they think so, of course they have a right to say so, and so vote. I do not question Mr. Lincoln's conscientious belief that the negro was made his equal, and hence is his brother, but for my own part, I do not regard the negro as my equal, and positively deny that he is my brother or any kin to me whatever. Lincoln has evidently learned by heart Parson Lovejoy's catechism."

Douglas understood Lovejoy's popularity, and its limits. Lovejoy was an asset to Lincoln in the areas where the Republicans where expected to win; Lovejoy was a detriment to Lincoln were he needed to win.

7. The First Debate

Douglas also, once again, attacked the "House Divided" speech. He described it as "revolutionary and destructive of the existence of this Government" and believed that, contrary to his opponent, the founding fathers had "provided that each State should retain its own Legislature, and its own sovereignty with the full and complete power to do as it pleased within its own limits." Following Lincoln's principles, Douglas predicted, would create a national uniformity, that, if established with the foundation of the republic, would have resulted in the "uniformity of slavery everywhere, or else the uniformity of negro citizenship and negro equality everywhere," two principles which Douglas knew were not acceptable to the majority in Illinois.

The Senator discussed other issues apart from the central ones. He contended that the Whig and the Democratic parties were united in their support of the Compromise of 1850, and that his "Kansas and Nebraska" bill was founded on the same principles. Douglas charged Lincoln and Trumbull with a conspiracy to dissolve both the Whig and Democratic parties in order to bring both members into an "Abolition party under the name and disguise of the Republican party." He made a passing reference to Lincoln's opposition to the Mexican War, claiming that his opponent had taken "the side of the common enemy against his own country"; he expressed his support for the Dred Scott decision and noted that Lincoln's support for "negro citizenship" explained his distaste for the Supreme Court's opinion.

Douglas also went on the offensive by putting several questions to Lincoln in rapid succession: Was Lincoln "in favor of the unconditional repeal of the fugitive slave law"? Was he opposed to the admission of additional slave states irrespective of the voters' opinion? Was he against the "admission of a new State into the Union with such a constitution as the people of that State may see fit to make"? Was he "pledged to the abolition of slavery in the District of Columbia"? Was he "pledged to prohibit slavery in all the territories of the United States"? And finally, was he "opposed to the acquisition of any more territory unless slavery is first prohibited" within the territory?

Unlike Douglas, at Ottawa, Lincoln followed a strategy that was, in fact, two-sided. Douglas had accurately represented Lincoln's views on the Declaration of Independence, and Lincoln wanted to publicly affirm these views. This was Lincoln the statesman.

Lincoln the politician knew what Douglas knew. He need not cater to voters in northern Illinois. Voters south of Chicago, south of Lovejoy's district, rejected his opinion on the Declaration of Independence and had no intention of ending slavery or conferring rights upon freed slaves. Lincoln made statements to appeal to their prejudices, claiming that the slave was not equal to "the white man" in all respects. This was Lincoln the politician. It was not the same Lincoln who had spoken so boldly in Chicago and Lewistown.[19]

Lincoln also recognized his weakness and sought to refute any radical propositions that Douglas might pin on him. He would not bring about racial equality, he stated, and "anything that argues me into his idea of perfect social and political equality with the negro, is but a specious and fantastic arrangement of words, by which a man can prove a horse-chestnut to be a chestnut horse."[20]

Lincoln countered those who argued that he intended to abolish slavery in the South. He had "no purpose directly or indirectly to interfere with the institution of slavery in the States where it exists" because he had "no lawful right to do so" and "no inclination to do so."

His statesmanship was lacking, but his political intuition was obvious as he expounded on the question of race. He had "no purpose to introduce political and social equality between the white and the black races. There is a physical difference between the two, which in my judgment will probably forever forbid their living together upon the footing of perfect equality, and inasmuch as it becomes a necessity that there must be a difference, I, as well as Judge Douglas, am in favor of the race to which I belong, having the superior position."

This was a sharp departure from his Chicago and Springfield speeches, and generally a sharp departure from Lincoln's previous statements. In his Chicago speech on July 10, Lincoln attacked the idea of "superior" and "inferior" races by asking that the nation "discard all this quibbling about this man and the other man — this race and that race and the other race being inferior, and therefore they must be placed in an inferior position" and "discard all these things, and unite as one people throughout this land, until we shall once more stand up declaring that all men are created equals." At Springfield on July 17, he had moved slightly away from his Chicago position when he spoke in favor of the "separation of the white and black races," but he had dismissed the issue

7. The First Debate

of racial superiority with the question, "Who shall say, 'I am the superior, and you are the inferior?'" Now, a little over a month after these two speeches, Lincoln was changing his public political philosophy. The Lincoln of Ottawa was now contradicting the Lincoln of Chicago and Springfield, abandoning his egalitarianism, and appearing far more as a politician than a statesman.

Despite these comments, Lincoln, as he struggled over the ideal of a statesman and that of a politician, could not pass on the opportunity to speak up on behalf of the Declaration of Independence, no matter how contrary his statements on that document were in comparison to his previous statements. Although he had argued for the concept of "superior" and "inferior" among the races, he argued that there was "no reason in the world why the negro is not entitled to all the natural rights enumerated in the Declaration of Independence, the right to life, liberty, and the pursuit of happiness." His egalitarianism had limits, and the following sentences reflected Lincoln's careful balancing act. He asserted that the "negro" was "as much entitled to these [rights] as the white man," and while he agreed with Douglas that the "negro" was not his "equal in many respects—certainly not in color, perhaps not in moral or intellectual endowment," he was in "the right to eat the bread, without the leave of anybody else, which his own hand earns." In this respect, Lincoln argued, the "negro" was his "equal and the equal of Judge Douglas, and the equal of every living man."

The slave is our equal, sometimes. This was the middle road that Lincoln intended to follow between the philosophies of Lovejoy and Davis, between the ideals of a statesman and the immediate goals of a politician.

Lincoln recognized the critical impact that the former Whigs, who had not joined the Republicans, the Democrats, or the Know-Nothings, would hold in the election and he realized that Crittenden's letter to Dickey was a direct appeal to former Whigs to support Douglas. He also recognized that their hero, above all others, was Henry Clay, the man who many considered the greatest Whig of them all. Clay's death in 1852 had left the Whigs leaderless. Lincoln described Clay as his "ideal of a statesman," both because this represented his personal view and because he knew that the dissatisfied Whigs would support the candidate that they believed was following in Clay's footsteps. Lincoln further referred to Clay as the one for whom he "fought" throughout his life. He claimed that Clay had described politicians such as Douglas as those "who would repress all tendencies to liberty and ultimate emancipation," who would "blow out the moral lights around us" and would "eradicate there the love of liberty; and then and not till then, could they perpetuate slavery in this country! To my thinking, Judge Douglas is, by his example and vast influence, doing that very thing in this community, when he says that the negro has nothing in the Declaration of Independence."

Henry Clay would have supported the Republicans, Lincoln contended. Clay desired slavery's end, and if Douglas were elected that hope would be dashed. Douglas, Lincoln asserted, was "going back to the era of our Revolution, and to the extent of his ability, muzzling the cannon which thunders its annual joyous return. When he invites any people, willing to have slavery, to establish it, he is blowing out the moral lights around us. When he says he 'cares not whether slavery is voted down or voted up'—that it is a sacred right of self-government—he is in my judgment penetrating the human soul and eradicating the light of reason and the love of liberty in this American people. And now I will only say that when, by all these means and appliances, Judge Douglas shall succeed in bringing public sentiment to an exact accordance with his own views—when these vast assemblages shall echo back all these sentiments—when they shall come to repeat his views and to avow his principles, and to say all that he says on these mighty questions—then it needs only the formality of the second Dred Scott decision, which he endorses in advance, to make Slavery alike lawful in all the States—old as well as new, North as well as South."

This was a rare example of Lincoln referring to his "House Divided" speech without actually mentioning it. He was still running away from it, but he hoped that the voters could see a link between his philosophy and that of Clay's philosophy.

Of the minor issues, Lincoln disavowed the Republican conventions and resolutions that Douglas had claimed best reflected Lincoln's philosophy. He insisted that there was "no substance" to Douglas's charge that he and Trumbull had conspired to create an abolition party by the destruction of the Democrats and Whigs. Lincoln rejected Douglas's interpretation of his actions in respect to the Mexican War, asserting that

7. The First Debate

he had opposed the manner by which the Democratic president had commenced the war, and had never taken any stance in opposition to the soldiers. He renewed his belief that Pierce, Buchanan, Taney, and Douglas had conspired to make slavery national, even if they had not met. They had created policy based on a mutual understanding, Lincoln charged. And he renewed his criticism of Douglas for opposing Chase's antislavery amendment.

Douglas had displayed remarkable consistency in his Ottawa remarks as compared with those he had delivered in Chicago, Bloomington and Springfield. In all four of these speeches, he had attacked the "House Divided" speech, defended the Kansas-Nebraska Act, and assailed the concept, that he ascribed to Lincoln, of African American equality. Not only was Douglas predictable in terms of the topics he discussed, but also the manner in which he discussed them. He attacked the "House Divided" speech for justifying belligerent action against the South. He used the concept of popular sovereignty to defend the Kansas-Nebraska Act, and he refuted African American equality with his interpretation of the Declaration of Independence. This consistency reflected his astute political skill and ability, and his decades of experience in politics. He had carved out his positions years before and was determined to maintain them, much as he had stubbornly stood before that angry Chicago mob years before.

Lincoln, in contrast, was wholly inconsistent, especially on the vital issue of the Declaration of Independence. Sometimes, as a statesman, he defended it; at other times, like a politician, he demurred. He made no overt mention of the document in the "House Divided" speech, boldly asserted the inclusion of all in Chicago, and then declared the caveat at Springfield that African Americans might not be equal in all respects. At Lewistown, he sounded the same theme as he did in Chicago, but at Ottawa, in Lovejoy's district, with Lovejoy on the platform, in a strong Republican district, he thought it necessary to embrace the concept of "superior" and "inferior" races, something he had specifically rejected in Chicago. While Douglas had developed a cohesive, universal strategy, Lincoln had none.

The Lincoln-Douglas Debates and the Making of a President

Lincoln's struggles reflected the conflict between his personal beliefs—that the Declaration of Independence applied to all men—and his perception of the public's attitude toward African Americans, especially in central Illinois. His speeches show that he believed a choice between these two opposite opinions was necessary, that a campaign based on his own unrefined personal ideas would fail.

In other respects, the debate could not be considered a positive for Lincoln's campaign either. The most honest analysis of the first debate came from Lincoln himself. A day after Ottawa he wrote: "Douglas and I, for the first time this canvass, crossed swords here yesterday; the fire flew some, and I am glad to know I am yet alive."[21] He had a penchant for understatement, and to say that the "fire flew some" exemplified Lincoln's ability for understatement.

In fact, he was shocked. Douglas had shown far more force in his remarks than Lincoln had expected. The lawyer had anticipated an exchange of ideas on the nation's future to be conducted in the manner that one would expect in a courtroom, not what one would expect in a saloon. But Douglas intended to carry the debates both by the force of his argument and by the force of his voice.

Lincoln needed help, and he knew it. He wrote to two of his most respected advisors for advice. They gathered a group of Republicans in Chicago five days after the Ottawa debate, and they provided him with precisely the advice that he so desperately required.

8

The Second Debate: Freeport, Illinois

August 27, 1858

Lincoln headed north, while his philosophy headed south. Between August 21 and August 27, he traversed a considerable distance measured both in miles and in the change of his public statements. In making the journey from Ottawa to Freeport, Lincoln left behind a companion he had known for years, one that had provided him with guidance, hope and direction, one that had made his nation unique, special and morally strong. In traveling to Freeport, Lincoln left behind the Declaration of Independence.

This abandonment exemplified Lincoln's skills as an astute politician. Although Freeport was a safe Republican area, the next two debates sites—Jonesboro and Charleston—were not. He was preparing his campaign for the future, hoping that his political career would have a future.

Freeport was a turning point for Lincoln in another respect as well. Recognizing his lack of debating experience when compared to his opponent, he requested, and received, valuable suggestions from his advisors in Chicago. This time he intended to follow the advice, unlike his solicitation before the "House Divided" speech. The recommendations enabled him to ask questions of Douglas, which gave him, for the first time in the campaign, the initiative and momentum.

The questions Lincoln asked of Douglas are important, but not as crucial as Lincoln's failure to mention the Declaration of Independence. That is the most important aspect of the Freeport debate, because it indicated that Lincoln, at this point in the campaign, was willing to compromise on his most dearly held principle. His omission was of far greater consequence than what he included.

Lincoln wrote two letters, one to Judd, and another to an associate, requesting advice for the Freeport debate. The Judd letter has never been found, but the second letter provides some indication as to the contents of the first:

> I have just written Judd that I wish him and you to meet me at Freeport next Friday to give me the benefit of a consultation with you. Douglas is propounding questions to me, which perhaps it is not quite safe to wholly disregard. I have my view of the mode to dispose of them, but I also want yours and Judd's. I have written more at length to Judd, and would to you, but for lack of time. See Judd, you and he keep the matter to yourselves, and meet me at Freeport without fail.
> Your as ever
> Lincoln[1]

Lincoln's advisors, six of them including Judd and Joseph Medill, the editor of the *Tribune*, convened, and from that meeting Medill wrote him a letter marked "*Confidential*" and addressed to "Friend Lincoln."

According to Medill, the group focused on four main questions that Lincoln should ask of Douglas, knowing that these would put Douglas where Lincoln needed him, on the defensive: "Put a few ugly questions at Douglas," such as "Do you care whether slavery be voted up or down?" This question would force Douglas to admit whether he was concerned over the institution. Lincoln's advisors were confident that Douglas was not.

His advisors also recommended that he ask his opponent: "Will you stand by the adjustment of the Kansas question on the basis of the English bill compromise?" The English bill required that the admission of Kansas be decided by a vote of the territorial residents. The enactment of this bill had resulted in the overwhelming defeat of the Lecompton Constitution, which had allowed slavery, ensuring that Kansas would be admitted as a free state. This was in apparent opposition to the Supreme Court's Dred Scott decision that permitted slavery in Kansas. The question would force Douglas to choose between his popular sovereignty doctrine or Taney's determination, between the residents' right to decide their state's constitution or the Supreme Court's right to allow slavery where the Missouri Compromise had banned it. The next two

8. The Second Debate

recommended questions were intended to complete the trap: "Having given your acquiescence and sanction to the Dred Scott decision that destroys popular sovereignty in the Territories, will you acquiesce in the other half of that decision when it comes to be applied to the states, by the same court? What becomes of your vaunted popular Soveignty [*sic*] in Territories since the Dred Scott decision?"

Medill offered advice as to which questions Lincoln should ask, and how he should ask them: "Put your questions in as sharp pointed and *offensive* a form as possible, and *note down* his replies, for your rejoinder."

Medill's letter also contained guidance for the use of time: "Dont [*sic*] let the foregoing occupy over *half* an *hour*. Employ your best hour in pitching into Dug.[2] Make your assertions *dogmatically* and *unqualifiedly*. Be saucy with the 'Catiline' & permit no browbeating — in other words give him h--l."[3]

Lincoln was to show that Douglas was doing the "treasonable work of the slave holders, betraying & humbugging Illinois." It was imperative that Lincoln not be "on the *defensive* at all" and Medill recommended that he "hold Dug up as a "traitor," as a "conspirator," as "a proslavery, bamboozelling demagogue." Lincoln should "wind up" his last half hour "with a *peroration* to the Declaration of Independence such as your Lewistown speech."

Medill urged Lincoln that above "all things be bold, *defiant* and *dogmatic*," for then "a great triumph" would await him. Douglas, in the antislavery area of northern Illinois, might attempt to claim support for "Negro" equality, Medill feared. In that case, Lincoln was to show that it was "*humbug, slang* and trash, uttered to deceive the ignorant and *swindle* foolish men out of their votes." Medill, knowing Lincoln's character, thought he should dispense with it: "For once leave modesty aside. You are dealing with a bold, brazen, lying rascal & you must *fight the devil with fire*."[4]

The questions were perfect, but Lincoln did not follow all the advice; he failed to act on one crucial recommendation.

Judd's and Medill's support for Lincoln did not pass without notice. One newspaper, the *Missouri Republican* of St. Louis, ironically a Democratic newspaper, used space to criticize Lincoln's supporters:

The Lincoln-Douglas Debates and the Making of a President

These lying reports have been devised by the Republican committee, which meets every evening at the office of the *Press and Tribune* for the purpose of squaring up the reports sent in by Lincoln's hired reporters, and to see that they tell the tale of his progress as Republican leaders can best afford to let the readers of their circulating mediums peruse them. I speak on no hypothesis, for it is beyond denial that the committee does so meet on nearly every evening, and that the Black Republican gubernatorial aspirant for 1860, Mr. Judd, is constantly running in to see that all goes on according to gunter.[5]

The crowd that assembled at Freeport on the 27th of August was even larger than that at Ottawa. Hundreds of people came from Chicago and many from the neighboring State of Wisconsin. Douglas came from Galena the night before the debate, and was greeted with a great torch-light procession. Lincoln came the following morning from Dixon, and was received at the railway station by a dense crowd, filling up all the adjacent streets, who shouted themselves hoarse when his tall form was seen emerging from the train. Here, again, the people had seized upon the platform, and all the approaches to it, an hour before the speaking began, and a hand-to-hand fight took place to secure possession.[6]
— Horace White

Friday was the day appointed for the joint discussion at Freeport between Douglas and Lincoln.
On Thursday night Judge Douglas reached Freeport from Galena, and was met at the depot by a vast multitude of persons. As he stepped upon the platform, he was greeted with tremendous shouts and cheers. A grand salute was fired at the same time, which, as it resounded through the city, gave notice to the people that the champion of popular rights had arrived, and thousands of persons flocked from the hotels and from all parts of the city swelling the assemblage to not less than five thousand persons.[7]
— *Chicago Times*

To-day was set apart as the occasion of the second discussion between Lincoln and Douglas, and Freeport has the distinguished honor. It is a day fruitful in debate, and abundantly refreshing to hotel and saloon keepers,

8. The Second Debate

who stand aghast at the multitudes to be fed. There is an immense throng here, larger than that at Ottawa, and larger, it is admitted, than at the great Freemont demonstration here, two years ago. By the Illinois Central and the Chicago and Galena railroads, by boats on the Pecatonic, and by divers vehicles, the masses have come. The Rockford train brought eighteen cars filled. The Dixon train brought twelve, and others in proportion. All prairiedom has broken loose. Banners waive unyielding devotion to "Old Abe Lincoln," and unfettering faith in "Douglas and Popular Sovereignty."[8]
— *Evening Post* of New York

There was not one congressional district in all of Illinois that tilted more heavily toward the Republicans than did the first, which contained all six of Illinois' northernmost counties. The Republican candidate had received over 70 percent of the vote in the 1856 election in all of these counties and three voted over 80 percent for the Republican. If Lincoln needed to reinvigorate his campaign, there was no better place for him to accomplish that goal than in this one.[9]

He stood at Freeport armed with the new questions that would change, at least for the moment, the momentum of the campaign. Lincoln made some slight changes in the wording to increase their potency. After answering some "interrogatories" that Douglas had previously asked of him, Lincoln proceeded to "propound to the Judge" his own interrogatories:

The first one is:

Question 1. If the people of Kansas shall, by means entirely unobjectionable in all other respects, adopt a State Constitution, and ask admission into the Union under it, before they have the requisite number of inhabitants according to the English bill — some ninety-three thousand — will you vote to admit them?

Q. 2. Can the people of a United States Territory, in any lawful way, against the wish of any citizen of the United States, exclude slavery from its limits prior to the formation of a State Constitution?

Q. 3. If the Supreme Court of the United States shall decide that States can not exclude slavery from their limits, are you in favor of acquiescing in, adopting and following such decision as a rule of political action?

Q. 4. Are you in favor of acquiring additional territory, in disregard of how such acquisition may affect the nation on the slavery question?[10]

Lincoln also called on all those opposed to the Nebraska bill to unite, although there was little need for this encouragement before the Freeport audience. He was clearly addressing his comments to the future audiences in the central and southern areas. Lincoln declared that the "plain truth is this. At the introduction of the Nebraska policy, we believed there was a new era being introduced in the history of the Republic, which tended to the spread and perpetuation of slavery. But in our opposition to that measure we did not agree with one another in everything. The people in the north end of the State were for stronger measures of opposition than we of the central and southern portions of the State, but we were all opposed to the Nebraska doctrine. We had that one feeling and that one sentiment in common." Douglas, Lincoln asserted, was "afraid" that all the anti–Nebraska individuals would "pull together. This is what alarms him more than anything else. For my part, I do hope that all of us, entertaining a common sentiment in opposition to what appears to us as a design to nationalize and perpetuate slavery, will waive minor differences on questions which either belong to the dead past or the distant future, and all pull together in this struggle."

Since Douglas had continued his assaults on the "House Divided" speech, Lincoln felt compelled to defend it and admitted some frustration in having to tread this well worn path again. He acknowledged, perhaps reluctantly, that Douglas had "addressed himself to the abolition tendencies of a speech of mine, made at Springfield in June last" and he admitted that he had "so often tried to answer what he is always saying on that melancholy theme" that he almost turned "with disgust from the discussion—from the repetition of an answer to it." But Lincoln hoped that "nearly all of this intelligent audience have read that speech" and he left it to them to "inspect it closely, and see whether it contains any of those 'bugaboos' which frighten Judge Douglas."

Lincoln mentioned a few other issues. He claimed that Douglas, in opposition to his policy of popular sovereignty, had opposed an amendment that Senator Salmon P. Chase of Ohio had introduced, an amendment which would have permitted the people of a territory the right to determine slavery's legality within the territory. He continued his assertion that a conspiracy existed between "a large number of members of Congress, the Supreme Court and two Presidents" for the purpose of nationalizing slavery. And, in response to Douglas's charges concerning

8. The Second Debate

the various Republican resolutions, Lincoln admitted that there were differences among them, but that he did not hold to all provisions of all resolutions passed by all Republicans.

Douglas, exhibiting the boldness which had become his trademark, immediately answered Lincoln's questions. He constructed his replies in order to satisfy both those in northern and southern Illinois, and, in looking ahead to his expected 1860 presidential bid, those of the northern and southern United States. In respects to this last goal, he would fail. This was most visibly exhibited by the fact that Douglas won a majority in neither the northern nor southern states in that election. Douglas failed to realize that, on the slavery issue, the middle ground no longer existed, and his attempt to find the common ground fell far short. He reminded the audience that Lincoln desired to know "if the people of Kansas shall form a constitution by means entirely proper and unobjectionable and ask admission into the Union as a State, before they have the requisite population for a member of Congress, whether I will vote for that admission." Kansas had enough people to constitute a slave State, Douglas answered, and had enough to constitute a free State. Neither "Kansas, or any other territory, should be admitted until it has the requisite population."

These were sound, legal answers, but half the nation demanded that Kansas enter the Union as a slave state, while the other half demanded Kansas's entrance as a free state. Douglas's position, appearing neutral, satisfied neither North nor South and was unpopular on the national stage, although it had little effect within Illinois.

Douglas continued on to the next question. Lincoln had asked him if the "people of a territory in any lawful way against the wishes of any citizen of the United States [could] exclude slavery from their limits prior to the formation of the State Constitution."

This was the perfect trap. Douglas could either side with the Supreme Court's Dred Scott decision which allowed slavery in the territories, or he could hold that self-determination, the right of the citizens in a territory, trumped the Court. For Douglas, there was no escape. He answered "emphatically, as Mr. Lincoln has heard me answer a hundred times from every stump in Illinois, that in my opinion the people of a territory can, by lawful means, exclude slavery from their limits prior to the formation of a State Constitution." The Supreme Court was not the crucial factor, Douglas argued. The Court's decisions on the "abstract question whether slavery may or may not go into a territory under the constitution" was immaterial, because "the people have the lawful means to introduce it or exclude it as they please, for the reason that slavery cannot exist a day or an hour anywhere, unless it is supported by local police regulations."

For Douglas, self-determination of the citizens of the territory trumped the expressed opinion of the Supreme Court. This position would gradually lose Douglas support in the southern United States, as the slaveholders and those who believed their economic well-being was tied to slavery knew that the majority in Kansas would not support slavery. While this position appealed more to northern Illinois than central and southern Illinois in the 1858 campaign, it never proved to be the crucial issue.

Lincoln's third question focused on the apparent contradictions of popular sovereignty and the Supreme Court. He had asked of Douglas, "If the Supreme Court of the United States shall decide that a State of this Union cannot exclude slavery from its own limits will I submit to it?" Lincoln's advisors had drawn this question from the Supreme Court's Dred Scott decision, which some Republicans claimed made slavery legal throughout the nation, even in those states which had prohibited it by state law. Douglas simply answered that he would obey the Supreme Court, a position which further alienated him from those in northern Illinois and the northern United States.

Douglas, having been on the defensive when replying to the first three, regained the offensive by turning the fourth question back on the Republicans. Lincoln asked Douglas if he were in "favor of acquiring additional territory in disregard as to how such acquisition may effect the Union on the slavery questions." "This," Douglas admitted, was a question that was "very ingeniously and cunningly put." He answered by claiming that the "Black Republican creed lays it down expressly, that under no circumstances shall we acquire any more territory unless slavery is first prohibited in the country." The Senator turned the issue around and asked "Mr. Lincoln whether he is in favor of that proposition. Are you [addressing Mr. Lincoln] opposed to the acquisition of any more territory, under any circumstances, unless slavery is prohibited in it?" Douglas recognized that this was a question which Lincoln did "not like to answer. When I ask him whether he stands up to that article in the platform of his party, he turns, yankee-fashion, and without answering it, asks me whether I am in favor of acquiring territory without regard to how it may affect the Union on the slavery question." The Senator then expressed his overall hopes for his nation, hopes centered on American expansionism: "I answer that whenever it becomes necessary, in our growth and progress, to acquire more territory, that I am in favor of it, without reference to the question of slavery, and when we have acquired it, I will leave the people free to do as they please, either to make it slave or free territory, as they prefer. It is idle to tell me or you that we have territory enough. Our fathers supposed that we had enough when our territory extended to the Mississippi river, but a few years' growth and expansion satisfied them that we needed more, and the Louisiana territory, from the West branch of the Mississippi, to the British possessions, was acquired. Then we acquired Oregon, then California and New Mexico. We have enough now for the present, but this is a young and a growing nation." Defending the Kansas-Nebraska Act on the basis of manifest destiny, Douglas concluded his argument: "With our natural increase, growing with a rapidity unknown in any other part of the globe, with the tide of emigration that is fleeing from despotism in the old world to seek refuge in our own, there is a constant torrent pouring into this country that requires more land, more territory upon which to settle, and just as fast as our interests and our destiny require additional territory in the north, in the south, or on the islands of the ocean, I am for it, and when we acquire it, will leave the people, according to the Nebraska bill, free to do as they please on the subject of slavery and every other question."

Douglas made special mention of the "House Divided" speech by asserting that Lincoln's apocryphal statements proved Lincoln's intention to oppose the admission of any additional slave states. He asserted that the "true intent and inevitable conclusion to be drawn from his first Springfield speech is, that he is opposed to the admission of any more slave States under any circumstance. If he is so opposed why not say so? If he believes this Union cannot endure divided into free and slave States, that they must all become free in order to save the Union, he is bound, as an honest man, to vote against any more slave States. If he believes it he is bound to do it. Show me that it is my duty in order to save the

Union to do a particular act, and I will do it if the constitution does not prohibit it." Douglas, on the other hand, was "not for the dissolution of the Union under any circumstances" and would "pursue no course of conduct that will give just cause for the dissolution of the Union. The hope of the friends of freedom throughout the world rests upon the perpetuity of this Union. The down-trodden and oppressed people who are suffering under European despotism all look with hope and anxiety to the American Union as the only resting place and permanent home of freedom and self-government."

Frederick Douglass, an abolitionist, an African American, a former slave, a writer, and an orator, had been a hero to the abolitionists, and a lightning rod to many others. He was a valuable asset to the Senator's cause. Douglas used Douglass to his advantage and addressed the issue that he knew would determine the outcome of the campaign: the place of the "negro" in American society. The Senator realized that "some people in this country think that Fred. Douglass is a very good man" and recalled that the last time he had made a speech in this region, he had seen "a carriage, and a magnificent one it was, drive up and take a position on the outside of the crowd; a beautiful young lady was sitting on the box seat, whilst Fred. Douglass and her mother reclined inside, and the owner of the carriage acted as driver. I saw this in your own town. All I have to say of it is this, that if you, Black Republicans, think that the negro ought to be on a social equality with your wives and daughters, and ride in a carriage with your wife, whilst you drive the team, you have perfect right to do so.... All I have to say on that subject is that those of you who believe that the negro is your equal and ought to be on an equality with you socially, politically, and legally have a right to entertain those opinions, and of course will vote for Mr. Lincoln." This all bore evidence for Douglas's chief claims that, in 1854, "after the death of Clay and Webster, Mr. Lincoln on the part of the Whigs undertook to abolitionize the Whig party, by dissolving it, transferring the members into the Abolition camp."

Douglas also responded to Lincoln's assertions. As for the Chase amendment, the Nebraska bill permitted those in the territories to determine the legality of slavery while the Chase amendment had been offered for the sole purpose of enabling "demagogues in the country to try and deceive the people." He also flatly denied any conspiracy to nationalize slavery, calling such allegations "false" and an "infamous lie."

8. The Second Debate

In his comments, Douglas continued the strategy that he had employed at the first debate with attacks on the "House Divided," defense of the Kansas-Nebraska Act and the Dred Scott decision, while attacking African American equality. In terms of the four questions, Douglas had answered each one with the political skill and intelligence that he had long displayed, but the questions succeeded in their objective. For the first time in the campaign, Lincoln stood on equal footing with Douglas. The Senator's answers would not harm his current campaign, but they did further damage to his national standing, especially in the southern states.

The Freeport questions can be overemphasized, however. Lincoln did not consider these questions of great persuasion, at least when judged by the frequency of their repetition. He only repeated some of the questions at two other debates. At Jonesboro, he mentioned the first two questions, and added a fifth one, while at Galesburg, he repeated only the third question. Compared to other issues such as the Kansas-Nebraska Act, the Dred Scott decision, and the Declaration of Independence, the Freeport questions received far less attention from Lincoln, and can best be considered minor issues of the debates.[11]

Lincoln had exhibited political maturity when preparing for the Freeport debate by seeking, and then accepting, advice, something he failed to do when preparing the "House Divided" speech. Still, he had not followed all of Medill's suggestions. At the end of the letter, Medill had proposed: "And wind up your last half hour after noting his replies with a *peroration* to the Declaration of Independence such as your Lewistown speech."[12] Lincoln ignored this recommendation and made no mention of the Declaration of Independence. This was a shocking change, considering how important Lincoln believed this document was for his nation. For someone who, just five years later, would write his most famous speech, the Gettysburg Address, and refer to the Declaration of Independence as America's cornerstone in the opening line, "Four score and seven years ago" (1776), this exclusion was all the more surprising.

The omission is best explained as a political strategy by which Lincoln intended to appeal to southern and central Illinois, where the next two debates were scheduled. The Freeport debate was not an example of Lincoln's statesmanship, but rather his political skill. This was the first time in the campaign that Lincoln compromised on his most cherished principles for the sake of winning the election.

Whether this omission was an anomaly, or whether it indicated a permanent change in strategy, would be revealed at the next debate at Jonesboro, deep within southern Illinois. The next debate would show whether the Lincoln of Chicago and Lewiston, or the Lincoln of Freeport was dominant, whether Lincoln the politician, or Lincoln the statesman, was guiding the campaign.

9

The Third Debate: Jonesboro, Illinois

September 15, 1858

Lincoln headed south. Four hundred miles separated the northern Illinois city of Freeport from the southern Illinois city of Jonesboro. Freeport lay just twenty miles south of the fervently antislavery state of Wisconsin, while Jonesboro sat barely twenty miles from the slave state of Kentucky.

In making this journey, Lincoln cemented a significant change in strategy that he had made before Freeport: he once again left behind the Declaration of Independence. This decision, wise for a politician, disappointing for a statesman, had become the center of his campaign. Those who resided in this extreme southern portion of Illinois, known as Egypt, clung to a political philosophy that mirrored that of their neighbors on the opposite side of the Ohio River. The Republicans failed to field a candidate in the Jonesboro Congressional District. In this region, the party was resigned to defeat. Lincoln was not. He would not yield in any district or at any debate and was prepared to modify his public statements to match the public sentiments of the Jonesboro region.

The 1856 congressional election demonstrated overwhelming evidence of the Ninth Congressional District's bias. In the eighteen counties there, the Republican candidate gained a majority in only one, and that by just 51 percent. The Democrats garnered over 90 percent support in eight of them. For the district as a whole, 81 percent of the people of southern Illinois voted for the Democratic candidate. By any measure this constituted a landslide, and it was expected to be repeated again in 1858.[1] In fact, the disparity between the voter preferences of the

The Lincoln-Douglas Debates and the Making of a President

First Congressional District, where the Freeport debate had occurred, and the Ninth Congressional District was so substantial that the following appeared in an 1857 *Chicago Tribune* article: "There is not between South Carolina and Massachusetts ... a more deadly hostility than between the Ninth and First Congressional Districts in this State."[2]

Lincoln traveled throughout central Illinois in making his way to Jonesboro. On one trip, taking a train from his hometown of Springfield to Decatur, less than fifty miles east, he made a promise to Horace White which he was unable to keep:

> We left Springfield about nine o'clock in the evening for Decatur, where we were to change cars and take the north-bound train on the Illinois Central Railway. I was very tired and I curled myself up as best I could on the seat to take a nap, asking Mr. Lincoln to wake me up at Decatur, which he promised to do. I went to sleep, and when I did awake I had the sensation of having been asleep a long time. It was daylight and I knew that we should have reached Decatur before midnight. Mr. Lincoln's seat was vacant. When I was pulling myself together, the conductor opened the door of the car and shouted, "State Line." This was the name of a shabby little town on the border of Indiana. There was nothing to do but to get out and wait for the next train going back to Decatur. About six o'clock in the evening I found my way to Clinton. The meeting was over, of course, and the Chicago *Tribune* had lost its expected report, and I was out of pocket for railroad fares. I wended my way to the house of Mr. C.H. Moore, where Mr. Lincoln was staying, and where I, too, had been an expected guest. When Mr. Lincoln saw me coming up the garden path, his lungs began to crow like a chanticleer, and I thought he would laugh, sans intermission, an hour by his dial. He paused long enough to say that he had fallen asleep, also, and did not wake up till the train was starting from Decatur. He had very nearly been carried past the station himself, and, in his haste to get out, had forgotten all about his promise to waken me. Then he began to laugh again. The affair was so irresistibly funny, in his view....[3]
> — Horace White

Before Republican audiences, Lincoln still maintained his allegiance to the promises of the Declaration of Independence, although he

9. The Third Debate

acknowledged the difficulties of making such statements. At a speech at Clinton, a town in central Illinois, on September 2, he confessed personal frustration at the Democrats' attacks on the Declaration: "We can no longer express our admiration for the Declaration of Independence without their petty sneers." The Democrats were "fast bringing that sacred instrument into contempt" in their "desire that slavery should be perpetual and that we should not foster all lawful moves toward emancipation, and to gain their end they will endeavor to impress upon the public mind that the negro is not human, and even upon his own soil he has no rights which white men are bound to respect." To Lincoln, the great danger lay in Douglas's attempt to make the people "believe that slavery is a sacred right" by swallowing "Dred Scottism, that the right of property in negroes is not confined to those states where it is established by local law," and "if by special sophisms he can make you believe that no nation except the English are born equal and are entitled to life, liberty, and the pursuit of happiness ... then may we truly despair of the universality of freedom ... and give in our adhesion to the perpetuation and unlimited extension of slavery."[4]

There were those who wished he would drop his interpretation of the Declaration of Independence. On September 3, while in Bloomington, Lincoln met with David Davis, the only time during the campaign that they met. Davis's letters always recommended that Lincoln take a conservative stance on the slavery issue and that he make no comments suggesting that the "negro" be included in the Declaration of Independence. The Judge advised the candidate: "Among all the Kentuckians, it is industriously circulated that you favor negro Equality. All the orators should distinctly & emphatically disavow negro suffrage, negroes holding office, serving on juries & the like."[5] Davis would only accept statements that argued for slavery to remain confined. Any comments beyond that position would be considered political naiveté or political suicide.

On September 7, Lincoln and Lovejoy spoke at Paris, Illinois, a town in central Illinois near the Indiana border. Lovejoy had not wavered in his philosophy. In fact, the *Tribune* reported that Republicans and old-line Whigs responded to Lovejoy's speech with the words, "If that's what they call Abolitionism, I'm an Abolitionist."[6] White described the audience's reaction: "We were joined by Owen Lovejoy, who had never been in that part of the State before. The fame of Lovejoy as an Abolitionist had preceded him, however, and the people gathered around him in a curious and hesitating way, as though he were a witch who might suddenly give them lock-jaw or bring murrain on their cattle, if he were much provoked. Lovejoy saw this and was greatly amused by it, and when he made a speech in the evening, Mr. Lincoln having made his in the daytime, he invited the timid ones to come up and feel of his horns and examine his cloven feet and forked tail. Lovejoy was one of the most effective orators of his time. After putting his audience in good humor in this way, he made one of his impassioned speeches which never failed to gain votes where human hearts were responsive to the wrongs of slavery."[7]

Lincoln could not have met with two Republicans more opposite than these two individuals. He well understood their opposing views. While his "House Divided" speech expressed more Lovejoy than Davis, he was moving away from the advice of the Preacher to the advice of the Judge.

He did not accept the Judge's advice quickly. On September 11, at Edwardsville, Illinois, another town in central Illinois, in his concluding remarks, Lincoln spoke not as a politician, but as a statesman. He succinctly stated the division between the two parties in his opening comments: "The difference between the Republican and the Democratic parties on the leading issue of this contest, as I understand it, is that the former consider slavery a moral, social and political wrong, while the latter do not consider it either a moral, social or political wrong."[8]

In his closing paragraph, he spoke with a boldness he had not exhibited since the "House Divided" speech and Lewistown:

> Now, when by all these means you have succeeded in dehumanizing the negro; when you have put him down, and made it forever impossible for him to be but as the beasts of the field; when you have extinguished his soul, and placed him where the ray of hope is blown out in darkness like that which broods over the spirits of the damned; are you quite sure the demon which you have roused will not turn and rend you? What constitutes the bulwark of our own liberty and independence? It is not our frowning battlements, our bristling sea coasts, the guns of our war steamers, or the strength of our gallant and disciplined army. These are not our reliance against a resumption of tyranny in our fair land. All of them may

9. The Third Debate

be turned against our liberties, without making us stronger or weaker for the struggle. Our reliance is in the love of liberty which God has planted in our bosoms. Our defense is in the preservation of the spirit which prizes liberty as the heritage of all men, in all lands, everywhere. Destroy this spirit, and you have planted the seeds of despotism around your own doors. Familiarize yourselves with the chains of bondage, and you are preparing your own limbs to wear them. Accustomed to trample on the rights of those around you, you have lost the genius of your own independence, and become the fit subjects of the first cunning tyrant who rises.[9]

These speeches defined Lincoln's strategy. Before a Republican audience, he declared his full support of the Declaration as it applied to all men. Before a mixed audience that he faced during the debates, he demurred. Before the heavily pro–Democratic audience at Jonesboro, he would not speak so boldly.

From Edwardsville we went to the Jonesboro joint debate. The audience here was small, not more than 1,000 or 1,500, and nearly all Democrats. This was in the heart of Egypt. The country people came into the little town with ox teams mostly, and a very stunted breed of oxen, too. Their wagons were old-fashioned, and looked as though they were ready to fall in pieces. A train with three or four carloads of Douglas men came up, with Douglas himself, from Cairo. All who were present listened to the debate with very close attention, and there was scarcely any cheering on either side. Of course we did not expect any in that place....[10]
— Horace White

White's description of the Jonesboro area, and specifically the Ninth Congressional District appears accurate, especially when considering the statistics from the 1860 census. In that year, Illinois contained 1,182 farms which exceeded five hundred acres in size, but a mere twenty existed in the Ninth. The state averaged 37.4 percent of unimproved farm acreage; in the Ninth, the percentage was almost double, at 66 percent. As historian John Y. Simon concluded, the Ninth "was a region of subsistence farmers, southern in origin, Protestant in religion, and Democratic in politics."[11]

The Lincoln-Douglas Debates and the Making of a President

The only thing noteworthy that I recall at Jonesboro was not political and not even terrestrial. It was the splendid appearance of Donati's comet in the sky, the evening before the debate. Mr. Lincoln greatly admired this strange visitor, and he and I sat for an hour or more in front of the hotel looking at it.[12]
— Horace White

The pro–Lincoln *Chicago Journal* found the arrival of Douglas and his cannon worth noting. The *Journal* was compelled to "say something about the 'reception' Douglas and his cannon were honored with here." The reception "was highly amusing, and to the Senator himself, evidently a disappointment. When the train arrived at the Station, his cannon (he always carries it with him, on an extra wood car attached to the train) fired his own salute, and a crowd of about a hundred rushed to the cars." Douglas stepped forward, "waved his hand, and nobody appearing to take any particular notice of him —(they are a very *cool* set of people down here, notwithstanding the hot weather they are having)— he went to a carriage prepared for him and left. There was no cheering — no anything."[13]

The railroads, which strongly supported Douglas, provided him with a private railroad car, operated special trains to his campaign rallies, and freely advertised for him. One of the railroad officials who assisted the Senator was the vice president of the Illinois Central Railroad, George B. McClellan. These services were not free, though; Douglas did compensate the railroads for their assistance.[14]

Lincoln, on the other hand, when he traveled by train, simply used the regular passenger cars *sans* cannon.

The Jonesboro debate attracted the fewest people of all the debates. The *New York Evening Post* reported "the meeting, which was in a pleasant grove hard by the town, was very small, not over 1,200; and of these, probably a fourth were Republicans, another fourth Buchanan men, the

9. The Third Debate

rest Douglas men and women." The *Chicago Journal* concurred: "The town was exceedingly quiet, and the people scattered about here and there, until 2 o'clock when the crowd gathered in the grove near by, and the debate commenced."[15]

Lincoln framed his statements at Jonesboro to emphasize his conservatism. He knew that this was his only hope of appealing to southern Illinois. In reference to his years in southern Indiana, he reminded the audience that "I was raised just a little east of here. I am a part of this people." But he was not. His personal philosophy was far different from those in Jonesboro. His first sentences, claiming much greater common ground with Douglas than in fact existed, immediately set the tone: "Ladies and Gentlemen: There is very much in the principles that Judge Douglas has here enunciated that I most cordially approve, and over which I shall have no controversy with him. In so far as he has insisted that all the States have the right to do exactly as they please about all their domestic relations, including that of slavery, I agree entirely with him."[16]

Lincoln, on the defensive, returned to a topic about which Douglas had made ample mention during the campaign: the "House Divided" speech. He once again attempted to explain that his comments were consistent with the founding principles of the nation. Lincoln repeated Douglas's question, "'Why can't this Union endure permanently, half slave and half free?'" He reminded the audience that, on a previous occasion, he had answered that he "supposed it could not" but agreed "before this new audience, to give briefly some of the reasons for entertaining that opinion. Another form of his question is, 'Why can't we let it stand as our fathers placed it?' That is the exact difficulty between us." Douglas and his friends, Lincoln argued, "have changed them from the position in which our fathers originally placed it.... In the way our fathers originally left the slavery question, the institution was in the course of ultimate extinction, and the public mind rested in the belief that it was in the course of ultimate extinction." The founding fathers, Lincoln continued, had created a policy "to prohibit the spread of slavery into the new Territories of the United States, where it had not existed. But Judge

Douglas and his friends have broken up that policy and placed it upon a new basis by which it is to become national and perpetual."

Lincoln displayed more candor than political sense before this audience. He not only acknowledged the possibility that slavery, under Douglas, would spread throughout the nation, but also that its extinction might occur if Douglas could be stopped. Lincoln claimed that he had only asked or desired that slavery would be "placed back again upon the basis that the fathers of our Government originally placed it upon. I have no doubt that it would become extinct, for all time to come, if we but re-adopted the policy of the fathers by restricting it to the limits it has already covered — restricting it from the new Territories."

Lincoln was clearly trying to force Douglas to state whether the nation was established on the basis that slavery would eventually end. He reminded the audience that Congressman Preston Brooks, of South Carolina, who had "assaulted Senator Sumner on the floor of the Senate, and who was complimented with dinners and silver pitchers, and gold-headed canes, and a good many other things for that feat, in one of his speeches declared that when this Government was originally established nobody expected that the institution of slavery would last until this day." However, while Brooks willingly provided that opinion, "it was such an opinion as we can never get from Judge Douglas or anybody in favor of slavery in the North at all. You can sometimes get it from a Southern man. He said at the same time that the framers of our Government did not have the knowledge that experience has taught us — that experience and the invention of the cotton-gin have taught us that the perpetuation of slavery is a necessity. He insisted, therefore, upon its being changed from the basis upon which the Fathers of the Government left it to the basis of its perpetuation and nationalization."

In closing this argument, he defined the difference between him and his opponent, presenting himself as following in the footsteps of the Founding Fathers and contending that Douglas had altered the nation's course. The difference "between Judge Douglas and myself," Lincoln said, lay in Douglas's policy of helping make slavery national while Lincoln was insisting that this Government remain "where our fathers originally placed it."[17]

Yet, once again, he avoided any mention of the Declaration of Independence. He chose his remarks carefully, avoiding the more radical statements that Douglas enjoyed repeating.

9. The Third Debate

Douglas had one goal at Jonesboro: label Lincoln as an abolitionist. He claimed that Lincoln had transformed the Whigs into abolitionists, the Republicans were sectional, the Republicans were more concerned for the "negro" than for whites, and he could not pass up the opportunity to once again criticize one of his favorite topics, Lincoln's "House Divided" speech.

Douglas described the dissolution of the Whigs, and the rise of the Republicans as "a great revolution" that resulted in two parties which were "divided by a geographical line, a large party in the North being arrayed under the abolition or republican banner in hostility to the Southern States, Southern people, and Southern institutions." The Whig party had been "transformed into a sectional party" under the Republican name, while the Democratic party remained "the same national party it was at that day. All sectional men, all men of Abolition sentiments and principles, no matter whether they were old Abolitionists or had been Whigs or Democrats, rally under the sectional Republican banner," he declared.

Of all the Republicans, it was Lincoln who was especially responsible for this change, Douglas charged. Lincoln had been a Whig, but it was "beyond denial," Douglas argued, that Lincoln had "undertook to Abolitionize the Whigs and bring them into the Abolition camp." And now that the Whigs had been "abolitionized" into Republicans, they were taking orders from an individual that those in southern Illinois despised. The Republicans had Lovejoy as "one of their high priests" who "brought in resolutions defining the abolition creed, and required them to commit themselves on it by their votes."

Unlike the Democrats, the Republicans were also divided within the state of Illinois. They espoused "abolitionist" principles in Northern Illinois but a "little farther south they became bleached and grew paler just in proportion as public sentiment moderated and changed in this direction. They were Republicans or Abolitionists in the north, anti–Nebraska men down about Springfield, and in this neighborhood they contented themselves with talking about the inexpediency of the repeal of the Missouri compromise." Douglas accused his opponents of finding it necessary for "partizan [sic] effect, to change their colors in different counties in order to catch the popular breeze."

Douglas, knowing the "popular breeze" of southern Illinois, told the pro-slavery audience where the "negro" should be placed in American society. He held that a "negro is not and never ought to be a citizen of the United States. I hold that this Government was made on the white basis, by white men, for the benefit of white men and their posterity forever, and should be administered by white men and none others."

While Lincoln avoided mention of the Declaration of Independence, Douglas did not. He rejected any notion that the "Almighty made the negro capable of self-government. I am aware that all the abolition lecturers that you find traveling about through the country are in the habit of reading the Declaration of Independence to prove that all men were created equal and endowed by their Creator with certain inalienable rights, among which are life, liberty, and the pursuit of happiness." His opponent was "very much in the habit of following in the track of Lovejoy," as he would read "that part of the Declaration of Independence to prove that the negro was endowed by the Almighty with the inalienable right of equality with white men."

In countering this interpretation, the Senator argued that they had no intention of including the "negro" in any of the freedoms. These rights were explicitly intended for only those of European descent. Douglas claimed that the "signers of the Declaration had no reference to the negro whatever when they declared all men to be created equal. They desired to express by that phrase, white men, men of European birth and European descent, and had no reference either to the negro, the savage Indians, the Fejee, the Malay, or any other inferior and degraded race, when they spoke of the equality of men." "Every signer of the Declaration represented a slaveholding constituency, and we know that not one of them emancipated his slaves, much less offered citizenship to them when they signed the Declaration," Douglas asserted. If the signers had "intended to declare that the negro was the equal of the white man, and entitled by divine right to an equality with him," Douglas believed "they were bound, as honest men," to place "their negroes on an equality with themselves. Instead of doing so, with uplifted eyes to Heaven they implored the Divine blessing upon them, during the seven years' bloody war they had to fight to maintain that Declaration, never dreaming that they were violating divine law by still holding the negroes in bondage and depriving them of equality."

9. The Third Debate

Not only should the "negro" remain in bondage, Douglas declared, but "I, for one, am utterly opposed to negro suffrage anywhere and under any circumstances." He acknowledged that the Supreme Court had determined that a "State has a right to confer the privilege of voting upon free negroes" but he issued a warning: "I am not going to make war upon New York because she has adopted a policy repugnant to my feelings. But New York must mind her own business, and keep her negro suffrage to herself and not attempt to force it upon us." Douglas also noted that Maine had "decided that a negro may vote and hold office on an equality with a white man. I had occasion to say to the Senators from Maine in a discussion last session, that if they thought that the white people within the limits of their State were no better than negroes, I would not quarrel with them for it, but they must not say that my white constituents of Illinois were no better than negroes, or we would be sure to quarrel."

Douglas again referred to one of his favorite topics, the "House Divided" speech, for the third consecutive debate, and twisted it to remind the audience that the Republicans, and specifically Lincoln, modified their statements according to their latitude. In the northern part of the State, Douglas argued, Lincoln and the Republicans hold to "that abolition platform" and if they rejected it "in the south and in the center they present the extraordinary spectacle of a house divided against itself, and hence cannot stand. I now bring down upon him the vengeance of his own scriptural quotation, and give it a more appropriate application than he did, when I say to him that his party, abolition in one end of the State and opposed to it in the other, is a house divided against itself, and cannot stand, and ought not to stand, for it attempts to cheat the American people out of their votes by disguising its sentiments."

After quoting from specific passages of the "House Divided," Douglas characterized Lincoln's statements as encouraging civil war. He reminded the audience that Lincoln had stated that the "Republic cannot endure permanently divided into slave and free States, as our fathers made it. He says that they must all become free or all become slave, that they must all be one thing or all be the other, or this government cannot last. Why can it not last if we will execute the government in the same spirit and upon the same principles upon which it is founded? Lincoln, by his proposition, says to the South, 'If you desire to maintain your institutions as they are now, you must not be satisfied with minding your own business, but you must invade Illinois and all the other northern States, establish slavery in them and make it universal'; and in the same language he says to the North, 'You must not be content with regulating your own affairs and minding your own business, but if you desire to maintain your freedom you must invade the Southern States, abolish slavery there and everywhere, in order to have the States all one thing or all the other.'" This policy had one result, Douglas argued, it would invite "a warfare between the North and the South, to be carried on with ruthless vengeance, until the one section or the other shall be driven to the wall and become the victim of the rapacity of the other."

The Senator covered some other issues as well. He devoted some time to suggesting that there were significant problems with the relationship between Lincoln and Trumbull, and that Trumbull was in league with the abolitionists. Douglas also answered Lincoln's question concerning Congress's responsibility in determining the legality of slavery in the territories, by reiterating his policy that popular sovereignty, not Congress, should determine the issue. He also defended the Supreme Court's decision in the Dred Scott case, agreeing with the Court that slaves were property and should be treated in the same respect as other property.

Douglas handled the Jonesboro debate as a masterful politician. He freely quoted from Lincoln's most radical statements and placed them, and his opponent, firmly within the abolitionist camp. For the third consecutive debate, he had used the same strategy in terms of the "House Divided" speech, the Declaration of Independence, and popular sovereignty. Douglas was predictable and consistent.

Lincoln knew he was vulnerable to Douglas's attacks concerning the issue of race, especially in the crucial central Illinois area where he and his opponent would next debate. By ignoring the Declaration of Independence in the Freeport and the Jonesboro debates, he exhibited his understanding of the gap between his personal philosophy and that of the electorate. While it appeared that Lincoln had developed a consistent strategy, at the next debate, in Charleston, in central Illinois, he shifted his position once again. At Charleston, Lincoln completely abandoned his egalitarian philosophy, the Declaration of Independence, and the hope of his nation as he had never so blatantly done before.[18]

10

The Fourth Debate: Charleston, Illinois

September 18, 1858

Those who gathered for the fourth debate witnessed Lincoln the politician at his best, and Lincoln the statesman at his worst.

In describing the challenges for both Lincoln and Douglas, Herndon wrote to a Massachusetts friend: "If you remember, our State is a peculiar one politically: first, we have a north which is all intelligence, all for freedom. Secondly, we have a South, people from sand hills of the South, poor white folks. These are pro-slavery and ignorant 'up to the hub.' And thirdly, we have a belt of land, seventy-five miles in width, running from the east bank of the Mississippi to the Wabash — to Indiana; and running north and south, from Bloomington to Alton. In or upon this strip or belt of land this 'great battle' between Lincoln and Douglas is to be fought and victory won."[1] Charleston was the first debate held within this decisive "belt of land."

Lincoln knew those who resided in the Charleston area; he knew them well. When, at the age of twenty-one, his family had emigrated from Indiana to Illinois, it was near Charleston that his father had decided to build a farm. For a year, the last year he would live with his father and stepmother, Lincoln, using his renowned physical strength, helped the family establish a homestead. This year provided him with the invaluable opportunity to talk, learn, and discuss the issues of the day with the local population. He would draw on this experience when preparing his remarks at Charleston.

As Herndon described, Charleston was within the crucial central area. The voters in this region were more southern in their proclivities. They supported slavery where it then existed, but generally opposed the Kansas-Nebraska Act and, more importantly, despised abolitionists.

The votes in the 1856 congressional election supported Herndon's contention. The Republicans received just over 40 percent of the vote while the Democratic candidate received almost 60 percent. The vote closely followed geographic lines with the counties that provided the lowest Republican support in the extreme southern area of the district (22, 35 and 35 percent) while the Republicans polled a majority in only two of the counties, and those which were at the northern area of the district.[2]

To appeal to these voters, Lincoln would have to embrace their views and distance himself from the abolitionists. He would accomplish both. Once again, the Declaration of Independence would be absent from Lincoln's remarks.[3]

Only forty-eight hours separated the Jonesboro debate from the Charleston debate, the shortest time between any of the debates. This allowed Lincoln no opportunity to make any speeches, but he did compose two letters, one of which illustrates two aspects of Lincoln: his poor ability at extemporaneous speaking and his admirable character.

Lincoln wrote to Martin B. Sweet concerning a statement he made at Jonesboro:

> As my attention was divided, half lingering upon that case and half advancing to the next one, I mentioned your name, as Campbell's opponent, in a confused sentence, which, when I heard it myself, struck me as having something disparaging to you in it. I instantly corrected it, and asked the reporters to suppress it; but my fear now is that those villainous reporters Douglas has with him will try to make something out of it. I do not myself exactly remember what it was, so little connection had it with any distinct thought in my my [sic] mind, and I really hope no more may be heared [sic] of it; but if there should, I write this to assure you that nothing can be farther from me than to feel, much less, intentionally say anything disrespectful to you.
>
> I sincerely hope you may hear nothing of it except what I have written.[4]

Concerning Sweet, Lincoln had stated at Jonesboro, "and there was poor Martin P. Sweet standing on the platform, trying to help poor me

10. The Fourth Debate

to be elected." Lincoln began the letter by admitting that this was a "very trifling thing" which it so appears, but it exemplifies his character in that he believed that a letter was required.

Both Lincoln and Douglas left the train at Mattoon, distant some ten miles from Charleston, to accept the escort of their respective partisans. Mattoon was then a comparatively new place, a station on the Illinois Central Railway peopled by Northern men. Nearly the whole population of this town turned out to escort Mr. Lincoln along the dusty highway to Charleston. In his procession was a chariot containing thirty-two young ladies, representing the thirty-two States of the Union, and carrying banners to designate the same. Following this, was one young lady on horseback holding aloft a banner inscribed, "Kansas—I will be free." As she was very good looking, we thought she would not remain free always. The muses had been wide awake also, for, on the side of the chariot, was the stirring legend: "Westward the star of empire takes its way; The girls link-on to Lincoln, as their mothers did to Clay."

The Douglas procession was likewise a formidable one. He, too, had his chariot of young ladies, and, in addition, a mounted escort. The two processions stretched an almost interminable distance along the road, and were marked by a moving cloud of dust.[5]
— Horace White

The pro–Lincoln *Chicago Journal* had this to add to the description of the 32 ladies: "The Douglasites tried to get up a similar display, but, to do their best, couldn't find more than four women in the town who thought enough of Douglas to honor him in this manner."[6]

On Friday evening the hotels of the town were already crowded to excess, and the streets were hung with national flags, banners, and all manner of artistic devices which could be pressed into political service. Early on Saturday morning the town began to fill up with delegations of teams from the adjoining precincts and the surrounding counties. A special train from Indiana brought eleven car-loads of interested lookers-on from that

The Lincoln-Douglas Debates and the Making of a President

State. People came on horseback and mule-back, in wagons, in freight trains and on foot — some with badges and some with banners, some with their dinners and some without. At ten o'clock the streets and the sidewalks around the public square were almost impassable.[7]
— *Chicago Press and Tribune*

There were a variety of banners displayed by both sides: "Edgar County good for five hundred majority for the Little Giant," "This government was made for whitemen — Douglas for life," "Coles County Four Hundred Majority For Lincoln," "Coles County Goes For Lincoln."[8] One banner received special attention from the pro–Lincoln *Chicago Journal*:

> ... the Douglasites went to work and got a caricature painted — eminently characteristic of these low-lived politicians — representing a white man standing with a negro woman, and followed by a negro boy, with the inscription of "Negro Equality," over it. We take it from this, that the Douglas-worshipers of Charleston, like the Douglas editor of the DeKalb *Sentinel*, are in favor of Negro Equality. This is what their banner indicates surely.[9]

Saturday was at [sic] great day in Charleston. There were not less than twelve thousand people present, from the adjacent towns and counties, to hear the fourth debate between Lincoln and Douglas. The streets of the village were filled with a perfect tide of humanity, surging to and fro, and immediately after dinner the tide flowed out to the County Fair Grounds, where the debate took place.[10]
— *Chicago Journal*

The occasion drew together one of the largest gatherings of the people that has taken place this year. From twelve to fifteen thousand were present. The democracy [the Democrats] were out in their strength and struck terror into the hearts of their enemies.[11]
— *Chicago Times*

The correspondent for the *New York Evening Post* provided the best description of Illinois in 1858: "'The prairies are on fire' and all the parties partake of the general enthusiasm."[12]

10. The Fourth Debate

At Charleston, Douglas continued the strategy he had employed in previous debates. He once again attached the "abolitionist" label to Lincoln and the Republicans using several pieces of evidence to support his claim: Frederick Douglass, the African American orator, was speaking on Lincoln's behalf, the Republican party and Lincoln were inconsistent in their speeches, and the Republicans were wrong when they claimed that the Declaration of Independence applied to all men.

Douglas was especially careful in this former Whig bastion to tie the Whig party's former leaders, Henry Clay and Daniel Webster, and the Whig party's principles with those of the current Democratic party. Prior to 1854, the Senator recalled, "This country was divided into two great political parties, one the Whig, the other the Democratic. I, as a Democrat for twenty years prior to that time, had been in public discussions in this State as an advocate of Democratic principles, and I can appeal with confidence to every old line Whig within the hearing of my voice to bear testimony that during all that period I fought you Whigs like a man on every question that separated the two parties." Despite his attacks on the opposition, Douglas admitted that he had "the highest respect for Henry Clay as a gallant party leader, as an eminent statesman, and as one of the bright ornaments of this country; but I conscientiously believed that the Democratic party was right on the questions which separated the Democrats from the Whigs." However, Douglas maintained, there was no one "who can say that I ever personally assailed Henry Clay or Daniel Webster, or any one of the leaders of that great party, whilst I combatted with all my energy the measures they advocated. What did we differ about in those days? Did Whigs and Democrats differ about this slavery question?"[13]

The Senator answered in the negative, but acknowledged that Whig and Democrats had disagreements on other issues. The parties "differed about a bank, the tariff, distribution, the specie circular, the sub-treasury, and other questions of that description. Now, let me ask you, which one of those questions on which Whigs and Democrats then differed now remains to divide the two great parties?" All the questions which had divided the Whigs and Democrats, Douglas maintained, had "passed away, the country has out-grown them, they have passed into history.

Hence it is immaterial whether you were right or I was right on the bank, the sub-treasury, and other questions, because they no longer continue [as] living issues. What then has taken the place of those questions about which we once differed? The slavery question has now become the leading and controlling issue; that question on which you and I agreed, on which the Whigs and Democrats united, has now become the leading issue between the national Democracy on the one side, and the Republican or Abolition party on the other."

Douglas claimed that he was the political descendant of Clay. He asked the former Clay followers, "How is it that since that time so many of you Whigs have wandered from the true path marked out by Clay and carried out broad and wide by the great Webster? How is it that so many old line Democrats have abandoned the old faith of their party, and joined with Abolitionism and Freesoilism to overturn the platform of the old Democrats, and the platform of the old Whigs?"

Douglas admitted that it was his Kansas-Nebraska Act that had created a "great revolution" but that it was not the elements of this act that caused Democrats and Whigs to join the Republicans. It was the "disappointed politicians" such as the Senator William Seward of New York, a man often described as an abolitionist. "No sooner was the sod grown green over the grave of the immortal Clay, no sooner was the rose planted on the tomb of the god-like Webster, than many of the leaders of the Whig party, such as Seward, of New York and his followers, led off and attempted to abolitionize the Whig party, and transfer all your old Whigs, bound hand and foot into the abolition camp," the Senator argued. These abolitionists had seized "hold of the temporary excitement produced in this country by the introduction of the Nebraska bill, the disappointed politicians in the Democratic party united with the disappointed politicians in the Whig party, and endeavored to form a new party composed of all the abolitionists, of abolitionized Democrats and abolitionized Whigs, banded together in an abolition platform."

The abolitionists now had the most famous African American orator canvassing northern Illinois, a far too tempting target for Douglas. He reminded the audience that in the "northern part of the State I found Lincoln's ally, in the person of FRED. DOUGLASS, THE NEGRO, preaching abolition doctrines, while Lincoln was discussing the same principles down here.... They had the same negro hunting me down, and they now

10. The Fourth Debate

have a negro traversing the northern counties of the State, and speaking in behalf of Lincoln."

The Senator alleged that Lincoln was making speeches "in which he conjures all the friends of negro equality and negro citizenship to rally as one man around Abraham Lincoln, the perfect embodiment of their principles, and by all means to defeat Stephen A. Douglas." Lincoln's speeches, confined to the northern section of the state, were typical of the Republican party's inconsistent philosophy, Douglas claimed.

This inconsistency was not limited to the Republican's senatorial candidate, Douglas charged, it defined the entire party in Illinois. He recalled four years earlier when he had attended the State Fair in Springfield that he found the Republican leaders "all assembled together under the title of an Anti-Nebraska meeting. It was Black Republicans up north, and Anti-Nebraska at Springfield. I found Lovejoy, a high priest of Abolitionism, and Lincoln, one of the leaders who was towing the old line Whigs into the abolition camp." Douglas inquired as to what was the object of the "Black Republicans" strategy. He argued that they had "one name in the north, another in the center, and another in the South. When I used to practice law before my distinguished judicial friend, whom I recognize in the crowd before me, if a man was charged with horse stealing and the proof showed that he went by one name in Stephenson county, another in Sangamon, a third in Monroe, and a fourth in Randolph, we thought that the fact of his changing his name so often to avoid detection was pretty strong evidence of his guilt. I would like to know why it is that this great free soil abolition party is not willing to avow the same name in all parts of the State? If this party believes that its course is just, why does it not avow the same principles in the North, and in the South, in the East and in the West, wherever the American flag waves over American soil?"

To Douglas, the Republican "principles in the North are jet black, in the centre they are in color a decent mulatto, and in lower Egypt they are almost white." The Senator realized that Lincoln had displayed some inconsistency in his comments, although Douglas only made a passing reference to this point when he claimed that he had "admired many of the white sentiments contained in Lincoln's speech at Jonesboro, and could not help but contrast them with the speeches of the same distinguished orator made in the Northern part of the State." He noted that in the southern part of the state Lincoln "denies that the Black Republican party is opposed to the admission of any more slave States, under any circumstances, and says that they are willing to allow the people of each State when it wants to come into the Union, to do just as it pleases on the question of slavery.... Thus, while they avow one set of principles up there, they avow another and entirely different set down here." Douglas would wait until the next debate to fully develop this point which would become one of his favorite topics.

Douglas, once again, gave Lincoln's "House Divided" speech special attention. He reminded the audience that Lincoln had applied a scriptural quotation to the federal government, "that a house divided against itself cannot stand," and he wondered how Lincoln expected "this Abolition party to stand when in one-half of the State it advocates a set of principles which it has repudiated in the other half."

Douglas, hoping to alienate Lincoln from either the radical or the conservative wings of the Republican party, posed to Lincoln the question of "negro" equality. The Senator recalled that Lincoln stated in his "first remarks that he was not in favor of the social and political equality of the negro with the white man" but "up north he has declared that he was not in favor of the social and political equality of the negro, but he would not say whether or not he was opposed to negroes voting and negro citizenship. I want to know whether he is for or against negro citizenship?" Lincoln had provided the answer, Douglas claimed, but only in northern Illinois. The Senator accused Lincoln of dodging the question here, but he recalled that in every speech Lincoln had "made in the north he quoted the Declaration of Independence to prove that all men were created equal, and insisted that the phrase 'all men' included the negro as well as the white man, and that the equality rested upon Divine law."

Douglas saved his most extensive observations on the Declaration of Independence for the end of his remarks, knowing that these comments would be the most persuasive in bringing former Whigs into the Democratic fold. According to Lincoln, the Senator claimed, the "Declaration of Independence asserts that the negro is equal to the white man" but if this was Lincoln's true interpretation, then, Douglas continued, it would be "rational for him to advocate negro citizenship, which, when allowed, puts the negro on an equality under the law. I say

10. The Fourth Debate

to you in all frankness, gentlemen, that in my opinion a negro is not a citizen, cannot be, and ought not to be, under the Constitution of the United States.... I say that this Government was established on the white basis. It was made by white men, for the benefit of white men and their posterity forever, and never should be administered by any except white men." Following the same logic that Taney had employed in the Dred Scott decision, Douglas declared "that a negro ought not to be a citizen, whether his parents were imported into this country as slaves or not, or whether or not he was born here. It does not depend upon the place a negro's parents were born, or whether they were slaves or not, but upon the fact that he is a negro, belonging to a race incapable of self government, and for that reason ought not to be on an equality with white men."

At Charleston, Lincoln spoke as he had never spoken before. He made statements that radically diverged from the political philosophy that he had espoused throughout his life. He clothed himself in the racist beliefs of the audience. It was the not the true Lincoln that debated there, but Lincoln the politician. He opened the debate with a joke and then explained his stance on racial equality.

Lincoln had been at the hotel, he began, and an "elderly gentleman called upon me to know whether I was really in favor of producing a perfect equality between the negroes and white people [great laughter]." Lincoln restated his stance that he was not, "nor ever have been in favor of bringing about in any way the social and political equality of the white and black races [applause]—that I am not nor ever have been in favor of making voters or jurors of negroes, nor of qualifying them to hold office, nor to intermarry with white people; and I will say in addition to this that there is a physical difference between the white and black races which I believe will forever forbid the two races living together on terms of social and political equality. And inasmuch as they cannot so live, while they do remain together there must be the position of superior and inferior, and I as much as any other man am in favor of having the superior position assigned to the white race."

He further stated that while "the white man is to have the superior position" this should not deny the "negro" everything. "I do not understand that because I do not want a negro woman for a slave I must necessarily want her for a wife [cheers and laughter]. My understanding is that I can just let her alone. I am now in my fiftieth year, and I certainly never have had a black woman for either a slave or a wife. So it seems to me quite possible for us to get along without making either slaves or wives of negroes. I will add to this that I have never seen to my knowledge a man, woman or child who was in favor of producing a perfect equality, social and political, between negroes and white men."

He felt obliged to counter the charge that the Republicans were in favor of, or that their policies would result in, the mixing of the races. Lincoln had "never had the least apprehension that I or my friends would marry negroes if there was no law to keep them from it, but as Judge Douglas and his friends seem to be in great apprehension that they might, if there were no law to keep them from it, I give him the most solemn pledge that I will to the very last stand by the law of this State, which forbids the marrying of white people with negroes." He added that he did not believe that there was "any place where an alteration of the social and political relations of the negro and the white man can be made except in the State Legislature — not in the Congress of the United States — and as I do not really apprehend the approach of any such thing myself, and as Judge Douglas seems to be in constant horror that some such danger is rapidly approaching, I propose as the best means to prevent it that the Judge be kept at home and placed in the State Legislature to fight the measure."

The Charleston debate was unique in that both candidates devoted a considerable amount of time to an issue other than slavery, namely Senator Trumbull's veracity. Trumbull had recently accused Douglas of influencing the Toombs bill, one that would have brought Kansas into the Union as a slave state. Lincoln quoted Trumbull's charge that Douglas had participated in a plot to force a constitution on Kansas without granting the citizens of that state the opportunity to vote on it. Douglas had been responsible for removing a provision in the bill that would have properly submitted the constitution to a vote. Lincoln inferred that Douglas had called Trumbull a liar. Douglas responded to this charge by alleging that Trumbull knew this was a lie, that these were "petty, malicious assaults," and the accusations were "false." He also attacked

10. The Fourth Debate

Lincoln's idea that there was a conspiracy to nationalize slavery and to orchestrate the Dred Scott decision.

Lincoln's sudden and extensive preoccupation with the Trumbull issue seems surprising. The Senator, though, found a reason for this new tactic. Douglas accused Lincoln of concocting this issue because Douglas had been "showing up Lincoln's Abolitionism and negro equality doctrines," knowing that "white men would not support his rank Abolitionism" and so Trumbull "trumped up a system of charges" against him. Lincoln's "only reason" and "true reason" for occupying the "whole of his first hour in this issue between Trumbull" and himself, Douglas argued, was because Lincoln wanted to "conceal from this vast audience the real questions which divide the two great parties."

Douglas's conclusion best explains Lincoln's Charleston strategy. The voters in this crucial district were not inclined to accept his egalitarian interpretation of the Declaration of Independence. Yet Lincoln needed to debate some issue, and he found a safe one with the Trumbull controversy. It held the potential of questioning Douglas's adherence to popular sovereignty, and it allowed him to avoid any issues of equality, slavery, or African American citizenship.

The Charleston debate marked a change in Douglas's strategy as well. For the first time in the debates, he failed to attack the "House Divided" speech. He had assailed the speech in Chicago, Springfield, Ottawa, Freeport and Jonesboro. This change was most likely not because the Senator found his criticisms poor material for the Charleston audience, but because Douglas recognized that Republican party's duplicity on the issue of race and the Declaration of Independence was far better material.

Lincoln's acceptance of the "superior" and "inferior" racial distinctions without mention of the Declaration was the most surprising change in his comments. At Chicago, he had specifically asked that the nation "discard all this quibbling about this man and the other man — this race and that race and the other race being inferior, and therefore they must be placed in an inferior position" and "discard all these things, and unite as one people throughout this land, until we shall once more stand up declaring that all men are created equals." At the first debate, in Ottawa, he had, for the first time, rejected his Chicago remarks when he had stated that he had "no purpose to introduce political and social equality between the white and the black races," because there was "a physical difference between the two" that would "probably forever forbid their living together upon the footing of perfect equality, and inasmuch as it becomes a necessity that there must be a difference, I, as well as Judge Douglas, am in favor of the race to which I belong having the superior position." At Ottawa though, he still embraced the Declaration of Independence. Now, at Charleston, he spoke only of "superior" and "inferior." This was Lincoln as a politician appealing to the voters whose support he required; he did not show the courage to speak as he believed. His ambition had supplanted any public expression of his personal beliefs. Ironically, he had criticized Douglas for steering the nation away from the Declaration of Independence, and now that he was engaged in a fiercely competitive campaign, he had decided to discard the Declaration as well. Had this been the last debate, had this been his last public comments in the campaign, Lincoln may well have been a far different president than we know him today, and the United States may have become a far different nation as well. Fortunately, there were three more debates, three more opportunities for Lincoln to redeem himself, three more opportunities for him to "return to the fountain whose waters spring close by the blood of the Revolution," as he had so eloquently spoke at Lewistown.

A few days after the Charleston debate, Davis, believing that Lincoln had finally accepted his point of view, wrote to him: "Your concluding speech on Douglas at Charleston was admirable."[14] The conservatives in the Republican party had reason to now rejoice in Lincoln. Their joy was short-lived. At the next debate, in Galesburg, Lincoln would attempt a new strategy where he sought to straddle the fence between the abolitionists and the conservatives.

This proved to be a crucial step. After Charleston, Lincoln's final transformation began. He would not only rise to the occasion, he would rise above it.

11

The Fifth Debate: Galesburg, Illinois

October 7, 1858

Lincoln continued to struggle with his political strategy, but Galesburg presented a new beginning. In the early months of his campaign, he had fully embraced the Declaration of Independence as applying to all men, but as he traveled south, he attempted to appeal to those in the south, and he left that philosophy behind. Now returning to the northern area of Illinois where he had strong support, the politician tried to straddle the fence. Lincoln would speak of the Declaration of Independence and he would quote from his Charleston comments. His remarks would contain something that he hoped would appeal to everyone.

Three weeks passed between the Charleston and Galesburg debates, the longest period of time between any of the encounters. During the interim, Lincoln traveled extensively—by boat, horse, and train. He delivered speeches at a variety of locations, but, regrettably, no verbatim copies of these speeches are known to exist. Fortunately, two of Lincoln's writings have survived, and shed light on the struggle within him that was nearing its climax.

Lincoln wrote two paragraphs for himself—taking an opportunity to compose his thoughts based on articles he read in the *Richmond (VA) Enquirer* and the *New York Day-book*, both pro–Democrat newspapers. In these paragraphs it is evident that Lincoln was returning to his core beliefs. There was a "larger issue" than the spread of slavery, Lincoln believed, namely, the interpretation of the Declaration of Independence. In these sentences, the statesman began challenging the politician. He recalled that Democratic senator John Pettit of Indiana had "declared the equality of men, as asserted in our Declaration of Independence, to be a 'self-evident lie.' In his numerous speeches now being made in Illinois, Senator Douglas regularly argues against the doctrine of equality of men; and while he does not draw the conclusion that the superiors ought to enslave the inferiors, he evidently wishes his hearers to draw that conclusion."

Lincoln the statesman must have realized that to accept the superiority of one race over another, as he had done at Charleston, implied that the superior would have the right to enslave the inferior. Lincoln the politician was not ready to surrender this point, and he would still make this argument at Galesburg.

In the final paragraph, Lincoln clearly stated the philosophy that would eventually dominate his campaign. This conviction led him to embrace his old companion, the Declaration of Independence, at Galesburg. It would be his first mention of the Declaration at any of the debates since the first one at Ottawa: "It is equally impossible to not see that that common object is to subvert, in the public mind, and in practical administration, our old and only standard of free government, that 'all men are created equal,' and to substitute for it some different standard. What that substitute is to be is not difficult to perceive. It is to deny the equality of men, and to assert the natural, moral and religious right of one class to enslave another."[1]

These paragraphs bear evidence to Lincoln's continuing inner conflict. This internal debate would continue until one side would rise victorious at the final debate.

During the three week interim between Charleston and Galesburg, on September 20, at Sullivan, Illinois, a violent incident occurred despite Douglas's and Lincoln's best efforts to prevent it. This incident is noteworthy because of its rarity and because it reflected the intense emotions of the campaign. Despite the barrage of newspaper attacks on the

11. The Fifth Debate

candidates, and the occasional interruption of a Lincoln or Douglas speech, the people of Illinois generally displayed great respect toward the candidates and their supporters. Yet at Sullivan a brawl occurred that highlighted the intense animosity between some Democrats and Republicans.

Anticipating the potential for violence, Lincoln wrote a short note, which, according to both Douglas's and Lincoln's supporters, was delivered to the Senator on September 20 before the two candidates were to deliver their speeches in the town. Lincoln understood "that Judge Douglas would speak before dinner" and that Lincoln would address his supporters at 2:00 P.M. Aware of the possibility of conflict between the candidate's supporters and no doubt desiring not to interrupt Douglas's speech, Lincoln noted that Douglas did "not begin till 1 o'clock" and he requested that his opponent make the announcement that Lincoln would not begin his speech until 3:00 P.M.[2]

Best evidence suggests that Douglas received this note and agreed to Lincoln's terms, but, in the highly charged atmosphere of the campaign, these efforts would not prove successful.[3]

"Almost a Riot.— Collision between the Parties.— Disgraceful Conduct of Lincoln and His Pack.— Meeting at Sullivan" was how one Democratic paper entitled their article. The *Times,* predictably, found fault with Lincoln for the confrontation. The reporter, when he reached Sullivan, "was astonished to find that Lincoln had an appointment for the same time and place" as Douglas. He was "much astonished" that Lincoln "should endeavor to impose himself upon a Democratic audience in quite so bold a manner." However, his surprise at Lincoln's plans subsided when he was present for the delivery of Lincoln's note to Douglas. After this agreement, "Mr. Douglas was escorted to the speaker's stand, erected in the court house square, around which he found an immense gathering of people, extending clear back to the court house on the one side and some hundreds of people being on the street at the rear of the stand." Before Douglas commenced his remarks, "he made the announcement stipulated for by Mr. Lincoln." The *Times* reporter believed this "contract" was unfair and believed that Lincoln had "no right to attempt to rob Douglas of his audience...."

Douglas had spoken for some time, presumably not longer than an hour, when "one of the fellows who was acting as marshal for the Black

Republican crew, rode up to the edge of the crowd, blue sash and all, and called out that Lincoln was waiting to be escorted by his friends." At this point, according to the reporter, "the Indiana band of music, imported at unheard of expense" commenced "blowing their mightiest to drown the voice of the Senator." A "few" individuals "with blue badges, inscribed 'A. Lincoln' who had been apparently listening to Douglas, "marched out of the crowd." After this interruption, the Senator was prepared to continue, "when the band marched" forward toward the crowd "with the evident intention of forcing a way through the Democratic meeting."

The reporter believed that Lincoln was with this procession. The Republicans "advanced round the square, taking all its sides, until they came to where the street was blocked by" the Democrats.

A Republican newspaper had a different account of the event. Describing October 20 as one of the "most exciting days that ever occurred in Sullivan," the reporter noted that Douglas began his speech at 1:00 P.M. and Lincoln "waited until a little past 3 P.M. when the Brass Band commenced playing and drew off about two-thirds of the Douglas hearers. The Lincoln procession then formed and started around the Public Square." As the Republicans approached the square, Lincoln "gave orders to his friends to stop the procession and turn it back."

The tension had risen to belligerent levels which neither Douglas nor Lincoln could control — not that either one of them lacked experience in physical altercations. Douglas, while campaigning in 1838, had once been assaulted by the opposing candidate, and in the scuffle bit the thumb of his opponent to the extent that the scar remained for years. Lincoln, in his pre–Springfield days in Illinois, had been involved in a wrestling match with Jack Armstrong, whose son's life he would later successfully defend in a murder case.[4]

This time a brawl ensued, although neither candidate took part. The "Border Ruffians" from the Democratic crowd charged the Republicans, throwing "rails in the spokes of the band wagon, clubbed and beat the horses most shamefully, and knocked the driver from his seat with a brick-bat, which struck him on the side of his head." The reporter indicated that "by this time we had all got mad, and the fight became general. Such yelling I never heard. It appeared as if all hell had been let loose." He noted that "six or seven" were "pretty badly hurt on both sides" before the band wagon passed through the crowd. After listening

11. The Fifth Debate

to Lincoln speak for "about two hours," the crowd received word from the "Douglasites" that the "Band should not pass around the square that evening." Some of the Republicans, instead of heeding the warning, "formed in procession, each man with a club in his hand," with the "Band playing Yankee Doodle," and "marched all around town." No further incident occurred, though, and fortunately, the incident at Sullivan proved an atypical incident of the campaign.[5]

A little over two weeks after Sullivan, Lincoln and Douglas met again at Galesburg:

> Here we had the largest audience of the whole series and the worst day, the weather being very cold and raw, notwithstanding which, the people flocked from far and near. One feature of the Republican procession was a division of one hundred ladies and an equal number of gentlemen on horseback as a special escort to the carriage containing Mr. Lincoln. The whole country seemed to be swarming and the crowd stood three hours in the college grounds, in a cutting wind, listening to the debate. Mr. Lincoln's speech at Galesburg was, in my judgment, the best of the series.[6]
> —Horace White

White's assertion that Galesburg was Lincoln's finest debate was probably due to the fact that Lincoln, for the first time since the first debate, argued that the Declaration of Independence applied to "all men." White was, by his own admission, more radical in his public statements than Lincoln, and was probably delighted that Lincoln returned to what White considered the fundamental issue of the campaign. However, in evaluating Lincoln's greatness at this debate, White was mistaken. Lincoln the politician would repeat the statements that he had made in Charleston at Galesburg. This was not Lincoln's finest debate; that one was still to come.

The *Chicago Times* concurred with White's description of the weather conditions: "The day was a most unpleasant one for speaking in the open air. A strong northwest wind was blowing, which rendered talking difficult; and although the stand was built on the east side of Knox College (the meeting being held in the college grounds), the current of air which swept around the building rendered it impossible for the speakers at times to make themselves heard at all. Besides this, the cold was intense."[7]

Just before the Galesburg debate, a reporter for the *Chicago Tribune*, possibly White, no doubt as a result of previous problems, made some recommendations:

> In this connection we desire to say a word to the Committee of Arrangements for the debate. At none of the previous discussions have there been any adequate accommodations for reporters. It is not a fact that two chairs and a wash-stand eighteen inches square are sufficient furniture for a half a dozen men to work on, nor is it always convenient to make a battle against a mob of excited politicians, when the fighting editor is at home. In behalf of ourselves and such other representatives of the press as may be represented, may we request that arrangements be made for at least six reporters—that the chairs and tables be placed where they will not be jarred or overthrown by the people on the platform and where there will be no room for persons to crowd between the reporters and the speakers— and that somebody with authority and physical strength enough to secure obedience, be appointed to keep loafers out of the reporting corner. These things are absolutely essential to the accuracy of the reports.[8]

It is not known whether the Committee followed this reporter's advice.

Lincoln's modification in strategy, a return to mentioning the Declaration of Independence, was, no doubt, a reflection of the area in which the fifth debate occurred. Galesburg, Illinois, was within Illinois' Fourth Congressional District and, unlike the locations of the two previous debates, had voted Republican in the 1856 congressional districts. It was not the overwhelming majority typical of northern Illinois; 51 percent of the votes had been cast for the Republican candidate and approximately

11. The Fifth Debate

46 percent for the Democratic. Resurrecting the phrase "all men are created equal" and repeating his Charleston remarks was a strategy that fit well with this closely divided population.[9]

Lincoln opened his comments with what he considered America's cornerstone.[10] Douglas, Lincoln explained, has "alluded to the Declaration of Independence, and insisted that negroes are not included in that Declaration; and that it is a slander upon the framers of that instrument, to suppose that negroes were meant therein; and he asks you: Is it possible to believe that Mr. Jefferson, who penned the immortal paper, could have supposed himself applying the language of that instrument to the negro race, and yet held a portion of that race in slavery? Would he not at once have freed them?"

Lincoln answered the question by asserting that this was a new interpretation with no historical basis. The "entire records of the world," Lincoln countered, "from the date of the Declaration of Independence up to within three years ago, may be searched in vain for one single affirmation, from one single man, that the negro was not included in the Declaration of Independence. I think I may defy Judge Douglas to show that he ever said so, that Washington ever said so, that any President ever said so, that any member of Congress ever said so, or that any living man upon the whole earth ever said so." This new interpretation had been invented because of the "necessities of the present policy of the Democratic party, in regard to slavery." As for Jefferson, Lincoln reminded his opponent and the audience that, "while Mr. Jefferson was the owner of slaves, as undoubtedly he was, in speaking upon this very subject, he used the strong language that 'he trembled for his country when he remembered that God was just'; and I will offer the highest premium in my power to Judge Douglas if he will show that he, in all his life, ever uttered a sentiment at all akin to that of Jefferson."

Lincoln's statements on the Declaration of Independence were not without qualification. He still heeded the advice of Davis and was not prepared to alienate those voters who were antislavery but not for racial equality. Lincoln the politician still held sway. Douglas would "have it that if we do not confess that there is a sort of inequality between the white and black races, which justifies us in making them slaves, we must, then, insist that there is a degree of equality that requires us to make them our wives." Lincoln claimed that if "it should be insisted that there was an equality between the white and black races that should produce a perfect social and political equality, it was an impossibility. This you have seen in my printed speeches, and with it I have said, that in their right to 'life, liberty and the pursuit of happiness,' as proclaimed in that old Declaration, the inferior races are our equals."

Lincoln was sensitive to Douglas's criticisms that he preached a different philosophy at different latitudes, and believed it necessary to respond. When Douglas claimed that he made "speeches of one sort for the people of the Northern end of the State, and of a different sort for the Southern people," Lincoln asserted that he incorrectly assumed that he did not realize that his "speeches will be put in print and read North and South." Lincoln fully knew that his Chicago, Jonesboro and Charleston comments would "all be put in print and all the reading and intelligent men in the community would see them and know all about my opinions."[11]

Lincoln devoted some time to other points. He argued against Douglas's proposition that the Nebraska bill was an extension of the Compromise of 1850. Lincoln believed it did not continue the policy but overturned it. He countered the charge that a conspiracy existed in Illinois between the Republicans and those Democrats who supported Buchanan and opposed Douglas. Lincoln also claimed that the resolutions which Douglas had attempted to associate with Lincoln were, in fact, frauds. And, Lincoln attacked the Dred Scott decision as a product of the Democratic party.

Douglas covered four main topics in this debate, three of which had been a staple part of his comments. He defended the Kansas-Nebraska Act based on popular sovereignty, attacked the "House Divided" speech, and ridiculed Lincoln's interpretation of the Declaration of Independence. However, he now focused on a new issue. Douglas had many times criticized the Republican party for its inconsistent comments in northern and southern Illinois, but the Senator now, after the Charleston debate, could, for the first time, make the same charge against Lincoln.[12]

Douglas opened his remarks with a defense of self-determination

11. The Fifth Debate

and popular sovereignty. He remembered that he had in 1854 "appeared before the people of Knox county for the purpose of defending my political action upon the compromise measures of 1850 and the passage of the Kansas-Nebraska bill. Those of you before me, who were present then, will remember that I vindicated myself for supporting those two measures by the fact that they rested upon the great fundamental principle that the people of each State and each territory of this Union have the right, and ought to be permitted to exercise the right of regulating their own domestic concerns in their own way, subject to no other limitation or restriction than that which the Constitution of the United States imposes upon them." Douglas had, after creating this policy, asked "the people of Illinois to decide whether that principle of self-government was right or wrong. If it was, and is right, then the compromise measures of 1850 were right, and, consequently, the Kansas and Nebraska bill, based upon the same principle, must necessarily have been right." Before this audience, in a strong Republican area, Douglas did not craft his comments to their political persuasion. He argued that his "Kansas and Nebraska bill" was not meant to "legislate slavery into any State or territory, nor to exclude it therefrom, but to leave the people thereof perfectly free to form and regulate their domestic institutions in their own way, subject only to the Constitution of the United States."

He later switched his focus from defending his policies to attacking his opponent's party: "Now, let me ask you whether the country has any interest in sustaining this organization known as the Republican party?" The Republican party was not similar to the Whig party, Douglas argued. The later had a national following, the former, only a sectional one. The Republicans, Douglas claimed, were "unlike all other political organizations in this country. All other parties have been national in their character — have avowed their principles alike in the slave and the free States, in Kentucky as well as in Illinois, in Louisiana as well as in Massachusetts. Such was the case with the old Whig party, and such was and is the case with the Democratic party. Whigs and Democrats could proclaim their principles boldly and fearlessly in the north and in the south, in the east and in the west, wherever the constitution ruled and the American flag waved over American soil." But the Republicans were nothing more than a "sectional organization, a party which appeals to the northern section of the Union against the southern, a party which appeals to northern passion, northern pride, northern ambition, and northern prejudices, against southern people, the southern States and southern institutions." The Republican leaders had one hope, Douglas believed, that they would be able to "unite the northern States in one great sectional party," and if they did, since the North was "the strongest section," the Republicans would be "enabled to out vote, conquer, govern, and control the South."

Douglas expanded on this point as a pretext to take another swipe at the "House Divided" speech. He claimed that, if Lincoln's policy had been followed by the founders at the formation of the nation, the "twelve slaveholding States" would have out-voted the "one free State," which would have legalized slavery in North and South. Such a division had been avoided, Douglas argued, only because the Americans had pursued a "path of peace" that allowed a division between free and slave, "allowing each State to decide for itself whether it wants slavery or not. If Illinois will settle the slavery question for herself, mind her own business and let her neighbors alone, we will be at peace with Kentucky, and every other Southern State." This was a perfect articulation of Douglas's conception of popular sovereignty.

The Senator knew that Lincoln's true weakness lay in his interpretation of the Declaration of Independence. Douglas pounded away at this vulnerability in several paragraphs. The Senator reminded the Galesburg audience that at Chicago Lincoln had declared the "negro and the white man are made equal by the Declaration of Independence and by Divine Providence." This, Douglas claimed, was a "monstrous heresy. The signers of the Declaration of Independence never dreamed of the negro when they were writing that document. They referred to white men, to men of European birth and European descent, when they declared the equality of all men." Surely, Douglas argued, Thomas Jefferson, if he had believed as Lincoln asserted he did, would not have been an owner of a large number of slaves. The Senator rhetorically asked whether Jefferson intended "to say in that Declaration that his negro slaves, which he held and treated as property, were created his equals by Divine law, and that he was violating the law of God every day of his life by holding them as slaves? It must be borne in mind that when that Declaration was put forth every one of the thirteen colonies were slaveholding colonies, and every man who signed that instrument represented a slaveholding

11. The Fifth Debate

constituency. Recollect, also, that no one of them emancipated his slaves, much less put them on an equality with himself, after he signed the Declaration." These slaveholders, instead of emancipating their slaves, Douglas recalled, continued to hold their slaves throughout the Revolutionary War. He asked, "Now, do you believe — are you willing to have it said — that every man who signed the Declaration of Independence declared the negro his equal, and then was hypocrite enough to continue to hold him as a slave, in violation of what he believed to be the divine law? And yet when you say that the Declaration of Independence includes the negro, you charge the signers of it with hypocrisy." Douglas "frankly" admitted that in his "opinion this government was made by our fathers on the white basis. It was made by white men for the benefit of white men and their posterity forever, and was intended to be administered by white men in all time to come."

At Galesburg, Douglas exploited the new weakness he had discovered in his opponent, one that he had touched on briefly at Charleston, but now fully developed. He had attacked the Republicans for their duplicity on the issue of race, as they spoke differently in northern, central and southern Illinois, but now, after the fourth debate, he found that the Republicans' senatorial candidate was following the same strategy. Lincoln's Charleston remarks were far different from his Chicago remarks, and Douglas brought this contradictory point home to the audience. Lincoln, he maintained, finds it "extremely difficult to manage a debate in the centre part of the State, where there is a mixture of men from the North and the South." Douglas found it interesting that Lincoln, "in the extreme northern part of Illinois," proclaimed as "bold and radical abolitionism as ever Giddings, Lovejoy, or Garrison enunciated," but when he traveled "a little further South" he claimed that he was an "old line Whig, a disciple of Henry Clay," declaring that he still adhered to the "old line Whig creed, and has nothing whatever to do with Abolitionism, or negro equality, or negro citizenship." Douglas found it odd that Lincoln's supporters were cheering for their candidate even though he "stood up for negro equality" in one area of the state and "in another part for political effect, discarded the doctrine and declared that there always must be a superior and inferior race. Abolitionists up north are expected and required to vote for Lincoln because he goes for the equality of the races, holding that by the Declaration of

Independence the white man and the negro were created equal and endowed by the Divine law with that equality." However, when Lincoln traveled "down south" Douglas noted that his opponent told "the old Whigs, the Kentuckians, Virginians, and Tennesseeans, that there is a physical difference in the races, making one superior and the other inferior, and that he is in favor of maintaining the superiority of the white race over the negro." Douglas questioned, "Now, how can you reconcile those two positions of Mr. Lincoln? He is to be voted for in the south as a pro-slavery man, and he is to be voted for in the north as an Abolitionist."

Later, in his rebuttal, Douglas's returned to the issue of Lincoln's duplicity on race, an issue that was rapidly becoming Douglas' favorite topic, even supplanting the Senator's previous interest in the "House Divided" speech:

> Why, the reason I complain of him is because he makes one speech north and another south. Because he has one set of sentiments for the abolition counties and another set for the counties opposed to abolitionism. My point of complaint against him is that I cannot induce of him to hold up the same standard, to carry the same flag in all parts of the State. He does not pretend, and no other man will, that I have one set of principles for Galesburg and another for Charleston. He does not pretend that I hold one doctrine in Chicago and to an opposite one in Jonesboro. I have proved that he has a different set of principles for each of these localities.[13]

Douglas, to emphasize this point, recalled again that Lincoln had asserted at Galesburg, "as he did at Chicago, that the negro was included in that clause of the Declaration of Independence which says that all men were created equal and endowed by the Creator with certain inalienable rights, among which are life, liberty and the pursuit of happiness. If the negro was made his equal and mine, if that equality was established by Divine law, and was the negro's inalienable right" Douglas wanted to know why Lincoln stated "at Charleston to the Kentuckians residing in that section of our State, that the negro was physically inferior to the white man, belonged to an inferior race, and he was for keeping him always in that inferior condition?"

The Senator reminded the assemblage that at Charleston Lincoln "gave the people to understand that there was no moral question involved, because the inferiority being established, it was only a question of degree

11. The Fifth Debate

and not a question of right." However, before the Galesburg audience, in more northern Illinois, Lincoln had, "instead of making it a question of degree," made it "a moral question, says that it is a great crime to hold the negro in that inferior condition. Is he right now or was he right in Charleston?" Lincoln, Douglas charged, "can trim his principles any way in any section, so as to secure votes. All I desire of him is that he will declare the same principles in the South that he does in the North."[14]

Lincoln would not fulfill Douglas's desire at the next debate, at Quincy. The pro–Douglas *Chicago Times* summed up Lincoln's campaign strategy in an article entitled "The Mottled Candidate":

> At Charleston he declares negroes to be inferior in the eyes of God and man, and should be treated — as "inferiors"— men outside of the political party — and at Galesburg he asserts that God created them the political equals of the white race, and that it is inhuman and anti–Christian to deny them that equality. Such is the mottled candidate. Such are the mottled principles, and such the mottled exhibition presented to the people of Illinois in the person of Abraham Lincoln.[15]

However, the next debate would mark the last time that Lincoln would appear as a "mottled candidate."

12

The Sixth Debate: Quincy, Illinois

October 13, 1858

In the sixth debate, Lincoln and Douglas returned to central Illinois, the crucial belt of land that both candidates desperately needed to win the election in November.

The divisiveness of the Fifth Congressional District was reflected in the 1856 congressional election returns. Of the eight counties, the Republican candidate had prevailed in only one, with almost 45 percent of the vote. Although the Democratic candidate won the remaining seven counties, his support ranged from 50 percent to 57 percent in all, except one, the southernmost county in the district, where he garnered over 70 percent. Overall, the Democrats received 52 percent of the votes, reflecting the sharp divide within this district.

Judging by his performance at Charleston, the last time Lincoln debated in this region, one would have expected that he would follow the same strategy of abandoning the Declaration of Independence and speaking in favor of "superior" and "inferior." Yet Lincoln, continuing his unpredictability, pursued a strategy that he had not employed throughout the entire campaign. For the first time, and the only time in the debates, Lincoln spoke the same philosophy at two consecutive debates. His Quincy comments were strikingly similar to his words at Galesburg.

His strategy of continuing to straddle the fence reflected Lincoln's inner struggle between statesman and politician. He spoke of the Declaration of Independence, claiming that all men are created equal, but

The Lincoln-Douglas Debates and the Making of a President

he also spoke of the superiority of white over black. He could not free himself from catering to what he believed the electorate wanted to hear.

Making his way to Quincy, Lincoln visited a variety of towns around Galesburg and even found time to cross the Mississippi to spend a day in Burlington, Iowa, the only time during the campaign that he departed Illinois. At Monmouth, on October 11, the *Chicago Tribune* reported that, due to rain, his scheduled speech was cancelled. The presence of a large crowd caused Lincoln to change his plans and he gave his speech despite the unfavorable conditions, and then he traveled to Quincy where he was expected to arrive on October 13.

Two of the Quincy newspapers, the *Whig*, a Republican paper, and the *Herald*, the Democratic paper, urged their followers to participate in the upcoming festivities:

> Great preparations are being made for the Grand debate to come off in this city on Wednesday next, the 13th. inst. It is expected that one of the largest crowds that ever assembled in Quincy, will be present. Our friends, in all parts of the country, promise to be on hand.
> Again we urge upon Republicans to come, and hear the great champion of Freedom.
> — *Quincy (IL), Whig*

JUDGE DOUGLAS COMING TONIGHT
Grand Torchlight Procession
The friends of Judge Douglas will meet at The Court House,
THIS EVENING AT 8 O'CLOCK

> where a grand procession with transparencies, torchlights, music, and live Democrats, will be formed ... and marched to the railroad depot, where Judge Douglas will arrive by the nine o'clock train.
> Let every Democrat in the city be on hand at the hour — the procession will move at precisely half past 8 o'clock — to extend to our distinguished Senator a hearty and enthusiastic welcome.
> — *Quincy (IL), Herald*

TORCH-LIGHT PROCESSION!
> On Wednesday night, the Republicans intend to have a grand torch-light procession. The most extensive preparations are being made.

12. The Sixth Debate

LINCOLN BADGES

Messrs. Laage & Barnum are prepared to furnish persons with any number of Lincoln Badges. We hope our Republican friends will not fail to get one, and turn out with the procession tomorrow.
—*Quincy (IL), Whig*

JUDGE DOUGLAS RECEPTION
The Torch-Light Procession

The most magnificent display that has ever been made in this city, was made by the Democracy on Tuesday last, on the occasion of the reception of Judge Douglas. Our distinguished Senator was received at half past nine o'clock, at the railroad depot, amid the booming of cannon, and a most splendid display of torch lights and transparencies, accompanied by the welcoming, enthusiastic shouts of not less than three thousand live Democrats.— Four hundred blazing torches, and beautiful transparencies in proportion, with bands of music and a procession more than half a mile in length, — and the streets of the city literally thronged with people, in honor of the great statesman of the day....
—*Quincy (IL), Herald*

A gentleman informed us that he timed the two processions of Wednesday, as they passed his place of business. The Republican procession was 19½ minutes in passing, without any stoppages while the Douglas procession was 12½ minutes, including a brief stoppage. This would indicate that the Republican procession was the largest from 500 to 600.
—*Quincy (IL), Whig*

As to the weather conditions for the debate, the *Tribune* and the *Times* disagreed. The *Tribune* described "a clear sky and altogether an admirable day" while the *Times* thought the weather "unfavorable." Nevertheless, a local newspaper claimed that "long before the speaking commenced, the public square was literally swarmed with people. The number present is variously estimated from eight to fourteen thousand."[1]

The Lincoln-Douglas Debates and the Making of a President

The debate, according to Carl Schurz, occurred in an "open square, where a large pine-board platform has been built for the committee of arrangements, the speakers, and the persons they wished to have with them." Schurz noted that, while "thousands of people were assembled," the Republicans and Democrats stood "peacefully together, only chaffing one another now and then in a good-tempered way."

Schurz sympathized with Lincoln, but he admitted that his candidate did not have "any of those physical advantages which usually are thought to be very desirable, if not necessary, to the orator. His voice was not musical, being rather high-keyed and apt to turn into a shrill treble in moments of excitement." He further found Lincoln's gestures "awkward," as he "swung his long arms sometimes in a very ungraceful manner." To give a particular emphasis to a point, Lincoln "would bend his knees and body with a sudden downward jerk and then shoot up again with a vehemence that raised him to his tiptoes and made him look much taller than he really was...."

Douglas appeared far different. As compared to Lincoln's "tall, lank and ungainly form" the Senator "stood almost like a dwarf, very short of stature, but square-shouldered and broad-chested, a massive head upon a strong neck—the very embodiment of force, combativeness, and staying power." Before the audience at Quincy, Douglas appeared "well-groomed, being clothed in excellently fitting broadcloth and shining linen."

The Senator also exhibited substantial confidence. As Douglas listened to Lincoln's speech, "a contemptuous smile now and then flitted across his lips, and when he arose, the tough parliamentary gladiator, he tossed his mane with an air of overbearing superiority, of threatening defiance, as if to say: 'How dare any one dare stand up against me?'"[2]

At Quincy, Douglas repeated themes that he had previously articulated: Lincoln had been inconsistent in his statements, he was erroneous in his interpretation of the Declaration of Independence, America's guiding principle should be the right of self-government for all the states, and Lincoln's "House Divided" speech was an attack on the fundamental right of popular sovereignty.

The Senator reiterated the discrepancies between Lincoln's statements in northern Illinois and those in southern Illinois. He claimed that when he had inquired of Lincoln whether he would support admitting

12. The Sixth Debate

additional slave states, Lincoln had avoided the question "because up North, the abolition creed declares that there shall be no more slave States, while down south ... he and his friends are afraid to advance that doctrine. Therefore, he gives an evasive and equivocal answer, to be construed one way in the south and another way in the north...."[3] The Senator quoted from Lincoln's Chicago speech "to prove that he had one set of principles up north among the abolitionists, and from his Charleston speech to prove that he held another set down at Charleston and in southern Illinois." Lincoln used a vacillating campaign strategy, Douglas maintained, because Lincoln held to "one set of principles in the abolition counties, and a different and contradictory set in the other counties."

The important question, Douglas argued, was why his opponent modified his statements. Why could not Lincoln "avow his principles the same in the North as in the South — the same in every county, if he has a conviction that they are just?" Douglas replied that, if Lincoln was consistent, then "he would not be a Republican" because "his principles would apply alike in every part of the country." The Republicans, the Senator asserted, were "bounded and limited by geographical lines. With their principles they cannot even cross the Mississippi river on your ferry boats. They cannot cross over the Ohio into Kentucky. Lincoln himself cannot visit the land of his fathers, the scenes of his childhood, the graves of his ancestors, and carry his abolition principles, as he declared them at Chicago, with him." The Republican party "appeals to the North against the South; it appeals to northern passion, northern prejudice, and northern ambition, against southern people, southern States, and southern institutions, and its only hope of success is by that appeal."

Continuing a theme that he had employed from the beginning of the debates, Douglas attacked Lincoln's interpretation of "all men are created equal." It was a "falsification of the Declaration of Independence," Douglas argued, "to pretend that that instrument applied to and included negroes in the clause declaring that all men were created equal." In Chicago, the Senator reminded the assemblage, Lincoln had informed the "abolitionists" that "if the Declaration of Independence did not declare that the negro was created by the Almighty the equal of the white man, that you ought to take that instrument and tear out the clause which says that all men were created equal." Douglas then called the audience's attention to Lincoln's comments at Charleston, comments which Lincoln had repeated at Quincy, in which Lincoln "declared that the negro belongs to an inferior race; is physically inferior to the white man, and should always be kept in an inferior position." This was inconsistent of his opponent, Douglas charged, and later in the debate, believing this point was worthy of repetition, the Senator recalled that Lincoln, when addressing the "Chicago abolitionists," had "declared that all distinctions of race must be discarded and blotted out, because the negro stood on an equal footing with the white man; that if one man said the Declaration of Independence did not mean a negro when it declared all men created equal, that another man would say that it did not mean another man; and hence we ought to discard all difference between the negro race and all other races, and declare them all created equal."

Douglas, once again, assailed Lincoln's prophetic prediction. Lincoln, the Senator pointed out, thought that it was "his duty to preach a crusade in the free States, against slavery, because it is a crime, as he believes, and ought to be extinguished; and because the people of the slave States will never abolish it." The more fundamental question, Douglas believed, was how Lincoln intended to abolish slavery: "How is he going to abolish it? Down in the southern part of the State he takes the ground openly that he will not interfere with slavery where it exists, and says that he is not now and never was in favor of interfering with slavery where it exists in the States." If Lincoln was not in favor of interfering with southern slavery, Douglas asked, "how does he expect to bring slavery in a course of ultimate extinction? How can he extinguish it in Kentucky, in Virginia, in all the slave States by his policy, if he will not pursue a policy which will interfere with it in the States where it exists? In his speech at Springfield before the Abolition or Republican convention, he declared his hostility to any more slave States." The Senator recalled that at Springfield Lincoln had told his "Abolition friends that this Government could not endure permanently, divided into free and slave States as our fathers made it, and that it must become all free or all slave, otherwise, that the government could not exist." Douglas questioned, "How then does Lincoln propose to save the Union, unless by compelling all the States to become free, so that the house shall not be divided against itself?"

In his conclusion, Douglas once again defended his principle of

12. The Sixth Debate

self-government and criticized the "House Divided" speech. "Under the Constitution of the United States," he argued, "each State of this Union has a right to do as it pleases on the subject of slavery" and, in obvious deference to those who had crossed the river to attend the debate, Douglas asserted that it was "none of our business whether slavery exists in Missouri or not. Missouri is a sovereign State of this Union, and has the same right to decide the slavery question for herself that Illinois has to decide it for herself." He clung "firmly to that great principle which declares the right of each State and each territory to settle the question of slavery, and every other domestic question for themselves. I hold that if they want a slave State they have a right under the Constitution of the United States to make it so, and if they want a free State, it is their right to have it."

Douglas urged that "each State stand firmly by that great constitutional right" of self-government. If we "stand by that great principle," the Senator believed, "we can go on as we have done, increasing in wealth, in population, in power, and in all the elements of greatness, until we shall be the admiration and terror of the world." Referring to the idea of manifest destiny, the engine which he believed popular sovereignty would fuel, Douglas predicted a bright future in which the American people "can go on and enlarge as our population increases, and we require more room, until we make this continent one ocean-bound republic." By adhering to popular sovereignty, "the United States can perform that great mission, that destiny which Providence has marked out for us" and the nation "can receive with entire safety that stream of intelligence which is constantly flowing from the Old World to the New, filling up our prairies, clearing our wildernesses and building cities, towns, railroads and other internal improvements, and thus make this the asylum of the oppressed of the whole earth." The United States had "this great mission to perform," Douglas argued, "and it can only be performed by adhering faithfully to that principle of self-government on which our institutions were all established."[4]

Douglas mentioned a few other issues. He attempted to connect Lincoln with previous Republican convention platforms that tended to espouse abolitionist doctrine. The Senator refuted the existence of any conspiracy between him and President Buchanan, even taking time to criticize the President for his support of the Lecompton Constitution.

Douglas also defended his obedience of the Dred Scott decision by criticizing Lincoln for supposedly recommending disobedience of the Supreme Court. Douglas briefly referred to one of Lincoln's Freeport questions, restating his belief that he should not have to answer the question of whether a free state could prohibit slavery, describing that question as "ridiculous."[5]

Lincoln's strategy for the Quincy debate was similar to the Galesburg debate: defend himself against Douglas's charges of inconsistency by quoting from former speeches. In addition, he laid out his position on slavery but avoided any lengthy discussion of the Declaration of Independence.

Lincoln acknowledged that Douglas had called him "guilty of a species of double-dealing with the public — that I make speeches of a certain sort in the North, among the Abolitionists, which I would not make in the South, and that I make speeches of a certain sort in the south which I would not make in the North." Lincoln recalled that Douglas had "brought forward a quotation or two from a speech of mine delivered at Chicago, and then to contrast with it, he brought forward an extract from a speech of mine at Charleston, in which he insisted that I was greatly inconsistent ... that I was playing a double part, and speaking in one region one way and in another region another way." Lincoln refuted the charge by quoting his statement from the Charleston debate: "'I will say, then, that I am not, nor ever have been, in favor of bringing about in any way the social and political equality of the white and black races— that I am not nor ever have been in favor of making voters or jurors of negroes, nor of qualifying them to hold office, nor to intermarry with white people; and I will say in addition to this that there is a physical difference between the white and black races which will ever forbid the two races living together on terms of social and political equality. And inasmuch as they cannot so live, while they do remain together, there must be the position of superior & inferior. I am as much as any other man in favor of having the superior position assigned to the white race.'"

Lincoln further expounded on this issue later in the debate by quoting from an "old speech" of his, comments he admitted were also made at the first debate at Ottawa. He had declared that his "own feelings would not admit a social and political equality between the white and

12. The Sixth Debate

black races, and that even if my own feelings would admit of it, I still knew that the public sentiment of the country would not, and that such a thing was an utter impossibility." His former statements, he argued, had clearly stated his position that "any thing that argues me into his idea of perfect social and political equality with the negro, is but a specious and fantastical arrangement of words by which a man can prove a horse-chestnut to be a chestnut horse" and that he had "no purpose, directly or indirectly, to interfere with the institution in the States where it exists." Lincoln believed that he had "no right to do so" and had "no inclination to do so." He had "no purpose to introduce political and social equality between the white and black races," because he contended that there was "a physical difference between the two, which" in his judgment would "probably forever forbid their living together on the footing of perfect equality." Lincoln also noted that as it became "a necessity that there must be a difference" he and Douglas were both in favor of their race "having the superior position."

In regards to the Declaration of Independence, Lincoln followed at Quincy the same strategy that he had employed at the first debate, at Ottawa, and the most recent debate at Galesburg. To soften his previous statements on the racial question, he asserted that there was "no reason in the world why the negro is not entitled to all the rights enumerated in the Declaration of Independence — the right of life, liberty, and the pursuit of happiness." African Americans were as entitled to the rights of the Declaration of Independence "as the white man," Lincoln claimed. But he checked these statements by admitting that he held common ground with Douglas. Lincoln believed that "negro" was not equal in all respects, such as "color," but the "negro" had the "right to eat the bread without leave of anybody else which his own hand earns" and therefore the negro was his "equal and the equal of Judge Douglas, and the equal of every other man."

Lincoln ended his first speech at Quincy with an attack on slavery, a position on which most Republicans held common ground. He stated that slavery was a "wrong," a "moral, a social and a political wrong." His party considered it a "wrong not confining itself merely to the persons or the States where it exists" but in slavery's tendency to extend itself to the "existence of the whole nation." Because the Republicans believed slavery "wrong" they had proposed a "course of policy that shall deal with it as a wrong. We deal with it as with any other wrong, insofar as we can prevent its growing any larger, and so deal with it that in the run of time there may be some promise of an end to it." The Republicans also "oppose it as an evil so far as it seeks to spread itself. We insist on the policy that shall restrict it to its present limits." When Douglas states that "whoever, or whatever community, wants slaves, they have a right to have them, he is perfectly logical if there is nothing wrong in the institution; but if you admit that it is wrong, he cannot logically say that anybody has a right to do wrong." Lincoln contended that when he could "show what is the real difference between us" and have the "question distinctly stated—can get all these men who believe that slavery is in some of these respects wrong, to stand and act with us in treating it as a wrong—then, and not till then, I think we will in some way come to an end of this slavery agitation."[6]

Lincoln also mentioned three other points. In response to Douglas's strategy of linking him with other Republicans and their abolitionist statements, Lincoln simply declared that he should not be held responsible for what other members of his party had stated. He again attacked the Dred Scott decision, claiming that it would permit slavery nationally and reiterated his argument that Clay believed the Declaration of Independence applied to all men.

Quincy marked a turning point for the campaign, for the debates, and for Lincoln. This would be the last time he would speak both of racial superiority and the Declaration of Independence within the same speech.

13

The Last Debate: Alton, Illinois

October 15, 1858

Something changed in Lincoln. What caused the transformation is not known. After debating at Quincy, he made no speeches, and wrote no letters. The only recorded event is a steamboat ride to Alton.[1]

Perhaps it was that steamboat journey on the Mississippi that precipitated Lincoln's final conversion. Perhaps that voyage caused him to reminisce about other river journeys he had taken, such as his two flatboat trips to Louisiana on the Mississippi. Perhaps he reminisced about the adventure of navigating the wide river on a small packet boat, past side-wheelers, rocks, and submerged logs. He would have remembered New Orleans, the diversity of people, the different languages, the food, the architecture, and the slaves, as well as the slave owners, the slave pens and the slave auctions.

Or maybe he reminisced about another river journey, this one on the Ohio River, one that he had described in a letter to a friend. Lincoln writing in 1855, fourteen years after the event, still remembered that "In 1841 you and I had together a tedious low-water trip, on a Steam Boat from Louisville to St. Louis. You may remember, as I well do, that from Louisville to the mouth of the Ohio there were, on board, ten or a dozen slaves, shackled together with irons. That sight was a continual torment to me; and I see something like it every time I touch the Ohio, or any other slave-border. It is hardly fair to you to assume that I have no interest in a thing which has, and continually exercises, the power of making me miserable." In referring to the slaves, he confessed that he hated "to see the poor creatures hunted down, and caught, and carried back to their stripes, and unrewarded toils; but I bite my lip and keep quiet."[2]

He would not bite his lip at Alton.

During the three days that separated the last two debates, Lincoln's civil war between the politician and the statesman ended, and the statesman would triumph.

However, the Alton area was not a region where it was politically wise for Lincoln to speak as a statesman. In the 1856 elections, of the nine counties that constituted Illinois' Eighth Congressional District, six voted Democratic, while only two, including the one in which Alton was located, voted Republican. Overall, the district averaged nearly 60 percent in favor of the Democrats.[3] This was not a strong Republican area, but was most similar to the Charleston area, and one would expect the politician to address the audience in a similar fashion. Yet, unlike Lincoln's approach in Charleston, at Alton there would be no mention of "inferior" races or "superior" races; instead, for the first time in the debates, Lincoln would stand firm on his interpretation that "all men are created equal" meant "all men," before an audience he knew opposed this interpretation, and whose support he needed to win the election. Lincoln would approach Alton as a lawyer. The jury was the American people, and the defendant was the Declaration of Independence.

> There was very little excitement manifest in the city during the forenoon, beyond the constant arrival of people from the country and neighboring towns. A train of eight or ten cars came down from Springfield, Carlinville, and other stations on the Alton and Chicago Railroad; and the steamer *White Cloud* brought up a full load from St. Louis. The whole number in attendance upon the discussion was probably between four and five thousand. By mutual agreement the friends of the respective candidates made no processions or other demonstrations of enthusiasm. The debate passed off with rather less than the ordinary amount of applause, but with unusually close attention on the part of the audience. The speaking commenced at 2 o'clock P.M., at the south front of the new City Hall.[4]
> — *Chicago Press and Tribune*

The *Chicago Press and Tribune* speculated that the small audience "may be attributed partly to the staid character of the population of

13. The Last Debate

Madison County — a considerable plurality of whom are old line Whigs." The newspaper apparently thought that the "old line Whigs" were conservative both in their politics and in their demeanor.

Douglas, his voice now hoarse from campaigning, and barely audible, opened his remarks with his favorite subject. He reminded the audience that Lincoln had begun the campaign with the proposition that "this government could not endure permanently divided into free and slave States, as our fathers made it; that they must all become free or all become slave."[5] Believing that those comments portrayed Lincoln as a radical, more in line with the abolitionists, he could not pass up an opportunity to once again quote from them.

The Senator reminded the audience that while Lincoln had been inconsistent in his campaign statements, he himself had not. He admitted that there were differences between the candidates, but he had "never intended to waver one hair's breadth" in either "the north or the south." Douglas believed that if he ever adopted a political philosophy that he could not proclaim "in the same terms not only in the northern but the southern part of Illinois, not only in the northern but the southern States, and wherever the American flag waves over American soil" then "there must be something wrong" with that philosophy.[6]

The right of self-government, Douglas maintained, was the foundation of the nation, the most sacred principle, which far exceeded the importance of "negroes." The founding fathers had made "this government divided into free and slave States" and did not "abolish it in any of them" but formed a government that guaranteed "forever to each State the right to do as it pleased on the slavery question." Completely avoiding the question of slavery's morality, Douglas asserted that this government can exist as the founders made it, "divided into free and slave States, if any one State chooses to retain slavery." As for the territories, if Kansans wanted "a slave State they have a right, under the constitution of the United States, to form such a State" and Douglas would "let them come into the Union with slavery or without." The Senator firmly believed that it was "their business, not mine. It is none of your business in Missouri whether Kansas shall adopt slavery or reject it." While Lincoln looked "forward to a time when slavery shall be abolished everywhere," Douglas, in advocating for the right of self-government, looked "forward to a time when each State shall be allowed to do as it pleases.

If it chooses to keep slavery forever, it is not my business, but its own; if it chooses to abolish slavery, it is its own business—not mine. I care more for the great principle of self-government, the right of the people to rule, than I do for all the negroes in Christendom. I would not endanger the perpetuity of the Union. I would not blot out the great inalienable rights of the white man for all the negroes that ever existed...."[7]

Douglas, before this pro–Democrat assembly, made repeated attacks on Lincoln's interpretation of the Declaration of Independence. Lincoln, Douglas asserted, had "uttered sentiments in regard to the negro being on an equality with the white man. He adopted in support of this position the argument which Lovejoy and Codding,[8] and other Abolition lecturers had made familiar in the northern and central portions of the State, to wit: that the Declaration of Independence having declared all men free and equal, by Divine law, also that negro equality was an inalienable right, of which they could not be deprived. He insisted, in that speech, that the Declaration of Independence included the negro in the clause asserting that all men were created equal." The Senator further claimed that Lincoln stated "that all these distinctions between this man and that man, this race and the other race, must be discarded, and we must all stand by the Declaration of Independence, declaring that all men were created equal."

The Senator saved his most extensive comments on the Declaration of Independence for the conclusion of his opening speech. He questioned whether the Republicans "really think that under the Declaration of Independence the negro is equal to the white man, and that negro equality is an inalienable right conferred by the Almighty, and hence, that all human laws in violation of it are null and void. With such men it is no use for me to argue. I hold that the signers of the Declaration of Independence had no reference to negroes at all when they declared all men to be created equal. They did not mean negro, nor the savage Indians, nor the Fejee Islanders, nor any other barbarous race. They were speaking of white men. They alluded to men of European birth and European descent—to white men, and to none others, when they declared that doctrine. I hold that this Government was established on the white basis. It was established by white men for the benefit of white men and their posterity forever, and should be administered by white men, and none others." Douglas could not have stated his position more clearly.

13. The Last Debate

Douglas also insisted that Lincoln had failed to answer whether he would vote to admit a state if that state chose to enter the Union as a slave state. The Senator reminded the assembled crowd that Lincoln had considered the now popular Mexican war "unconstitutional, unnecessary and unjust." And, in recognition of the "great many old Clay Whigs down in this region," while Lincoln had claimed that he was an "old line Clay Whig," Douglas argued that this "old Clay Whig party" to which Lincoln referred was incongruous with the abolitionism of which Lincoln had often spoke.

The Senator also realized that there were "Danites" in the audience, Democrat supporters of President Buchanan who were now his enemies. Douglas admitted that, against the administration's wishes, he had vehemently opposed the Lecompton Constitution, a constitution that had been approved by Kansas slave interests. His opposition was not because the constitution would have brought Kansas into the union as a slave state, but because it was not the "act and deed of the people." It was "the act of a small, pitiful, minority acting in the name of the majority." His opposition to the constitution had resulted from his sense of duty, that he was "'accountable to Illinois, as my constituency, and to God, but not to the President, or to any other power on earth.'" Now the Buchanan administration conducted "warfare" on him. But Buchanan could not provoke him "to abandon one iota of Democratic principles." Douglas would stand by the "platform of the Democratic party, and by its organization, and support its nominees." The President had no right to instruct him how to vote, Douglas claimed, and if he did, then this government would be converted "from a republic into a despotism."

In his final comments of the last debate, comments that, due to Douglas's hoarse voice, were probably read far more than heard, the Senator made a final plea for the issue he held most dear, the issue of popular sovereignty. "My friends, if, as I have said before," if the Americans only "live up to this great fundamental principle" then "there will be peace between the North and the South." There was a danger that the "agitators" in the free States would unite and make "war" upon slavery. "The only remedy and safety," Douglas believed was by supporting "the constitution as our fathers made it, obey the laws as they are passed" and "sustain the decisions of the Supreme Court and the constituted authorities." His remarks summed up the three main issues that he had consistently espoused: the "House Divided" speech called for aggression against the South, the Kansas-Nebraska Act should be supported as a manifestation of the popular will, and popular sovereignty was the true national issue that should be supported by both North and South as the one issue upon which both sections could agree. Douglas, as should have been expected from a seasoned politician, had been remarkably consistent in his arguments. In fact, the only main issue that he added to his repertoire, that disrupted his consistency, was when he began asserting that his opponent was inconsistent.[9]

Lincoln, facing south with a slave state just across the Mississippi River to his right, acknowledged that this was Douglas territory. Douglas knows, Lincoln admitted, that the debate was taking place before an audience "having strong sympathies southward by relationship, place of birth, and so on." For this reason, Lincoln knew, Douglas intended to place him "in an extremely Abolition attitude."[10]

Douglas most frequently attempted to "abolitionize" Lincoln by quoting from the "House Divided" speech. Lincoln felt compelled to once again defend his speech as Douglas had forced him to do on so many previous occasions. Lincoln acknowledged that "Judge Douglas has again referred to a Springfield speech in which I said 'a house divided against itself cannot stand.' The Judge has so often made the entire quotation from that speech that I can make it from memory...." His remarks at Springfield had been "extremely offensive to Judge Douglas," such that he "has warred upon them as Satan does upon the Bible."

Lincoln took the opportunity to defend his speech and to shift the focus to what he considered the two major issues of the day: slavery and the Declaration of Independence. Lincoln defended his "House Divided" speech by quoting directly from it, a new approach that he had not used at any of the previous debates. To Lincoln, there were two forces in operation in America: one that sought to make slavery national and another that sought to restrict it where it then existed so that it might end. There was no middle ground between these two philosophies, and there was no hope that an easy compromise might be found. The slavery "agitation," Lincoln argued, "would not cease until a crisis should have been reached and passed." He further acknowledged that he had stated the manner in which slavery would be passed, that it would either "go one way or the other. We might, by arresting the further spread of

13. The Last Debate

it and placing it where our fathers originally placed it, put it where the public mind should rest in the belief that it was in the course of ultimate extinction. Thus the agitation may cease." However, slavery might expand into the territories and the northern states "until it shall become alike lawful in all the States, old as well as new, North as well as South. I have said, and I repeat, my wish is that the further spread of it may be arrested, and that it may be placed where the public mind shall rest in the belief that it is in the course of ultimate extinction...."

To Lincoln, slavery was the key issue that divided the American people. And for the first time in the campaign, at the only debate where he spoke of the Declaration of Independence without the encumbrances of "superior" and "inferior" races, he provided his definitions of politician and statesman: "But is it true that all the difficulty and agitation we have in regard to this institution of slavery springs from office seeking—from the mere ambition of politicians? Is that the truth?" The institution of slavery, a "mighty, deep seated power," had caused the great agitation in the nation, had disturbed the "general peace of the country," and had threatened to split the national churches, Lincoln argued. Douglas had "intimated," Lincoln claimed, that all the nation's "difficulty in regard to the institution of slavery" was nothing more than the "mere agitation of office seekers and ambitious Northern politicians." But Northern politicians had not caused the problem of slavery, Lincoln argued. Politicians, by Lincoln's definition, were the ones who avoided discussing slavery. It was the pro-slavery forces, or as Lincoln put it, that "irresistible power" which, for fifty years, had "agitated the people to be stilled and subdued by pretending that it [slavery] is an exceedingly simple thing" that should not be discussed. He questioned where was the "statesmanship" that assumed "that you can quiet that disturbing element in our society which has disturbed us for more than half a century, which has been the only serious danger that has threatened our institutions—I say, where is the philosophy or the statesmanship based on the assumption that we are to quit talking about it [slavery], and that the public mind is all at once to cease being agitated by it? Yet this is the policy here in the north that Douglas is advocating — that we are to care nothing about it! I ask you if it is not a false philosophy?"

Lincoln accused Douglas and his followers of "false statesmanship" for creating "a policy upon the basis of caring nothing about *the very thing that every body does care the most about*—a thing which all experience has shown we care a very great deal about."

To Lincoln, this was the vital issue facing America, and the vital issue of the debates. He discounted the possibility that "good" and "bad" politicians existed; there were only politicians and statesmen, those for slavery and those against it. Douglas, by calling on the Americans to ignore slavery, defined the politicians, while the statesmen were those individuals who asserted that slavery was immoral and that the Declaration of Independence was inclusive of all men. It was true statesmanship to Lincoln to speak of slavery as a wrong. "The real issue in this controversy," Lincoln argued, "the one pressing upon every mind, is the sentiment on the part of one class that looks upon the institution of slavery as a wrong, and of another class that does not look upon it as a wrong. The sentiment that contemplates the institution of slavery in this country as a wrong is the sentiment of the Republican party. It is the sentiment around which all their actions, all their arguments, circle— from which all their propositions radiate. They look upon it as being a moral, social and political wrong...." Lincoln's opposition held to a different philosophy which "is a sentiment which treats it as not being a wrong. This is the Democratic sentiment of this day."

The slavery issue was a struggle that had been waged for centuries, a struggle in which Lincoln had been privileged to have partaken. The "real issue," Lincoln restated, "the issue that will continue in this country when these poor tongues of Judge Douglas and myself shall be silent," is the "eternal struggle between these two principles—right and wrong— throughout the world":

> They are the two principles that have stood face to face from the beginning of time; and will ever continue to struggle. The one is the common right of humanity and the other the divine right of kings. It is the same principle in whatever shape it develops itself. It is the same spirit that says, "You work and toil and earn bread, and I'll eat it." No matter in what shape it comes, whether from the mouth of a king who seeks to bestride the people of his own nation and live by the fruit of their labor, or from one race of men as an apology for enslaving another race, it is the same tyrannical principle. I was glad to express my gratitude at Quincy, and I re-express it here to Judge Douglas—that he looks to no end of the institution of slavery. That will help the people to see where the struggle really is. It will hereafter place with us all men who really do wish the wrong may have an end. And

13. The Last Debate

whenever we can get rid of the fog which obscures the real question — when we can get Judge Douglas and his friends to avow a policy looking to its perpetuation — we can get out from among them that class of men and bring them to the side of those who treat it as a wrong. Then there will soon be an end of it, and that end will be its "ultimate extinction."

But it was Lincoln's defense of the Declaration of Independence that made his Alton speech unique. He correctly stated that the interpretation of the Declaration of Independence was the crux of the controversy between the two candidates. Those who gathered on the banks of the Mississippi that day, who listened and watched, saw a different man on that platform, one whom no one had seen since the early stages of the campaign, a free man, clothed no longer as a politician beholden to the electorate, but as one beholden to none other than his own convictions of what was right, of what was ethical, of what was moral. At this juncture, Lincoln came of age. In this debate, more than any other, Lincoln, speaking before a hostile audience, held up the Declaration of Independence as his nation's best hope. Three years before, there had never been a man, Lincoln argued, "so far as I knew or believed, in the whole world, who had said that the Declaration of Independence did not include negroes in the term 'all men.' I re-assert it to-day. I assert that Judge Douglas and all his friends may search the whole records of the country, and it will be a matter of great astonishment to me if they shall be able to find that one human being three years ago had ever uttered the astounding sentiment that the term 'all men' in the Declaration did not include the negro." Lincoln knew his interpretation was not accepted by all, and recalled the "shameful though rather forcible declaration of Petit of Indiana, upon the floor of the United States Senate, that the Declaration of Independence was in that respect 'a self-evident lie,' rather than a self-evident truth. But I say, with a perfect knowledge of all this hawking at the Declaration without directly attacking it, that three years ago there never had lived a man who had ventured to assail it in the sneaking way of pretending to believe it and then asserting it did not include the negro. I believe that the first man who ever said it was Chief Justice Taney in the Dred Scott case, and the next to him was our friend Stephen A. Douglas. And now it has become the catch-word of the entire party."

There was a great danger, Lincoln believed, in this interpretation taking hold, and becoming permanent. Whenever this "new principle — this new proposition that no human being ever thought of three years ago — is brought forward, I combat it as having an evil tendency, if not an evil design; I combat it as having a tendency to dehumanize the negro — to take away from him the right of ever striving to be a man. I combat it as being one of the thousand things constantly done in these days to prepare the public mind to make property, and nothing but property, of the negro in all the States of this Union."

Douglas had argued that the founders had not intended the Declaration to include all men. Lincoln, directly quoting from his June 26, 1857, speech, countered with his belief that the "authors of that notable instrument intended to include all men, but they did not mean to declare all men equal in all respects." Lincoln noted that the founding fathers "did not mean to say all men were equal in color, size, intellect, moral development or social capacity. They defined with tolerable distinctness in what they did consider all men created equal — equal in certain inalienable rights, among which are life, liberty and the pursuit of happiness. This they said, and this they meant. They did not mean to assert the obvious untruth, that all were then actually enjoying that equality, nor yet, that they were about to confer it immediately upon them. In fact they had no power to confer such a boon."

Describing the Declaration of Independence as a noble goal, and not an immediate condition, Lincoln argued that the authors had "meant simply to declare the right so that the enforcement of it might follow as fast as circumstances should permit."[11] Equality did not have to exist in the late eighteenth century for the phrase to be considered universally egalitarian. Rather, Lincoln interpreted the founding fathers as intending to "set up a standard maxim for free society which should be familiar to all: constantly looked to, constantly labored for, and even, though never perfectly attained, constantly approximated and thereby constantly spreading and deepening its influence and augmenting the happiness and value of life to all people, of all colors, every where."[12]

Here Lincoln shed the self-imposed chains, which had bound him since the campaign's beginning, by boldly speaking of the Declaration of Independence and, for the first time in three debates, he made no mention of "superior" and "inferior"; he did not repeat his Charleston

13. The Last Debate

comments on race relations. This omission is all the more significant in that he had apparently, as he had done at the first debate, exhausted his material before his time expired. At the end of the paragraph which began with the words "This is the real issue," a paragraph that appears to have been his intended conclusion, he admitted, "I understand I have ten minutes yet" and, following the advice that Medill had given him in regards to using his full allotment of time, he proceeded into another discussion of the Dred Scott decision. He could have easily quoted his Charleston comments on "superior" and "inferior" as he had done at the previous two debates, but he did not.

When Davis read the Alton text, he must have shaken his head in disbelief, and Lovejoy must have smiled.

Why Lincoln suddenly and dramatically changed strategy at this late juncture in the campaign, at the very last debate, is not easily explained, especially when one considers his previous speeches and his remarks at the previous debates. Lincoln began the campaign speaking as a statesman, but moved away from that position as he catered his remarks to the prejudices of the audiences he faced. In the first speech of the campaign, the "House Divided" speech, he not only spoke of the possibility that the nation might become all slave, but that it also might become all free. At Chicago, the following month, he spoke even more boldly on the egalitarianism of the Declaration of Independence, and had argued against any discussion of "superior" and "inferior" races. However, when he next spoke at Springfield, just seven days after his Chicago speech, his courage began to fail, or his political wisdom had begun to take hold. There he claimed that African Americans were not equal in all respects. At the first debate, at Ottawa, Lincoln's descent continued. For the first time in the campaign, he embraced the "superior" and "inferior" concept while also arguing for his interpretation of the Declaration of Independence. When he traveled to Freeport in a strong Republican area though, he dropped the Declaration completely. He maintained this strategy at the southernmost debate, Jonesboro, but at the Charleston debate, in the crucial central area of Illinois, he moved even further from his Chicago remarks by catering to the audience's prejudices. He again advocated the division of the races based on "superior" and "inferior" lines, but without any mention of the Declaration. At Galesburg, in a more northern area, for the first time since Ottawa, he once again referred to the Declaration of Independence but he still advocated for the division of the races. Finally, at Quincy, at the second to last debate, he displayed consistency that had been absent in his remarks when he made the same arguments as he had at Galesburg. However, at Alton, he spoke as if he was facing a Chicago audience as opposed to the Democratic one that was before him.

Several theories may be offered to explain Lincoln's Alton remarks. First, Lincoln was unaware of the audience's opinions. This is easily dismissed by Lincoln's comments that he was aware of the difference between the Alton crowd's philosophy and his. Second, Lincoln knew he was defeated, and dispensed with any political maneuvering. His writings and speeches at the end of the campaign provide no evidence for this explanation.[13] Third, he was exhausted from the campaign and this affected his judgment. However, those who observed Lincoln and Douglas at Alton claim that Lincoln appeared stronger, as if the campaigning actually increased his stamina.

The most logical answer can be found in Lincoln's career and his personal philosophy. He had been a lawyer for decades and was experienced and comfortable in a courtroom setting where he could persuade the audience through the logic of his argument. It seems likely that, instead of simply adapting the prejudices of the assemblage, he decided that he would attempt to convince them that "all men are created equal" truly meant "all men."

This still does not answer the more fundamental question of *why* Lincoln decided to convince the audience to accept a philosophy he knew they did not share. The answer to this question lies in one's interpretation of *who* Lincoln was. Some believe that he changed over time; as illustrated by his many speeches which culminated with his last speech advocating the right to vote for some African Americans. Others have contended that Lincoln was a keen politician who adjusted his comments to suit his audience and simply seized on an available issue, the hatred of the Kansas-Nebraska Act, to advance his political career. Another theory is that Lincoln always personally believed in full

13. The Last Debate

egalitarianism regardless of race, but that he believed this goal could only be attained over time.

The individual debates provide support for all of these interpretations. In the first debate he spoke of the Declaration and unequal races while at the last debate he spoke only of the Declaration. This suggests that he changed over time. His vacillating position on the issue of the Declaration and race at each debate would suggest that he was simply a politician who modified his position to cater to the electorate. The theory that he believed in egalitarianism could be supported by the Alton debate as well as his Chicago and Lewistown speeches.

To answer this difficult question, the historian must lay down the microscope and pick up the telescope in order to understand Lincoln not by individual speeches but by the philosophy that he espoused over time. In this respect, the best explanation of who Lincoln was lies in one document, the Declaration of Independence. To Lincoln, this was America's cornerstone that functioned as a permanent guard against despotism, and as the guide for America's leaders. He often referred to the Declaration before the debates, and after them. The Gettysburg Address stands as the most popular example, when in the opening line, "Four score and seven years ago," he cleverly pointed the Americans back to 1776, to the Declaration, to the phrase "all men are created equal." This was the true Lincoln, Lincoln the statesman, and the Lincoln we remember today.

The consideration of *who* he was is the most likely reason that precipitated Lincoln's change in strategy at Alton. He must have, through a process of self-examination, considered *who* he was and *how* he wished to be remembered, and what had motivated him to reenter politics. Undoubtedly, he wanted to be remembered as an advocate for the Declaration of Independence, and he would have admitted to himself that he had returned to politics because the Kansas-Nebraska Act had reversed America's antislavery course, which had been so powerfully stated in the Declaration. He must have realized how incongruous his "superior" and "inferior" comments were when compared with "all men are created equal." And so, at the last debate, he ignored the known sympathies of the audience, ignored his political instinct, ignored the advice of Davis, and acted like Lovejoy, standing there not as a politician solely seeking votes, but as a statesman standing for what he had always believed, and always would.

One week before the election, the worst fears of Lincoln's supporters were realized. The rumors were true. Senator John J. Crittenden, to whom the former Whigs, the orphaned voters, had looked for guidance and direction, had written a letter endorsing Douglas. Crittenden used Douglas's vehement defense of popular sovereignty, and his opposition to the Lecompton Constitution, as proof of Douglas's statesmanship.

On October 26, the pro–Douglas *Chicago Times* published an article entitled "Crittenden for Douglas" which was prefaced with the sentence, "The Hon. John J. Crittenden in his letter to the Hon. T.L. Dickey of this State, thus speaks of Douglas and his services to Illinois and to the Union." Crittenden recalled that he did, in a previous conversation, "speak of Judge Douglas in high and warm terms." He believed "that the people of Illinois little know how much they really owed" Douglas because he "had the courage and patriotism to take an elevated, just and independent position on the Lecompton question, at the sacrifice of interesting social relations as well as old party ties and associations, and in defiance of the power and patronage of an angry Administration supported by a dominant party and disbursing a revenue of some $80,000,000 a year." For Douglas "noble conduct" had caused him to be "almost overwhelmed with denunciation," while the "attacks made upon him in the debates in the Senate were frequent, personal and fierce." Throughout the entire legislative session, Douglas "must have felt the consciousness that he was in daily danger of being so assailed in debate, as to force him into altercations and quarrels, that must in their consequences involve the loss of his honor, or the hazard of his life." Douglas had maintained his course "steadily and firmly," Crittenden argued, and "throughout the whole struggle he had borne himself gallantly." There was to Crittenden "a heroism" in Douglas's course "that deserved approbation, if not applause."[14]

Douglas's supporters were elated; Lincoln's supporters were devastated.[15]

13. The Last Debate

Four days later, in the last speech of the campaign, of which only a fragment exists, two paragraphs provide insight into Lincoln's reaction to this letter, and on the previous five months of the campaign. With the Crittenden letter and Dickey's defection in mind, he acknowledged that "in some respects the contest has been painful to me." He noted that "myself, and those with whom I act have been constantly accused of a purpose to destroy the union; and bespattered with every imaginable odious epithet; and some who were friends, as it were but yesterday, have made themselves most active in this." Lincoln confessed that he had, in reaction to these accusations, "cultivated patience, and made no attempt at a retort." He also recalled the cause which had brought him to the contest: "Ambition has been ascribed to me. God knows how sincerely I prayed from the first that this field of ambition might not be opened. I claim no insensibility to political honors; but today could the Missouri restriction be restored, and the whole slavery question replaced on the old ground of 'toleration[']' by necessity where it exists, with unyielding hostility to the spread of it, on principle, I would, in consideration, gladly agree, that Judge Douglas should never be out, and I never in, an office, so long as we both or either, live."[16]

On November 2, the people of Illinois went to the polls. The northern Illinois districts went solidly for the Republicans, the southern Illinois districts, with two exceptions, voted overwhelmingly for the Democrats. The central area of Illinois proved the decisive one, and the Democrats won all the districts, with the exception of two, including the district containing Charleston. In that central district where Lincoln had spoken of the "inferior" and "superior" races, the Republicans won a majority. In the central district containing Alton where Lincoln had spoken of "all men" applying to "all men," the Democrats had prevailed.

Determining the cause of Lincoln's defeat is difficult. The Republicans attributed defeat to numerous factors. Some of Lincoln's supporters blamed the lack of money, the unfair apportionment of delegates, or even the weather, apparently believing that Democrats were more likely to travel through rain than Republicans.[17] However, while none of the reasons provided by the Republicans can be substantiated, three individuals, all of whom had an intimate view of the campaign, agree on one factor that severely impacted Lincoln's chances: Crittenden's endorsement of Douglas.

Two days after the election, Lincoln wrote to Crittenden: "The emotions of defeat, at the close of a struggle in which I felt more than a merely selfish interest, and to which defeat the use of your name contributed largely, are fresh upon me; but, even in this mood, I can not for a moment suspect you of anything dishonorable."[18]

Lincoln's supporters were not so gracious when commenting on the actions of the Kentucky senator. Davis did believe that William H. Seward and Horace Greeley, two leading eastern Republicans, had failed to properly support Lincoln, but he placed most of his blame for Lincoln's defeat on Dickey: "The lever of Judge Dickey's influence has been felt. He drew the letter out of Mr. Crittenden, & I think, in view of every thing that it was perfectly outrageous in Mr. Crittenden to have written anything."

Davis also found it "very shameful" that Dickey, who had received the Crittenden letter on August 1, had waited until a week before the election to have it published.[19] This strategy, Davis, knew, had prevented the Republicans from responding.

Herndon was even more critical. He described Illinois as having "three distinct phases of human development: the extreme north, the middle, and the extreme south. The first is intelligence, the second timidity, and the third ignorance on the special issue, but goodness and bravery. If a man spoke to suit the north — for freedom, justice — this killed him in the center, and in the south. So in the center, it killed him north and south. So in the south, it surely killed him north and south. So in the south, it surely killed him north. Lincoln tried to stand high and elevated, so he fell deep."

Herndon also faulted Greeley for not providing "one single solitary, manly lift" and the pro-slavery men who "went to a man for Douglas." Displaying an anti–Catholic fervor that was distinctly lacking in his law

13. The Last Debate

partner, he blamed "thousands of roving, robbing, bloated, pockmarked Catholic Irish" who "were imported upon us from Philadelphia, New York, St. Louis, and other cities." But like Lincoln and Davis, he recognized that "Crittenden wrote letters to Illinois urging Americans and Old Line Whigs to go for Douglas, and so they went 'helter-skelter.' Thousands of Whigs dropped us just on the eve of the election, through the influence of Crittenden."[20]

The observations of Lincoln, Davis and Herndon, along with Dickey's contention that he had always opposed the opening paragraph of the "House Divided" speech, all suggest that Lincoln lost the election with the first few sentences of that speech. It proved to be the first domino that sent the central district of Illinois falling for Douglas. Lincoln became a political martyr for daring to speak of a time when his nation might be all free. A Chicago newspaper described it best: "Thus was Lincoln slain in Old Kentucky."[21]

For Judd, this defeat must have been especially painful. Years before, when he served as a state legislator, he, and his four other supporters, had prevented Lincoln from receiving the majority he needed to win election as senator. Now, he had worked tirelessly for Lincoln's election, only to watch him lose. Judd, with a certain degree of guilt, could only look back and know that if had supported him in 1855, Lincoln would not have had to campaign in 1858. To his depressed supporter Lincoln wrote, "You are feeling badly. 'And this too shall pass away.' Never fear. Yours as ever A. Lincoln."[22]

The next time I saw Mr. Lincoln, after the election, I said to him that I hoped he was not so much disappointed as I had been. This, of course, "reminded him of a little story." I have forgotten the story, but it was about an over-grown boy who had met with some mishap, "stumped" his toe, perhaps, and who said that "it hurt too much to laugh, and he was too big to cry."[23]
— Horace White

The Lincoln-Douglas Debates and the Making of a President

Seventeen days after the election, Lincoln wrote:

I am glad that I made the late race. It gave me a hearing on the great and durable question of the age, which I could have had in no other way; and though I now sink out of view, and shall be forgotten, I believe I have made some marks which will tell for the cause of civil liberty long after I am gone.[24]

Epilogue

Heroes sometimes fail us, let us down, disappoint. At Jonesboro and Charleston, Lincoln did just that. But then there are the times when they stand firm and true to what is right, the times when we call them heroes. The Lincoln of Lewistown and Chicago showed us a glimpse of that, but it was truly the Lincoln of Alton who earned the epitaph of hero, an American hero, *the* American hero, by ignoring sound advice, by parting with common sense, by saying what he should not have said.

Or, to view it from a different perspective, by stating what he *should* have said.

Before a hostile audience, with the election on the line, the apparent culmination of his political career in his hands, he told the majority before him that he did not believe as they did, that he did not believe in their bigotry, their hatred, their beliefs, or that the cornerstone of our nation was slavery or westward expansion, but that it was the Declaration of Independence, that "all men" meant all men, that this nation was different, special, that this nation was the "last, best hope on earth."

Appendix A: After '58

David Davis (1815–1886) helped orchestrate Lincoln's presidential nomination.

Davis originally approved of the Emancipation Proclamation, and Lincoln appointed him to the Supreme Court. When Davis later recommended that Lincoln alter the Emancipation Proclamation, Lincoln refused.

Davis served on the Supreme Court until 1877, served in the United States Senate for one term, and retired to Bloomington, Illinois.

Theophilus Lyle Dickey (1811–1885) maintained his hatred of abolitionists and his belief that Lincoln was one. He supported Douglas in the 1860 Presidential campaign, speaking throughout Illinois on Douglas's behalf but, like Douglas, he opposed secession, and served as a colonel with the Fourth Illinois Cavalry during the Civil War, and eventually became a member of General Ulysses S. Grant's staff. He served in the Grant administration as assistant attorney general from 1868 to 1870 and was elected a justice of the Illinois Supreme Court in 1875, serving in that position until his death in 1885.

Stephen Arnold Douglas (1813–1861) was nominated for president by the Democratic party in 1860, but relatively early in the campaign he turned his focus to the southern states and campaigned not so much for himself, but against secession, his greatest fear.

He continued his indifference toward slavery by hoping to avoid dissolution of the Union with a compromise that Crittenden had written. The compromise would have allowed slavery into the territories, but Lincoln refused to compromise.

As for Lincoln's Inaugural Address, Douglas stated, "I indorse it," and he made two famous quotes in the last year of his life.

Appendix A

In Chicago, he replied to those who wished to know where he stood on secession:

"There are only two sides to the question. Every man must be for the United States or against it. There can be no neutrals in this war, only patriots—or traitors."

As he was dying, his wife asked him if he had any words for his sons, he told her:

"Tell them to obey the laws and support the Constitution of the United States."

Four hours later, he died.

William Henry Herndon (1818–1891) became more radical on abolition as the war progressed. He eventually wrote, with Jesse W. Weik, a biography on Lincoln entitled *Herndon's Lincoln: The True Story of a Great Life*.

Norman Buel Judd (1815–1878), like Davis, worked tenaciously to secure Lincoln's nomination for president in 1860 and accompanied Lincoln on his railroad trip to Washington, D.C. Lincoln nominated him as United States Minister to Prussia, and after his return to the United States Judd was elected to the United States House of Representatives in 1866 and 1868.

Owen Lovejoy (1811–1864) won reelection to the United States House of Representatives in 1858, 1860, and 1862 and remained a steadfast opponent of slavery, an unswerving advocate of full equality, and a supporter of Lincoln.

After Lovejoy died, Lincoln wrote that "he was my most generous friend."

Joseph Meharry Medill (1823–1899) strongly supported Lincoln's nomination for president, but became critical over what he perceived as Lincoln's slow effort to attack slavery. His criticisms declined sharply after the issuance of the Emancipation Proclamation.

After the great fire of 1871, Medill became mayor of Chicago for two years, helped create Chicago's first public library, and continued to devote his time to the *Chicago Tribune*, of which he became the dominant partner in 1874.

Roger Brooke Taney (1777–1864) favored peaceful separation of the nation in 1861 and consistently opposed the Lincoln administration, believing that Lincoln had established a military tyranny. His death provided Lincoln the opportunity to nominate a chief justice to the Supreme Court who was opposed to the Dred Scott decision.

Horace White (1834–1916) became the *Chicago Tribune's* Washington correspondent from 1861 to 1863 and, as he remembered it, the story of his falling asleep on the train was "so irresistibly funny" to Lincoln that he "told the incident several times in Washington City when I chanced to meet him, after he became President, to any company who might be present, and with such contagious drollery that all who heard it would shake with laughter." When Herndon, in his 1888 biography on Lincoln, came to the chapter on the Lincoln-Douglas debates, he turned it completely over to White. White served as an editor of the *Chicago Tribune* from 1864 to 1874.

Abraham Lincoln (1809–1865) became the sixteenth president of the United States, and led the ship of state through the storm of civil war by the moral compass of the Declaration of Independence.

Appendix B: The Last Rebuttal

The fight must go on. The cause of civil liberty must not be surrendered at the end of one or even one hundred defeats. Douglas had the ingenuity to be supported in the late contest both as the best means to break down, and to uphold the Slave interest. No ingenuity can keep those antagonistic elements in harmony long. Another explosion will soon come.— November 19, 1858

Five years to the day after Lincoln wrote that sentence, the ideals of his nation, over which he had argued with Douglas throughout 1858, were succinctly summarized in another speech given at the cemetery dedication in Gettysburg, Pennsylvania.

Four score and seven years ago our fathers brought forth upon this continent, a new nation, conceived in Liberty, and dedicated to the proposition that all men are created equal.

Now we are engaged in a great civil war, testing whether that nation, or any nation so conceived, and so dedicated, can long endure. We are met on a great battle-field of that war. We have come to dedicate a portion of that field, as a final resting place for those who here gave their lives, that that nation might live. It is altogether fitting and proper that we should do this.

But, in a larger sense, we can not dedicate — we can not consecrate — we can not hallow — this ground. The brave men, living and dead, who struggled here, have consecrated it, far above our poor power to add or detract. The world will little note, nor long remember, what we say here, but it can never forget what they did here. It is for us, the living, rather, to be dedicated here to the unfinished work which they who fought here, have,

The Last Rebuttal

thus far, so nobly advanced. It is rather for us to be here dedicated to the great task remaining before us — that from these honored dead we take increased devotion to that cause for which they gave the last full measure of devotion — that we here highly resolve that these dead shall not have died in vain — that this nation, under God, shall have a new birth of freedom — and that, government of the people, by the people, for the people, shall not perish from the earth.

Chapter Notes

Chapter 1

1. Roy Basler, ed., *The Collected Works of Abraham Lincoln* (New Brunswick, NJ: Rutgers University Press, 1953), 2: 459.
2. Basler, *Collected Works*, 4:67.
3. *Ibid.*, 2:282 and 4:67.
4. *Ibid.*, 2:249–276.
5. Lincoln to William H. Henderson, February 21, 1855. Basler, *Collected Works*, 2:306–307. In conclusion, he commended the addressee's son, whom Lincoln respected because he had "kindly and firmly stood by me from first to last; and for which he has my everlasting gratitude." Lincoln wrote of forty-four, but he also had the support of the speaker of the House, which brought his total to forty-five. Thanks to Wayne Temple for his assistance with this question.
6. Basler, *Collected Works*, 2:323.
7. William Herndon and Jesse W. Weik, *Abraham Lincoln: The True Story of a Great Life* (New York: D. Appleton, 1896), 2:34.
8. Advertisement published in *Western Citizen*, June 1, 1843. Edward Magdol, *Owen Lovejoy: Abolitionist in Congress* (New Brunswick, NJ: Rutgers University Press, 1967), 42.
9. *Ibid.*, 49–50.
10. Willard L. King, *Lincoln's Manager: David Davis* (Cambridge, MA: Harvard University Press, 1960), 51.
11. *Ibid.*, 112–113.
12. Isabel Wallace, *The Life and Letters of General W.H.L. Wallace* (Carbondale, Southern Illinois University Press, 2000), 72.
13. William F. Moore and Jane Ann Moore, *Owen Lovejoy: His Brother's Blood; Speeches and Writings, 1838–1865* (Chicago: University of Illinois Press, 2004), 131.
14. King, *Lincoln's Manager*, 114.
15. Wallace, *Life and Letters of General Wallace*, 73–74.
16. Dickey to Herndon, December 8, 1866. Herndon-Weik Papers. Letter published in Douglas Wilson and Rodney Davis, eds., *Herndon's Informant's: Letters, Interviews and Statements about Abraham Lincoln* (Urbana: University of Illinois Press, 1998), 504–505. It is also noted in Don E. Fehrenbacher's *Prelude to Greatness: Lincoln in the 1850s* (Stanford, CA: Stanford University Press, 1962), 91.
17. Basler, *Collected Works*, 2:382–383.
18. As to the question of whether Taney's opinion should be considered as the Court's decision, and therefore law, is best answered by Fehrenbacher: "And yet the Taney opinion is, for all practical purposes, the Dred Scott decision and therefore a historical document of prime importance." Don Fehrenbacher, *The Dred Scott Case: Its Significance in American Law and Politics* (New York: Oxford University Press, 1978), 337.
19. Fehrenbacher, *The Dred Scott Case*, 341.
20. *Ibid.*, 343.
21. Fehrenbacher, *The Dred Scott Case*, 351. The *Chicago Tribune* bristled at the ruling: The Court ruled that a "negro cannot sue in the United States Courts; that he is not a citizen of the United States. Of course this should have been the end of

the case. The Court had no occasion, had no right to go a step further." Paul Finkelman, *Dred Scott v. Sandford: A Brief History with Documents* (New York: Bedford/St. Martin's, 1997), 156.

22. Robert W. Johannsen, *Stephen A. Douglas* (Chicago: University of Illinois Press, 1997), 569.

23. Johannsen, *Stephen A. Douglas*, 570, and Joseph Fort Newton, *Lincoln and Herndon* (Cedar Rapids, IA: The Torch Press, 1910), 117.

24. Fehrenbacher, *The Dred Scott Case*, 524–525.

25. Two justices filed dissenting opinions on the Dred Scott decision: Judge Benjamin R. Curtis and Judge John McLean. The year 1857 would be Curtis's last term on the court; he would resign due to an ongoing dispute with Taney over the Dred Scott decision. Ironically, although Lincoln agreed with Curtis, the justice would not agree with Lincoln. Curtis would oppose the Emancipation Proclamation and the Lincoln administration while serving as a lawyer in Civil War era Washington.

26. For a discussion of Lincoln's views on colonization, see Phillip Shaw Paludan's thorough essay, "Colonization: Policy or Propaganda," in the *Journal of the Abraham Lincoln Association* 25, no. 1 (Winter 2004): 23–37.

27. Basler, *Collected Works*, 2:398–409.

28. Lincoln would also occasionally include President Franklin Pierce in the conspiracy for working with Douglas to pass the Kansas-Nebraska Act.

29. Robert W. Johannsen, *Stephen A. Douglas*, 582–583, 608–610, and Albert Kirwan, *John J. Crittenden: The Struggle for the Union* (Lexington: University of Kentucky Press, 1962), 328–332.

Chapter 2

1. Roy Basler, ed., *The Collected Works of Abraham Lincoln* (New Brunswick, NJ: Rutgers University Press, 1953), 2: 434–436.

2. Lincoln to Ward H. Lamon, June 11, 1858, in Basler, *Collected Works*, 2:458–459.

3. As quoted in William F. Moore and Jane Ann Moore, *Owen Lovejoy: His Brother's Blood; Speeches and Writings, 1838–1864* (Chicago: University of Illinois Press, 2004), 159–160.

4. Herndon and Weik, *Abraham Lincoln: The True Story of a Great Life*, 2: 68.

5. Basler, *Collected Works*, 2:461–469.

6. Lincoln to John L. Scripps, June 23, 1858. Basler, *Collected Works*, 2:471.

7. Dickey to Herndon, December 8, 1866, in Herndon-Weik Papers. Letter published in Douglas Wilson and Rodney Davis, eds., *Herndon's Informant's: Letters, Interviews and Statements about Abraham Lincoln* (Urbana: University of Illinois Press, 1998), 505.

8. Lincoln to John J. Crittenden, July 7, 1858, in Basler, *Collected Works*, 2:483–484.

9. John J. Crittenden to Lincoln, July 29, 1858. Abraham Lincoln papers, Library of Congress, Washington, D.C.

10. *Ibid*.

11. Owen Lovejoy to Abraham Lincoln, August 4, 1858, in Abraham Lincoln Papers, Library of Congress, Washington, D.C.

12. *Chicago Times*, August 12, 1858. Abraham Lincoln Presidential Library, Springfield, Illinois.

Chapter 3

1. Roy Basler, ed., *The Collected Works of Abraham Lincoln* (New Brunswick, NJ: Rutgers University Press, 1953), 2:476–481.

2. Howard A. Allen and Vincent A. Lacey, eds., *Illinois Elections, 1818–1990: Candidates and County Returns for President, Governor, Senate, and House of Representatives* (Carbondale: Southern Illinois University Press, 1992), 142.

3. *Chicago Press and Tribune*, July 10, 1858. Abraham Lincoln Presidential Library, Springfield, Illinois.

4. *Chicago Times*, July 10, 1858, as quoted in Edwin Erle Sparks, *The Lincoln-Douglas Debates of 1858* (Springfield: Illinois State Historical Library, 1908), 33–35.

5. Under the title of "A Ridiculous Falsehood" the *Chicago Press and Tribune*

of July 12, 1858, printed the following: "The Times gravely states that there were over 30,000 persons to hear Douglas on Friday night and only 3,000 to hear Lincoln on Saturday night! There are not 30,000 adult males living in Chicago, and the number that assembled to see the Douglas show certainly did not exceed 15,000[;] 12,000 would be nearer the mark. If there were 30,000 people to see Douglas there were fully 25,000 to hear Lincoln demolish him. We put the number of the latter however at 10,000 to 12,000 auditors." Abraham Lincoln Presidential Library, Springfield, Illinois.

6. Paul M. Angle, ed., *The Complete Lincoln-Douglas Debates of 1858* (Chicago: University of Chicago Press, 1991), 12–22.

7. *Chicago Press and Tribune*, July 12, 1858, as quoted in Sparks, *The Lincoln-Douglas Debates*, 39.

8. Basler, *Collected Works*, 2:484–501. In response to the Chicago speeches, the pro-Republican *Chicago Press and Tribune* wrote on July 12, 1858: "It was conceded yesterday, by nine men out of every ten that Lincoln demolished Douglas; that he 'knocked him higher than a kite.' No candid, intelligent man or woman, who read his two speeches, can help admitting that Lincoln overthrew every position assumed by Douglas; that he completely exposed his sophistries and pulverized his arguments. If a jury should be empanelled today composed of the first twelve intelligent men met on the streets, and if put on their oaths, they would decide unanimously, in ten minutes after hearing both speeches read, that Lincoln had the best of the argument; that he beat Douglas, and beat him badly. If any of the *little* giant's friends doubt this statement, they can be convinced by asking the private and candid opinion of the first score or hundred men of common sense they may meet on the streets." Abraham Lincoln Presidential Library, Springfield, Illinois.

Chapter 4

1. Robert W. Johannsen, *Stephen A. Douglas* (Urbana: University of Illinois Press, 1997), 656.

2. *Chicago Times*, July 22, 1858. The *Chicago Press and Tribune* printed some of the *Times*' description of Douglas's journey, but added the following below the article: "The above telegram was written by the editor of the Chicago *Times*, who accompanies Douglas to write his puffs, and manufacture enthusiasm for him." *Chicago Press and Tribune*, July 19, 1858, in the Abraham Lincoln Presidential Library, Springfield, Illinois.

3. Paul M. Angle, ed., *The Complete Lincoln-Douglas Debates of 1858* (Chicago: University of Chicago Press, 1991), 24–25.

4. Stephen A. Douglas, "The Issues of 1858." This speech was delivered at Bloomington, Illinois, July 16, 1858. Abraham Lincoln Presidential Library, Springfield, Illinois.

5. *Ibid.*, 4.

6. *Ibid.*, 6. Before criticizing the "House Divided" speech, Douglas, as he had at Chicago, took time to compliment Lincoln. He described his opponent as "a kind-hearted, amiable gentleman, a right good fellow, a worthy citizen, of eminent ability as a lawyer," and a person of "sufficient ability to make a good Senator."

7. *Ibid.*, 7. Douglas claimed that Lincoln "never intended to convey the idea that he wished the 'people of the free States to enter into the Southern States, and interfere with slavery.'" The Republicans' "mode of making war," Douglas argued, was "not to enter into those States where slavery exists, and there interfere, and render themselves responsible for the consequences" but to "stand on this side of the Ohio River and shout across. They stand in Bloomington and shake their fists at the people of Lexington; they threaten South Carolina from Chicago. And they call that bravery!"

8. *Ibid.*, 9–12.

9. Returning to the fear of amalgamation and miscegenation, Douglas alleged that Lincoln would allow African Americans to "marry whom they please.... If the Divine law declares that the white man is the equal of the negro woman–that they are on perfect equality," which substantives the "right of the negro woman to

marry the white man. In other words, his doctrine that the negro, by Divine law, is placed on a perfect equality with the white man, and that that equality is recognized by the Declaration of Independence, leads him necessarily to establish negro equality under the law...."

10. *Ibid.*, 15. After substantiating that only "white" men were granted America's freedoms, Douglas also tackled the question concerning the extent to which any rights and privileges should be granted to African Americans. Popular sovereignty was the solution to this predicament: "My answer is that that is a question which each State and each Territory must decide for itself." Illinois had determined, the Senator replied, "that in this State the negro shall not be a slave, but that he shall enjoy no political rights–that negro equality shall not exist. I am content with the positions. My friend Lincoln is not. He thinks that our policy and our laws on that subject are contrary to the Declaration of Independence. He thinks that the Almighty made the negro his equal and his brother."

11. *Ibid.*, 15–16.

12. *Bloomington (IL) Pantagraph*, July 17, 1858, as quoted in Edwin Erle Sparks, *The Lincoln-Douglas Debates of 1858* (Springfield: Illinois State Historical Library, 1908), 51.

Chapter 5

1. Howard A. Allen and Vincent A. Lacey, eds., *Illinois Elections, 1818–1990: Candidates and County Returns for President, Governor, Senate, and House of Representatives* (Carbondale: Southern Illinois University Press, 1992), 142.

2. *Chicago Press and Tribune*, July 19, 1858 and *Chicago Times*, July 22, 1858. Abraham Lincoln Presidential Library, Springfield, Illinois.

3. Paul A. Angle, ed., *The Complete Lincoln-Douglas Debates of 1858* (Chicago: University of Chicago Press, 1991), 44.

4. Douglas's defeat of the Lecompton Constitution had driven the "enemies of the principle of popular sovereignty" from their "effort to force the Lecompton Constitution upon the people of Kansas." The Senator and his supporters had "compelled them to abandon the attempt and to refer that constitution to that people for acceptance or rejection." They had "obtained a concession of the principle" that he had maintained throughout the crisis. Angle, *Complete Debates*, 45.

5. Angle, *Complete Debates*, 60–61. Douglas had mentioned Maine and New York at Bloomington, but provided a more extensive discussion at Springfield.

6. Angle, 62.

7. *Ibid.*, 48–66.

8. *Chicago Press and Tribune*, July 20, 1858. Abraham Lincoln Presidential Library, Springfield, Illinois.

9. Basler, *Collected Works*, 2:505. In the July 20 edition, the same edition in which the *Chicago Press and Tribune* printed Lincoln's speech, it included the following article from the pro-Republican *Lincoln (IL) Herald*: "Great crises demand great men. And there is some wise overruling Power that sends the man for the occasion, and prepares the heart of the people for his reception. In the hour of her peril, England had her Alfred — Scotland her Wallace — Switzerland her Tell — France her Bonaparte — Columbia her Bolivar — America her Washington — and there seems something not not [sic] less over-ruling in the miraculous unanimity with which the people of Illinois have risen in favor of Abraham Lincoln, as the fit man to heal the wounds inflicted on the peace and tranquility of the country by the 'ruthless hand' that repealed the Missouri Compromise." Abraham Lincoln Presidential Library, Springfield, Illinois.

10. Basler, *Collected Works*, 2:505–521.

Chapter 6

1. Douglas traveled in a private railroad car, which provided fodder for Republican criticism. Lincoln rode in the same train, but in a regular passenger car. Albert J. Beveridge, *Abraham Lincoln, 1809–1865*, vol. 2 (Houghton Mifflin Company, 1928), 610.

2. Edwin Erle Sparks, *The Lincoln-Douglas Debates of 1858* (Springfield: Illinois State Historical Library, 1908), 39.

3. *Ibid.*, 56–58.

4. The *Missouri Republican* ran this article on June 24, 1858: "Vote on the Presidency.— The vote among the Republican Delegates to the Illinois State Convention and passengers on the morning train, indicating their preference for the Presidency, stood as follows: William H. Seward —139, John C. Freemont [*sic*]— 32, John McLean —13, Lyman Trumbull — 7, S.P. Chase — 6, W.H. Bissell — 2, Scattering — 26." From Sparks, 24. There is no mention of Lincoln among the Illinoisans.

5. Roy Basler, ed., *The Collected Works of Abraham Lincoln* (New Brunswick, NJ: Rutgers University Press, 1953), 2:522.

6. Johannsen wrote, "Lincoln could only gain from a series of debates, while Douglas had little to gain, and possibly much to lose." From Robert W. Johannsen, *Stephen A. Douglas*, 663, and David Herbert Donald, *Liberty and Union* (Washington, D.C. and Toronto: Heath, 1978), 211. Douglas's reluctance is also discussed in Albert J. Beveridge, *Abraham Lincoln, 1809–1865*, vol. 2 (Houghton Mifflin Company, 1928), 629.

7. Basler, *Collected Works*, 2:528.

8. *Ibid.*, 528–530. Lincoln was incensed by one comment that Douglas had made: "For you to say that we have already spoken at Chicago and Springfield, and that on both occasions I had the concluding speech, is hardly a fair statement. The truth is rather this. At Chicago, July 9th, you made a carefully prepared conclusion on my speech of June 16th.; twentyfour [*sic*] hours after I made a hasty conclusion on yours of the 9th.; you had six days to prepare, and concluded on me again at Bloomington on the 16th.; twentyfour [*sic*] hours after I concluded on you again at Springfield. In the meantime you had made another conclusion on me at Springfield, which I did not hear, and of the contents of which I knew nothing when I spoke; so that your speech made in day-light, and mine at night of the 17th at Springfield were both made in perfect independence of each other. The dates of making all these speeches, will show, I think, that in the matter of time and preparation, the advantage has all been on your side; and that none of the external circumstances have stood in my advantage."

9. *Ibid.*, 531–532.

10. *Ibid.*, 531. Lincoln to Stephen A. Douglas, July 31, 1858.

Chapter 7

1. William Herndon and Jesse W. Weik, *Abraham Lincoln: The True Story of a Great Life* (New York: D. Appleton, 1896), 2:10–11.

2. *Ibid.*, 11.

3. Robert W. Johannsen, *Stephen A. Douglas* (Urbana: University of Illinois Press, 1973), 429.

4. For Douglas, the debates of 1858 were just another battle, a continuation of a war that he had waged since 1844 when he had first introduced a bill for the organization of the Nebraska Territory.

5. Johannsen, *Stephen A. Douglas*, 399–400.

6. Roy Basler, ed., *The Collected Works of Abraham Lincoln* (New Brunswick, NJ: Rutgers University Press, 1953), 2:546–547.

7. *Ibid.*, 545.

8. After the campaign, when considering the publication of the debates, Lincoln noted that Douglas "would have the right to correct typographical errors in his" but Lincoln did not believe that the Senator would have as great a need for correction because Douglas "had two hired reporters traveling with him, and probably revised their manuscripts before they went to press." Lincoln, on the other hand, had not been so fortunate. He "had no reporter" of his own "but depended on a very excellent one sent by the Press & Tribune; but who never waited to show me his notes and manuscripts; so that the first I saw of my speeches, after delivering them, was in the Press & Tribune precisely as they now stand." The reporter to which Lincoln referred was Robert H. Hitt, who recorded Lincoln's speeches at the debates.

9. *Chicago Press and Tribune*, August 18, 1858, as quoted in Edwin Erle Sparks, *The Lincoln-Douglas Debates of 1858* (Springfield: Illinois State Historical Library, 1908), 85.

10. *Ibid.*, 85–86.

11. Herndon and Weik, *Abraham Lincoln*, 2:104–105.

12. For a complete discussion of this methodology and its antithesis, see "The Lincoln-Douglas Debates" in Douglas W. Wilson's *Lincoln before Washington: New Perspectives on the Illinois Years* (Chicago: University of Illinois Press, 1997), 151–165.

13. For a detailed essay on the differences in the political ideologies of Lincoln and Douglas, see chapter 14, "The Universal Meaning of the Declaration of Independence," in Harry V. Jaffa's *The Crisis of the House Divided: An Interpretation of the Issues of the Lincoln-Douglas Debates* (Chicago: University of Chicago Press, 1982), 308–329.

14. Howard W. Allen and Vincent A. Lacey, eds., *Illinois Elections, 1818–1990: Candidates and County Returns for President, Governor, Senate and House of Representatives* (Carbondale: Southern Illinois University Press, 1992).

15. *Chicago Times*, August 26, 1858. Abraham Lincoln Presidential Library, Springfield, Illinois.

16. *Chicago Press and Tribune*, August 23, 1858, as quoted in Sparks, *The Lincoln-Douglas Debates*, 86.

17. *Ibid.*, 141.

18. Basler, *Collected Works*, 3:5–9. At Ottawa, Douglas opened, Lincoln followed, and Douglas closed the debate.

19. The *Tribune's* August 23, 1858, headline reflected the same partisanship as its competitor: "GREAT DEBATE BETWEEN LINCOLN AND DOUGLAS AT OTTAWA" and "Twelve Thousand Persons Present.—The Dred Scott Champion Pulverized.—Verbatim Report of Douglas' Speech.—Lincoln's Reply and Douglas' Rejoinder." Sparks, *The Lincoln-Douglas Debates*,133.

20. Basler, *Collected Works*, 3:16–37.

21. *Ibid.*, 37. Lincoln to Joseph O. Cunningham, August 22, 1858.

Chapter 8

1. Lincoln to Ebenezer Peck, a Chicago Republican, August 23, 1858, as quoted in Don Fehrenbacher, *Prelude to Greatness: Lincoln in the 1850s* (Stanford, CA: Stanford University Press, 1962), 125.

2. "Dug" was Medill's short name for Douglas.

3. Catiline, to which Medill compares Douglas, was a Roman politician who, after failing to obtain a governing position by lawful means, concocted a conspiracy to seize it by unlawful means.

4. Joseph Medill to Abraham Lincoln, August 27, 1858. Abraham Lincoln Papers at the Library of Congress, Washington, D.C.

5. *St. Louis Missouri Republican*, August 31, 1858, as quoted in Edwin Erle Sparks, *The Lincoln-Douglas Debates of 1858* (Springfield: Illinois State Historical Library, 1908), 193–194. Gunter in this context means "according to plan."

6. William H. Herndon and Jesse W. Weik, *Abraham Lincoln: The True Story of a Great Life* (New York: D. Appleton, 1896), 2:110.

7. *Chicago Times*, September 2, 1858. Abraham Lincoln Presidential Library, Springfield, Illinois.

8. *New York Evening Post*, September 2, 1858, as quoted in Sparks, 192.

9. Howard W. Allen and Vincent A. Lacey, eds., *Illinois Elections, 1818–1990: Candidates and County Returns for President, Governor, Senate, and House of Representatives* (Carbondale: Southern Illinois University Press, 1992), 139.

10. Roy Basler, ed., *The Collected Works of Abraham Lincoln* (New Brunswick, NJ: Rutgers University Press, 1953), 3:43–72. At Freeport, Lincoln opened, Douglas followed, and Lincoln closed the debate.

11. Don Fehrenbacher, *Prelude to Greatness: Lincoln in the 1850s* (Stanford, CA: Stanford University Press, 1962), 121–142, has an excellent discussion of the Freeport questions. See also Basler, *Collected Works*, 3:128, 132, 230.

12. Joseph Medill to Abraham Lincoln, August 27, 1858. Abraham Lincoln Papers at the Library of Congress.

Chapter 9

1. Howard A. Allen and Vincent A. Lacey, eds., *Illinois Elections, 1818–1990: Candidates and County Returns for President, Governor, Senate, and House of Representatives* (Carbondale: Southern Illinois University Press, 1992), 140–141.
2. Don Fehrenbacher, *Prelude to Greatness: Lincoln in the 1850s* (Stanford, CA: Stanford University Press, 1962), 6.
3. William H. Herndon and Jesse W. Weik, *Abraham Lincoln: The True Story of a Great Life* (New York: D. Appleton, 1896), 2:111–112.
4. Roy Basler, ed., *The Collected Works of Abraham Lincoln* (New Brunswick, NJ: Rutgers University Press, 1953), 3:80–81.
5. As quoted in Willard L. King, *David Davis: Lincoln's Manager* (Cambridge, MA: Harvard University Press, 1960), 123.
6. Edward Madgol, *Owen Lovejoy: Abolitionist in Congress* (New Brunswick, NJ: Rutgers University Press, 1967), 216.
7. Herndon and Weik, *Abraham Lincoln*, 2:112–113. Lovejoy was always a favorite target of the *Times*. The following was published in the August 5 issue: "The *Bloomington Pantagraph*, a Republican paper, describing a meeting at that place, says: 'One of the audience then called for "Three cheers for the Hon. Owen Lovejoy." They also were given at once.' We are glad to hear that Mr. Lovejoy had three friends trained well enough to cheer together." Abraham Lincoln Presidential Library, Springfield, Illinois.
8. Basler, *Collected Works*, 3:92.
9. *Ibid.*, 95.
10. Herndon and Weik, *Abraham Lincoln*, 2:118.
11. John Y. Simon, "Union County in 1858 and the Lincoln-Douglas Debate," *Journal of the Illinois State Historical Society* 62 (Autumn 1969), 272.
12. Herndon and Weik, *Abraham Lincoln*, 2:119.
13. Edwin Erle Sparks, *The Lincoln-Douglas Debates of 1858* (Springfield: Illinois State Historical Library, 1908), 264–265.
14. Robert W. Johannsen, *Stephen A. Douglas* (Urbana: University of Illinois Press, 1973), 659.
15. Sparks, 261, 262, 265.
16. Basler, *Collected Works*, 3:116–140. At Jonesboro, Douglas opened, Lincoln followed, and Douglas closed the debate.
17. Lincoln covered other issues as well. He defended Trumbull and described Douglas's charges in relation to a deal between Lincoln and Trumbull as having not a "word of truth." Lincoln also argued against the Dred Scott decision, claiming that Douglas's assertion was false, that if Congress could not outlaw slavery then the territorial governments could not prohibit slavery, either, based on the opinion of the Taney court. Lincoln took a page from Douglas's strategy and dug up some old resolutions from previous Democratic conventions and Democrats to highlight discrepancies among the Democrats and Douglas.
18. One day before the Charleston debate, after only sixteen months of freedom, Dred Scott, the man whose case Lincoln and Douglas debated more than any other issue, passed away.

Chapter 10

1. Herndon to Theodore Parker, August 31, 1858, as quoted in Joseph Fort Newton, *Lincoln and Herndon* (Cedar Rapids, IA: The Torch Press, 1910), 203.
2. Howard W. Allen and Vincent A. Lacey, eds., *Illinois Elections, 1818–1990: Candidates and County Returns for President, Governor, Senate, and House of Representatives* (Carbondale: Southern Illinois University Press, 1992), 140.
3. Donald astutely notes that, when considering the southern proclivities of the audience, Lincoln's statements were "politically expedient" but he further admits that Charleston was the "lowest point in his campaign." Donald, *Lincoln*, 220–221.
4. Roy Basler, ed., *The Collected Works of Abraham Lincoln* (New Brunswick, NJ: Rutgers University Press, 1953), 3:144.
5. William H. Herndon and Jesse W. Weik, *Abraham Lincoln: The True Story of*

a Great Life (New York: D. Appleton, 1896), 2:121.

6. *Chicago Journal*, September 20, 1858, as quoted in Edwin Erle Sparks, *The Lincoln-Douglas Debates of 1858* (Springfield: Illinois State Historical Library, 1908), 322–325.

7. *Chicago Press and Tribune*, September 21, 1858, as quoted in Sparks, 313–314.

8. Sparks, 312, 323.

9. *Chicago Journal*, September 20, 1858, as quoted in Sparks, 324.

10. *Chicago Journal*, September 21, 1858, as quoted in Sparks, 327.

11. *Chicago Times*, September 23, 1858. Abraham Lincoln Presidential Library, Springfield, Illinois.

12. *New York Evening Post*, September 21, 1858, as quoted in Sparks, 319.

13. Basler, *Collected Works*, 3:168–178. At Charleston, Lincoln opened, Douglas followed, and Lincoln closed the debate.

14. Davis to Lincoln, September 25, 1858, in Robert Todd Lincoln Papers, Library of Congress, Washington, D.C.

Chapter 11

1. Roy Basler, ed., *The Collected Works of Abraham Lincoln* (New Brunswick, NJ: Rutgers University Press, 1953), 3:205.

2. Ibid., 201.

3. Ibid., 202.

4. Robert W. Johannsen, *Stephen A. Douglas*, 66. The person with whom Douglas scuffled was John Todd Stuart, Lincoln's first law partner. For several reasons, including the wrestling incident with Armstrong, Lincoln was inducted into the National Wrestling Hall of Fame in 1992.

5. Angle, 276–281, and Edwin Erle Sparks, *The Lincoln-Douglas Debates of 1858* (Springfield: Illinois State Historical Library, 1908), 557–563.

6. William H. Herndon and Jesse W. Weik, *Abraham Lincoln: The True Story of a Great Life* (New York: D. Appleton, 1896), 2:123.

7. *Chicago Times*, October 9, 1858, as quoted in Sparks, 381.

8. *Chicago Press and Tribune*, October 5, 1858, as quoted in Sparks, 330–331.

9. Howard W. Allen and Vincent A. Lacey, eds., *Illinois Elections, 1818–1990: Candidates and County Returns for President, Governor, Senate, and House of Representatives* (Carbondale: Southern Illinois University Press, 1992), 139–140.

10. Some emphasized the crucial issue of the debates in unique ways. Before the debate Lincoln was presented with an American shield inscribed on one side with the words "Presented to the Hon. A. Lincoln by the Republican Ladies of Galesburg, Oct. 7th, 1858," and on the other side the Declaration of Independence on a scroll. Herman Mitgang, ed., *Abraham Lincoln: A Press Portrait* (Athens: University of Georgia Press), 124.

11. Basler, *Collected Works*, 3:220–221.

12. The October 9, 1858, headline for the pro-Democratic *Chicago Times*, in using "Democracy," the common term of the time for the Democratic party, read: "Immense Concourse of People Present.—Upwards of 20,000 on the Ground.—Great Revolution in Popular Sentiment in Knox County.—Black Republicanism Beaten in Its Stronghold and Outnumbered by the Democracy.—Splendid Reception of Senator Douglas.—Interesting Debate.—Lincoln Again Defeated before the People," as quoted in Sparks, 380.

13. Basler, *Collected Works*, 3: 237.

14. Ibid., 3:213–238. Of the other issues, Douglas allotted a considerable amount of time to discussing his defense of the Lecompton Constitution, stating once again that his opposition to it had resulted from the undemocratic manner in which it had been forced on the Kansans, not because the constitution favored slavery. He also expressed his opposition to the English Bill, due to its inequities in requiring Kansas to have only 35,000 people to be admitted as a slave state, but three times that population if Kansas desired to enter the Union a free state.

Douglas also repeated his charge that Lincoln should be evaluated on the basis of other Republican conventions, an obvious attempt to tie Lincoln to the more abolitionist elements of the Republican Party.

15. *Chicago Times*, October 13, 1858, as quoted in Sparks, 386–387.

Chapter 12

1. Edwin Erle Sparks, *The Lincoln-Douglas Debates of 1858* (Springfield: Illinois State Historical Library, 1908), 390–396, 435–439.
2. Carl Schurz, as recorded in *McClure's Magazine*, January 1907, and quoted in Sparks, 447–448.
3. At Quincy, Lincoln opened, Douglas followed, and Lincoln closed the debate.
4. Roy Basler, ed., *The Collected Works of Abraham Lincoln* (New Brunswick, NJ: Rutgers University Press, 1953), 3:262–275.
5. The headline for the *Tribune* on October 15, 1858, read: "Twelve Thousand Persons Present!—Great Triumph of the Republicans of the Fifth District.—Lincoln 'Concludes' on the 'Artful Dodger' with a Vengeance.—Verbatim Report of Speeches," as quoted in Sparks, 435.
6. Basler, *Collected Works*, 3:247–257. The continuing accusations between the Democratic and Republican papers was highlighted once again during the campaign in the October 13 edition of the pro–Republican *Galesburg Democrat*: "Douglas has put out a lying document composed of extracts from the speeches of Lincoln & Douglas at the joint debates. The extracts from Lincoln's speeches are all emasculated and perverted just as his speech here was. They have been secretly scattered by the thousands ... and they are probably distributed throughout the State, excepting such places as Chicago, where the fraud would recoil upon their heads too quickly. What language can portray the depravity of the man who will resort to means so base for the accomplishment of his end?"—as quoted in Sparks, 591.

Chapter 13

1. The steamboat on which Lincoln and Douglas traveled was named the *City of Louisiana*, most likely after the city of Louisiana, Missouri. It was a side-wheel, wood hull packet built in St. Louis, Missouri, in 1857. It operated between Keokuk, Iowa, and St. Louis. Like one of her notable passengers in 1858, she served the United States government during the Civil War. In 1862 the U.S. chartered the steamboat and, after her modification, transformed her into a hospital ship serving the United States Sanitary Commission. The *City of Louisiana* was present at the battles of Pittsburg Landing and Island No. 10, and transported 3,389 wounded to Northern hospitals after the Battle of Shiloh. From Frederick Way, Jr., *Way's Packet Directory, 1848–1894: Passenger Steamboats of the Mississippi River System since the Advent of Photography in Mid-Continent America* (Athens: Ohio University Press, 1994), 93.
2. Roy Basler, ed., *The Collected Works of Abraham Lincoln* (New Brunswick, NJ: Rutgers University Press, 1953), 2:320.
3. Howard W. Allen and Vincent A. Lacey, eds., *Illinois Elections, 1818–1990: Candidates and County Returns for President, Governor, Senate, and House of Representatives* (Carbondale: Southern Illinois University Press, 1992), 139–141.
4. *Chicago Press and Tribune*, October 18, 1858.
5. Basler, *Collected Works*, 3:284. The *Chicago Times* headline for Alton read: "Douglas and Lincoln at Alton.—5,000 to 10,000 Persons Present!—Lincoln Again Refuses to Answer Whether He Will Vote to Admit Kansas if Her People Apply with a Constitution Recognizing Slavery.—Appears in His Old Character of the 'Artful Dodger.'—Tries to Palm Himself off to the Whigs of Madison County as a Friend of Henry Clay and No Abolitionist, and Is Exposed.—Great Speeches of Senator Douglas.—People of Illinois, Read and Be Convinced." *Chicago Times*, October 17, 1858, as quoted in Edwin Erle Sparks, *The Lincoln-Douglas Debates of 1858* (Springfield: Illinois State Historical Library, 1908), 497.
6. Basler, *Collected Works*, 3:284. At Alton, Douglas opened, Lincoln followed, and Douglas closed the debate.
7. *Ibid.*, 289, 322.
8. Codding, like Lovejoy, was a minister and considered radically antislavery.
9. Basler, *Collected Works*, 3:284–325.

The pro-Republican *Chicago Press and Tribune*, in attempting to find some way to criticize Douglas for his consistency, wrote on October 18, 1858: "The fact that Douglas has only one speech — and that one committed to memory for rehearsal everywhere — hardly needed the evidence given in his mumblings at Alton." Abraham Lincoln Presidential Library, Springfield, Illinois.

10. Basler, *Collected Works*, 300. The *Chicago Press and Tribune* October 18, 1858, headline was: "Douglas's Seventh Rehearsal of 'That Speech.' — Admirable Summing Up of the Issues of the Campaign by Mr. Lincoln. — Verbatim Report of Mr. Douglas's Speech, Mr. Lincoln's Reply and Mr. Douglas's Rejoinder," as quoted in Sparks, 508. The last debate was the first time that Mary Todd Lincoln attended a debate. Accompanying her was the Lincolns' eldest son, Robert Todd.

11. Basler, *Collected Works*, 3:305–316. Lincoln also briefly discussed some other issues. He repeated that his opposition to the Dred Scott decision was based on its intention to make slavery national, not because it denied citizenship to the "negro." He claimed that Clay believed the "negro" was included in the Declaration of Independence and he argued that within the Constitution there was evidence of the founding fathers' opposition to slavery and their desire to place it on course for "ultimate extinction."

12. *Ibid.*, 301.

13. On October 18, just three days after the Alton debate, Lincoln wrote to Judd: "I now have a high degree of confidence that we shall succeed...." Basler, *Collected Works*, 3:329.

14. *Chicago Times*, October 26, 1858. Abraham Lincoln Presidential Library, Springfield, Illinois.

15. Several of Lincoln's supporters were so concerned about Crittenden's letter that they sent an emissary to find Crittenden for the purpose of receiving a statement from him that might counter the one Dickey had received. The emissary was unable to locate Crittenden. Saul Sigelschiffer, *The American Conscience: The Drama of the Lincoln-Douglas Debates* (New York: Horizon Press, 1973), 378.

16. Basler, *Collected Works*, 3:334. In the last weeks of the campaign, not even White could avoid becoming a political target. The *Chicago Times*, on October 28, under the title of "Who 'Dressed up' Lincoln's Speeches for the *Press and Tribune?*" wrote: "*To the editors of the Chicago Daily Times*: I see that a correspondent in the *Press and Tribune* of yesterday suggests that if it be true that an editor of that paper has dressed up and improved Lincoln's speeches, he should be nominated, and run, as the next Republican candidate for the United States Senate in the event of Mr. Lincoln's defeat. The gentleman connected with the *Press and Tribune* who corrected, dressed up, and put into remarkable shape Mr. Lincoln's speeches, is Mr. Horace White. Mr. Lincoln tried to revise the speech he made at Chicago on the night of the 10th of July, but could not make it read grammatically and sensibly, as all who read the published report of that speech in the *Press and Tribune* well know. He then admitted his inability to either speak or write correct English, and it was at his special request that Mr. White revised all his speeches made at the joint debates and published in the *Press and Tribune*. The correctness of this statement cannot be denied with truth."

In regards to the issue of the accuracy of the debates, White, writing decades later, took an objective perspective: "The volume containing the debates, published in 1860 by Follett, Foster & Co., of Columbus, Ohio, presents Mr. Lincoln's speeches as they appeared in the *Chicago Tribune*, and Mr. Douglas's as they appeared in the *Chicago Times*. Of course, the speeches of both were published simultaneously in both papers. The *Chicago Times*' reports of Mr. Lincoln's speeches were not at all satisfactory to Mr. Lincoln's friends, and this led to a charge that they were purposely mutilated in order to give his competitor a more scholarly appearance before the public–a charge indignantly denied by Sheridan and Binmore [the correspondents for the *Chicago Times*]." There was really no foundation for this charge. Of course Sheridan and Binmore took more pains with Mr. Douglas's speeches than with those of his opponent. That was their business. It was what they were paid for, and what they were expected to do. The debates were all held in the open air, on rude platforms hastily put together, shaky, and overcrowded with people. The reporters' tables were liable to be jostled and their manuscript agitated by the wind. Some gaps were certain to occur in the reporters' notes and these, when occurring in Mr. Douglas's speeches, would certainly be straightened out by his own reporters, who would feel no such responsibility for the rough places in Mr. Lincoln's. Then it must be added that there were fewer involved sentences in Mr. Douglas's *extempore* speeches than in Mr. Lincoln's. Douglas was the more practiced and more polished speaker of the two, and it was easier for a reporter to follow him. All his sentences were round and perfect in his mind before he opened his lips. This was not always the case with Mr. Lincoln.

17. For a detailed discussion of the Republicans' excuses, see Richard Allen Heckman, *Lincoln vs. Douglas: The Great Debates Campaign* (Washington, D.C.: Public Affairs Press, 1967), 137–140.

18. Basler, *Collected Works*, 3:335.

19. Davis to Lincoln, November 7, 1858, in Robert Todd Lincoln Papers, Library of Congress, as quoted in Willard L. King's *David Davis*, 126.

20. William H. Herndon to Theodore Parker, November 8, 1858, as quoted in Joseph Fort Newton's *Lincoln's Herndon* (Cedar Rapids, IA: The Torch Press, 1910), 234–235.

21. *Chicago Democrat*, November 9, 1858, as quoted in Heckman, 63.

22. Basler, *Collected Works*, 3:337. The *Chicago Times* had published the following in its October 7 issue: "It is very amusing to hear Judd calling upon Republicans to support 'honest Abe,' 'old Abe,' 'our Abe,' when everybody knows that when Lincoln, in 1855, was the regular caucus nominee of the Republicans, he, Judd, (or as he wishes to be called, Governor Judd) refused to vote for him, and actually defeated Lincoln. If Abe 'was the best man in the State for Senator,' why did Mr. Judd, aided by Peck, who was a lobby member, defeat Lincoln in 1855?" Abraham Lincoln Presidential Library, Springfield, Illinois.

23. William H. Herndon and Jesse W. Weik, *Abraham Lincoln: The True Story of a Great Life* (New York: D. Appleton, 1896), 2:127.

24. Lincoln to Anson G. Henry, November 19, 1858, in Basler, *Collected Works*, 3:339.

Bibliography

Books

Allen, Howard W., and Lacey, Vincent A., eds. *Illinois Elections, 1818–1990: Candidates and County Returns for President, Governor, Senate, and House of Representatives*. Carbondale: Southern Illinois University Press, 1992.
Angle, Paul M., ed. *The Complete Lincoln-Douglas Debates of 1858*. Chicago: University of Chicago Press, 1991.
_____. *Here I Have Lived: A History of Lincoln's Springfield, 1821–1865*. Springfield, IL: Abraham Lincoln Association, 1935.
Baringer, William E. *Lincoln's Rise to Power*. Boston: Little, Brown, 1937.
Basler, Roy. *Abraham Lincoln: His Speeches and Writings*. New York: Da Capo Press, 1949.
_____, ed. *The Collected Works of Abraham Lincoln*, New Brunswick, NJ: Rutgers University Press, 1953.
Beveridge, Albert. *Abraham Lincoln, 1809–1858*. Vols. 1 and 2. New York: Houghton Mifflin, 1928.
Boritt, Gabor. *Lincoln and the Economics of the American Dream*. Champaign: University of Illinois Press, 1994.
Brown, William Garrott. *Stephen A. Douglas*. Boston: Houghton, Mifflin, 1902.
Carr, Clark Ezra. *Stephen A. Douglas: His Life, Public Services, Speeches and Patriotism*. Chicago: A.C. McClurg, 1909.
Coleman, Charles Hubert. *The Lincoln-Douglas Debate at Charleston, Illinois, September 18, 1858*. Charleston: Eastern Illinois University, 1957.
Crocker, Lionel. *Analysis of Lincoln and Douglas as Public Speakers*. Springfield, IL: Thomas, 1968.
Current, Richard N. *The Lincoln Nobody Knows*. New York: Hill and Wang, 1958.
Dennis, Frank L. *The Lincoln-Douglas Debates*. New York: Mason Lipscomb, 1974.
Donald, David Herbert. *Liberty and Union*. Washington, D.C. and Toronto: Heath, 1978.
_____. *Lincoln*. New York: Simon and Schuster, 1995.
_____. *Lincoln Reconsidered*. New York: Vintage, 1947.
_____. *"We Are Lincoln Men": Abraham Lincoln and His Friends*. New York: Simon and Schuster, 2003.
Fehrenbacher, Don. *The Dred Scott Case: Its Significance in American Law and Politics*. New York: Oxford University Press, 1978.
_____. *Prelude to Greatness: Lincoln in the 1850s*. Stanford, CA: Stanford University Press, 1962.

Bibliography

Fehrenbacher, Don, and Virginia Fehrenbacher, eds. *Recollected Words of Abraham Lincoln*. Stanford, CA: Stanford University Press, 1996.
Finkelman, Paul. *Dred Scott v. Sanford: A Brief History with Documents*. New York: Bedford/St. Martin's, 1997.
Foner, Eric. *Free Soil, Free Labor, Free Men: The Ideology of the Republican Party before the Civil War*. Oxford: Oxford University Press, 1970.
Franklin, John Hope. *From Slavery to Freedom*. New York: Alfred A. Knopf, 1965.
Freehling, William W. *The Road to Disunion: Secessionists at Bay, 1776–1854*. New York: Oxford University Press, 1990.
Gardner, William. *Life of Stephen A. Douglas*. Boston: Roxburgh, 1905.
Genovese, Eugene D. *Roll, Jordan, Roll: The World the Slaves Made*. New York: Vintage, 1976.
Guelzo, Allen C. *Abraham Lincoln: Redeemer President*. Grand Rapids, MI: Wm. B. Eerdmans, 1999.
Harper, Robert S. *Lincoln and the Press*. New York: McGraw-Hill, 1951.
Heckman, Richard Allen. *Lincoln vs. Douglas: The Great Debates Campaign*. Washington, D.C.: Public Affairs Press, 1967.
Herndon, William H., and Jesse W. Weik. *Abraham Lincoln: The True Story of a Great Life*. Vols. 1 and 2. New York: D. Appleton, 1896.
Holzer, Harold, ed. *The Lincoln-Douglas Debates: The First Complete, Unexpurgated Text*. New York: HarperCollins, 1993.
Jaffa, Harry V. *Crisis of the House Divided*. Chicago: University of Chicago Press, 1959.
Johannsen, Robert W. *The Frontier, the Union, and Stephen A. Douglas*. Urbana: University of Illinois Press, 1989.
_____. *The Lincoln-Douglas Debates of 1858*. New York: Oxford University Press, 1965.
_____. *Stephen A. Douglas*. Urbana: University of Illinois Press, 1973.
King, Willard L. *Lincoln's Manager: David Davis*. Cambridge, MA: Harvard University Press, 1960.
Kirwan, Albert D. *John J. Crittenden: The Struggle for the Union*. Lexington: University of Kentucky Press, 1962.
Kolchin, Peter. *American Slavery: 1619–1877*. New York: Hill and Wang, 1993.
Logsdon, Joseph. *Horace White, Nineteenth Century Liberal*. Westport, CT: Greenwood, 1971.
Magdol, Edward. *Owen Lovejoy: Abolitionist in Congress*. New Brunswick, NJ: Rutgers University Press, 1967.
McPherson, James M. *Abraham Lincoln and the Second American Revolution*. New York: Oxford University Press, 1991.
_____. *Battle Cry of Freedom: The Civil War Era*. New York: Oxford University Press, 1988.
_____. *The Negro's Civil War: How American Negroes Felt and Acted during the War for Union*. New York: Vintage, 1967.
Miers, Earl Schenck. *Lincoln Day by Day: A Chronology, 1809–1865*. Dayton, OH: Morningside, 1991.
Miller, William Lee. *Arguing About Slavery: The Great Battle in the United States Congress*. New York: Alfred A. Knopf, 1996.
Mitgang, Herbert, ed. *Abraham Lincoln: A Press Portrait*. Athens: University of Georgia Press, 1956.
Moore, William F., and Jane Ann Moore. *Owen Lovejoy: His Brother's Blood; Speeches and Writings, 1838–1864*. Chicago: University of Illinois Press, 2004.

Bibliography

Morgan, Edmund S. *American Slavery, American Freedom: The Ordeal of Colonial Virginia*. New York: W.W. Norton, 1975.
Neely, Mark E., Jr. *The Abraham Lincoln Encyclopedia*. New York: Da Capo, 1982.
Newton, Joseph Fort. *Lincoln and Herndon*. Cedar Rapids, IA: The Torch Press, 1910.
Nicolay, Helen. *Lincoln's Secretary: A Biography of John G. Nicolay*. New York: Longmans, Green, 1949.
Nicolay, John G., and John Hay, eds. *Complete Works of Abraham Lincoln*. Vols. 1–12. Harrogate, TN: Lincoln Memorial University, 1894.
Oakes, James. *Slavery and Freedom: An Interpretation of the Old South*. New York: Vintage, 1990.
Oates, Stephen. *With Malice Toward None: The Life of Abraham Lincoln*. New York: New American Library, 1977.
Pease, Theodore Calvin, and James G. Randall. *The Diary of Orville Hickman Browning*. Vol. 1, *1850–1864*. Springfield: Illinois State Historical Library, 1925.
Potter, David M. *The Impending Crisis: 1848–1861*. New York: Harper and Row, 1976.
Quarles, Benjamin. *Lincoln and the Negro*. New York: Oxford University Press, 1962.
Randall, J. G. *Lincoln: The Liberal Statesman*. New York: Dodd, Mead, 1947.
Ransom, Roger L. *Conflict and Compromise: The Political Economy of Slavery, Emancipation, and the American Civil War*. Cambridge: Cambridge University Press, 1990.
Roske, Ralph. J. *His Own Counsel: The Life and Times of Lyman Trumbull*. Reno: University of Nevada Press, 1979.
Shaw, Albert. *Abraham Lincoln: His Path to the Presidency*. The Review of Reviews Corporation, 1930.
Sigelschiffer, Saul. *The American Conscience: The Drama of the Lincoln-Douglas Debates*. New York: Horizon Press, 1973.
Shaw, Archer H. *The Lincoln Encyclopedia: The Spoken and Written Words of A. Lincoln*. New York: Macmillan, 1950.
Sparks, Edwin Erle. *The Lincoln-Douglas Debates of 1858*. Springfield: Illinois State Historical Library, 1908.
Stamp, Kenneth M. *The Peculiar Institution: Slavery in the Ante-Bellum South*. New York: Alfred A. Knopf, 1956.
Thomas, Benjamin. *Abraham Lincoln: A Biography*. New York: Alfred A. Knopf, 1952.
_____. *Portrait for Posterity: Lincoln and His Biographers*. New Brunswick: Rutgers University Press, 1947.
Turner, Justin G., and Linda Levitt Turner. *Mary Todd Lincoln: Her Life and Letters*. New York: Fromm International, 1987.
Wallace, Isabel. *Life and Letters of General W.H.L. Wallace*. Carbondale: Southern Illinois University Press, 2000.
Way, Frederick, Jr. *Way's Packet Directory, 1848–1894: Passenger Steamboats of the Mississippi River System since the Advent of Photography in Mid-Continent America*. Athens: Ohio University Press, 1994.
Wills, Gary. *Lincoln at Gettysburg: The Words That Remade America*. New York: Simon and Schuster, 1992.
Wilson, Douglas L. *Lincoln before Washington: New Perspectives on the Illinois Years*. Champaign: University of Illinois Press, 1997.
Wilson, Douglas L., and Rodney O. Davis. *Herndon's Informants: Letters, Interviews and Statements about Abraham Lincoln*. Urbana: University of Illinois Press, 1998.
Zarefsky, David. *Lincoln, Douglas and Slavery*. Chicago: University of Chicago Press, 1990.

Bibliography

Articles

Anderson, James W. "'The Real Issue': An Analysis of the Final Lincoln-Douglas Debate." *Lincoln Herald* 69 (Spring 1967): 27–39.

Auchampaugh, Philip G. "The Buchanan-Douglas Feud." *Journal of the Illinois State Historical Society* 25 (April-July 1932): 5–48.

Basler, Roy P. "Abraham Lincoln's Rhetoric." *American Literature* 11 (May 1939): 167–182.

Bauer, Marvin G. "Persuasive Methods in the Lincoln-Douglas Debates." *Quarterly Journal of Speech* 14 (February 1927): 29–39.

Beveridge, John W. "Lincoln's Views on Slavery and Blacks as Expressed in the Debates with Stephen A. Douglas." *Lincoln Herald* 83 (Winter 1981): 791–800.

Chu, James C.Y. "Horace White: His Association with Abraham Lincoln, 1854–1860." *Journalism Quarterly* 49 (Spring 1972): 51–60.

Clinton, Anita. "Stephen Arnold Douglas: His Mississippi Experience." *Journal of Mississippi History* 50 (June 1988): 56–88.

Collins, Bruce W. "The Lincoln-Douglas Contest of 1858 and Illinois Electorate." *Journal of American Studies* 20 (1986): 391–420.

Davis, Granville D. "Douglas and the Chicago Mob." *American Historical Review* 54 (April 1949): 553–56.

Fehrenbacher, Don E. "The Historical Significance of the Lincoln-Douglas Debates." *Wisconsin Magazine of History* 42 (Spring 1959): 193–199.

_____. "Lincoln, Douglas, and the 'Freeport Question.'" *American Historical Review* 66 (April 1961): 599–617.

Heckman, Richard Allen. "The Lincoln-Douglas Debates: A Case Study in 'Stump Speaking.'" *Civil War History* 12 (March 1966): 54–66.

Horner, Harlan Hoyt. "The Substance of the Lincoln-Douglas Debates: Part 1." *Lincoln Herald* 63 (Summer 1961): 89–98.

_____. "The Substance of the Lincoln-Douglas Debates: Part 2." *Lincoln Herald* 63 (Fall 1961): 139–149.

Jaffa, Harry V. "Value Consensus in Democracy: The Issue in the Lincoln-Douglas Debates." *American Political Science Review* 52 (September 1958): 745–753.

Johannsen, Robert W. "The Lincoln-Douglas Campaign of 1858: Background and Perspective." *Journal of the Illinois State Historical Society* 73 (Winter 1980): 242–262.

King, Willard L., and Allan Nevins. "The Constitution and Declaration of Independence as Issues in the Lincoln-Douglas Debates." *Journal of the Illinois State Historical Society* 52 (Spring 1959): 7–32.

Krug, Mark M. "Lyman Trumbull and the Real Issues in the Lincoln-Douglas Debates." *Journal of the Illinois State Historical Society* 57 (Winter 1964): 380–396.

Paludan, Phillip Shaw. "Colonization: Policy or Propaganda." *Journal of the Abraham Lincoln Association* 5 (Winter 2004): 36 pars.

Peck, Graham A. "Was Stephen A. Douglas Antislavery?" *Journal of the Abraham Lincoln Association* 26 (September 2005): 31 pars.

Simon, John Y. "Union County in 1858 and the Lincoln-Douglas Debate." *Journal of the Illinois State Historical Society* 62 (Autumn 1969): 267–292.

Stevenson, James A. "Lincoln vs. Douglas Over the Republican Ideal." *American Studies* 35 (Spring 1994): 63–89.

Zarefsky, David. "The Lincoln-Douglas Debates Revisited: The Evolution of Public Argument." *Quarterly Journal of Speech* 72 (May 1986): 162–84.

Index

Adams County, Illinois 85
Alton, Illinois 10, 84, 85, 163, 164, 173, 174, 175, 177, 181
Armstrong, William 88
Atlanta, Illinois 64, 83

Bloomington, Illinois 10, 12, 13, 50, 51, 52, 53, 63, 74, 79, 83, 101, 117, 183
Bloomington Pantagraph 61
Boston, Massachusetts 65
Brooks, Preston 122
Buchanan, James 15, 17, 18, 21, 37, 42, 101, 159, 167
Burlington, Iowa 154

California 111
Carlinville, Illinois 164
Charleston, Illinois 84, 85, 103, 126, 127, 131, 135, 136, 137, 138, 139, 140, 143, 145, 146, 149, 150, 151, 153, 157, 158, 160, 164, 172, 173, 177, 181
Chase amendment 112
Chase, Salmon Portland 108
Chicago, Illinois 16, 37, 38, 39, 40, 42, 51, 52, 53, 54, 57, 63, 65, 72, 74, 77, 79, 80, 81, 83, 89, 92, 98, 101, 102, 103, 106, 107, 137, 146, 149, 150, 157, 160, 173, 174, 175, 181, 184
Chicago and Rock Island R.R. 92
Chicago Journal 79, 120, 121, 129, 130
Chicago Press and Tribune 39, 45, 63, 70, 77, 78, 81, 91, 92, 93, 94, 95, 106, 116, 117, 130, 144, 153, 155, 164, 184, 185
Chicago Times 39, 40, 51, 52, 78, 79, 80, 81, 82, 84, 93, 95, 106, 130, 141, 143, 151, 155, 176
Clay, Henry 30, 31, 60, 99, 100, 112, 131, 132, 149, 162

Clinton, Illinois 80, 116, 117
Codding, Ichabod 166
Coles County, Illinois 85
Constitution of the U.S. 11, 16, 18, 19, 25, 27, 28, 41, 44, 53, 57, 59, 60, 61, 68, 69, 147, 159, 184
Cook County, Illinois 38
Crittenden, John Jordan 21, 30, 31, 32, 34, 52, 54, 77, 83, 176, 178, 179, 183
Curtis, Benjamin Robbins 18

Danites 21
Davis, David 10, 11, 12, 13, 23, 24, 50, 81, 99, 117, 118, 138, 173, 175, 178, 179, 183, 184
Decatur, Illinois 116
Declaration of Independence 6, 7, 14, 15, 16, 17, 18, 19, 20, 27, 34, 38, 40, 44, 45, 48, 49, 53, 57, 58, 59, 60, 61, 64, 67, 68, 70, 73, 74, 75, 90, 91, 94, 96, 97, 99, 101, 102, 103, 105, 113, 115, 116, 117, 119, 122, 124, 126, 128, 134, 137, 138, 139, 140, 143, 145, 146, 148, 149, 150, 153, 157, 158, 160, 161, 162, 164, 166, 168, 169, 170, 171, 172, 173, 174, 175, 185
DeKalb *Sentinel* 130
Dickey, Theophilus Lyle 11, 12, 13, 14, 23, 24, 25, 27, 30, 33, 34, 75, 77, 83, 87, 94, 176, 178, 183
Dixon, Illinois 106
Donald, David Herbert 83
Donati's comet 120
Douglas, Stephen Arnold 5–8, 14, 16, 18, 19, 20–23, 25, 28, 30–33, 37–41, 43–48, 50, 51–61, 63–75, 77–85, 87–93, 95–102, 103–113, 117, 119–126, 129–138, 140–143, 145–151, 153–157, 158–162, 165–172, 174, 176–179, 183, 186

Index

Douglass, Frederick 112, 131, 132
Dred Scott decision 15, 16, 17, 18, 20, 28, 40, 44, 47, 48, 53, 56, 57, 58, 64, 66, 67, 71, 72, 100, 104, 105, 109, 113, 126, 135, 137, 146, 160, 162, 171, 173

Edwardsville, Illinois 118
Emancipation Proclamation 183
English Bill 104, 107

Fehrenbacher, Don E. 16
Fort Snelling 15
Freeport, Illinois 84, 85, 103, 104, 106, 114, 115, 116, 126, 137, 173
Frémont, John Charles 13, 14, 37, 107

Galena, Illinois 106, 107, 143
Galesburg, Illinois 84, 85, 139, 140, 143, 144, 149, 151, 154, 160, 161, 174
Garrison, William Lloyd 149
Gettysburg Address 113, 175
Giddings 149
Grant, Ulysses S. 183
Greeley, Horace 178

Herndon, William Henry 9, 25, 127, 128, 178, 179, 184
Hillsboro, Illinois 85
"House Divided" speech 23, 25–26, 29–30, 34, 37, 38, 40, 43, 45, 49, 52, 53, 55, 66, 70, 74, 75, 77, 87, 92, 97, 100, 101, 103, 108, 111, 113, 118, 121, 123, 125, 126, 134, 146, 148, 150, 159, 168, 173, 179

Illinois 55, 58, 67, 69, 74, 81, 123, 147
Illinois State Journal 79, 85
Illinois State Register 80, 85
Illinois Supreme Court 183
Indiana 130

Jefferson, Thomas 6, 59, 145, 148
Joliet, Illinois 51, 92, 94
Jonesboro, Illinois 84, 85, 103, 114, 115, 116, 119, 120, 121, 126, 128, 133, 137, 146, 173, 181
Journal and Courier (Lowell, Mass.) 80
Judd, Norman Buel 79, 81, 82, 83, 104, 106, 179, 184

Kansas 7, 21, 31, 40, 41, 53, 54, 66, 107, 109, 110, 165, 167
Kansas-Nebraska Act 5, 6, 8, 9, 17, 18, 20, 27, 38, 40, 41, 42, 43, 44, 65, 66, 70, 72, 81, 82, 83, 89, 101, 111, 112, 113, 132, 146, 147, 168, 174, 175
Kentucky 55, 69, 115, 147, 148, 157, 158
Know-Nothing party 9, 14
Knox College 144
Knox County, Illinois 85, 147

La Porte, Indiana 39
La Salle County, Illinois 85
Lecompton Constitution 21–22, 31, 40–42, 45–46, 52–54, 64, 70–72, 104, 159, 167, 176
Lewistown, Illinois 90, 98, 101, 105, 114, 118, 138, 175
Lincoln, Abraham 5–22, 23–26, 28–30, 32, 35, 37, 40, 43–48, 52, 53, 55–59, 61, 63–74, 75, 77–85, 87, 88–93, 95–102, 103–114, 115–126, 127–138, 139–151, 153–154, 156–162, 163–180, 181, 183–186
Lincoln, Illinois 64, 83
Louisiana 147, 163
Louisiana Purchase 15
Louisville, Kentucky 163
Lovejoy, Owen 9–14, 23, 24, 32, 38, 68, 94, 96, 99, 117, 118, 149, 166, 173, 176, 184

Madison County, Illinois 85, 164
Maine 67, 125
Massachusetts 116, 147
Mattoon, Illinois 129
McClellan, George Brinton 120
Medill, Joseph Meharry 104, 113, 173, 184
Michigan City, Indiana 39
Minnesota 15
Mississippi 61
Missouri 15, 159, 165
Missouri Compromise of 1820 5, 6, 15, 17, 20, 66, 72, 82, 104
Missouri Republican 105
Monmouth, Illinois 154
Monroe County, Illinois 133
Monticello, Illinois 80
Moore, C.H. 116

Nebraska 6, 7, 41
New Mexico 111
New Orleans, Louisiana 163
New York 68, 125
New York, New York 179

Index

New York Day-book 139
New York Evening Post 107, 120, 130
New York Herald 80

Oregon 111
Ottawa, Illinois 84, 85, 87, 92, 93, 94, 95, 97, 101, 102, 103, 106, 107, 137, 138, 140, 160, 173, 174

Paris, Illinois 117
Peoria, Illinois 6
Petit, John 140, 171
Philadelphia, Pennsylvania 179
Philadelphia Press 80
Pierce, Franklin 101

Queen Victoria 25
Quincy, Illinois 84, 85, 153, 154, 156, 158, 161, 162, 163, 170, 174
Quincy *Herald* 154, 155
Quincy *Whig* 154, 155

Randolph County, Illinois 133
Richmond Enquirer 139
Rock Island County, Illinois 38
Rockford, Illinois 107

St. Louis, Missouri 163, 164, 179
Sangamon County, Illinois 63, 133
Schurz, Carl 156
Seward, William Henry 27, 29, 178
Simon, John Y. 119
South Carolina 116

Springfield, Illinois 6, 18, 23, 49, 63, 64, 74, 75, 77, 79, 81, 98, 101, 108, 116, 133, 158, 164, 173
Stephenson County, Illinois 85
Sullivan, Illinois 140, 141, 142, 143
Sweet, Martin B. 128

Taney, Roger 15, 16, 18, 19, 21, 22, 28, 65, 101, 104, 134, 171, 184
Toledo, Ohio 39
Toombs bill 136
Tremont House 38, 39, 45, 78
Trumbull, Lyman 8, 72, 97, 100, 126, 136, 137

Underground Railroad 10
Union County, Illinois 85
United States Supreme Court 15, 16, 17, 18, 44, 47, 56, 57, 66, 104, 107, 108, 109, 110, 125, 160, 167, 183

Virginia 158

Washington, George 145
Webster, Daniel 60, 112, 131, 132
Weik, Jesse William 184
White, Horace 91, 92, 93, 106, 116, 117, 119, 120, 129, 143, 144, 179, 185
Williamsville, Illinois 64
Wilmington, Illinois 51
Wisconsin 115

Yale University 10